MAP *of* ANOTHER TOWN

MAP *of* ANOTHER TOWN

A Memoir of Provence

by M. F. K. FISHER

with map and drawings by
Barbara Westman

Little, Brown and Company · Boston · Toronto

Published simultaneously in Canada
by Little, Brown & Company (Canada) Limited

PRINTED IN THE UNITED STATES OF AMERICA

For Nan Newton

Contents

Introduction   3

Aix-en-Provence   5

St. Sauveur   8

Main Street   20

The Two Havens   29

The Gypsy Way   47

The Foreigner   59

17 Rue Cardinale   69

Oath to Asclepius   101

The Sound of the Place   128

The University   132

The Man and the Words   138

A Familiar   146

The Unwritten Books   163

The Din   175

The Hôtel de Provence   188

Men and Women Mendicants   199

The Outlook Across   216

The Almond Blossoms   234

Correction on the Map   241

The Royal Game of Tennis   254

The Velvet Tunnel   264

MAP *of* ANOTHER TOWN

> . . . it is very probable that if I had
> to draw the portrait of Paris, I would,
> one more time, draw it of myself.
>
> JEAN GIONO, 1961

O FTEN in the sketch for a portrait, the invisible lines that
bridge one stroke of the pencil or brush to another are
what really make it live. This is probably true in a word picture too. The myriad undrawn unwritten lines are the ones
that hold together what the painter and the writer have tried
to set down, their own visions of a thing: a town, one town,
this town.

Not everything can be told, nor need it be, just as the artist
himself need not and indeed cannot reveal every outline of his
vision.

There before us is what one human being has seen of something many others have viewed differently, and the lines held
back are perhaps the ones most vital to the whole.

Here before me now is my picture, my map, of a place and
therefore of myself, and much that can never be said adds to its
reality for me, just as much of its reality is based on my own
shadows, my inventions.

Over the years I have taught myself, and have been taught,
to be a stranger. A stranger usually has the normal five senses,
perhaps especially so, ready to protect and nourish him.

Then there are the extra senses that function only in subcon-
sciousness. These are perhaps a stranger's best allies, the ones

that stay on and grow stronger as time passes and immediacy dwindles.

It is with the invisible ink distilled from all these senses, then, that I have drawn this map of a town, a place real in stone and water, and in the spirit, which may also be realer.

Aix-en-Provence

... 177 meters above sea level; 52,217 inhabitants; former capital of Provence; seat of an archbishopric since the fifth century, and of the departmental law courts and prison, and the schools of Law and Letters of the University of Aix-Marseille; one of the most beautiful art centers of Europe.

The town was founded in 123 B.C. by the Roman consul Sextius Calvinus, and was made into a prosperous colony by Julius Caesar. Between the fifth and twelfth centuries it lost much of its political importance to the town of Arles, although it was once more made the capital in the twelfth century under the Counts of Provence.

During the fifteenth century, before joining France, it became the hub of European culture under the benevolent administration of King René and his two queens.

Le Guide Bleu: France, 1960

So HERE IS the town, founded more than two thousand years ago by the brash Roman invaders, on much older ruins which still stick up their stones and artifacts. I was as brash a newcomer to it, and yet when I first felt the rhythm of its streets and smelled its ancient smells, and listened at night to the music of its many fountains, I said, "Of course," for I was once more in my own place, an invader of what was already mine.

Depending upon one's vocabulary, it is facile enough to speak of *karma* or atavism or even extrasensory memory. For me, there was no need to draw on this well of casual semantics, to recognize Aix from my own invisible map of it. I already knew where I was.

I had been conditioned to this acceptance by a stay in another old town on the northward Roman road, when I was younger and perhaps more vulnerable. I lived for some time in Dijon in my twenties, and compulsively I return to it when I can, never with real gratification. And I dream occasionally of it, and while the dream-streets are not quite the same as in waking life (the Rue de la Liberté swings to the right toward the railroad yards instead of going fairly straight to the Place d'Armes and the Ducal Palace, for instance, but I always know exactly where *I* am going), still I am a remote but easy visitor, happier as such than as a visible one.

I do not, in my imagination, feel as easy there as in Aix. I have long since made my own map of Dijon, and it is intrinsic to my being, but the one of Aix is better, a refuge from any sounds but its own, a harbor from any streets but its own: great upheavals and riots and pillages and invasions and liberations and all the ageless turmoil of an old place.

I feel somewhat like a cobweb there. I do not bother anyone. I do not even wisp myself across a face, or catch in the hair of a passerby, because I have been there before, and will be again, on my own map.

I can walk the same streets, and make my own history from them, as I once did in a lesser but still structural way in Dijon, my first return to the past, forever present to me.

The town was put on its feet by a Roman whose elegant bathing place still splutters out waters, tepid to hot and slightly stinking, for a ceaseless genteel flow of ancient countesses and their consorts and a quiet dogged procession of arthritic postal clerks and Swiss bankers and English spinsters suffering from indefinable malaises usually attributed to either their native climates or their equally native diets. This spa, more ancient than anyone who could possibly stay in it except perhaps I myself, is at the edge of the Old Town, at the head of the Cours

Sextius, and more than one good writer has generated his own acid to etch its strange watery attraction.

Countless poems have been written too, in wine rather than acid, and countless pictures have been painted, about the healing waters and the ever-flowing fountains of the place. They will continue as long as does man, and the delicate iron balconies will cling to the rose-yellow walls, and if anyone else, from 200 B.C. to now, ever marked the same places on the map, in acid or wine or even tears, his reasons would not be mine. That is why Aix is what it is.

St. Sauveur

Almost thou persuadest me to be a
Christian.

The Acts of the Apostles, xxvi, 28

i *THE BEGINNING*

The structure of the baptistry of the Cathedral of St.
Sauveur (end of the fourth, beginning of the fifth centuries) is strongly influenced by the liturgy of primitive
baptism: immersion, conferred by a bishop upon adults once
yearly during the night before Easter. To this sacramental
rite of purification, performed behind curtains to protect
the naked participants, two symbolisms are added: the passing from shadow to light (the water flows from east to
west; two granite columns serve as entrance to the east,
facing six of green marble; steps descend into the pool from
the east . . .), and the resurrection and new life, symbolized
by the figure 8, the primitive symbol for Sunday, the eighth
day (the original baptistry was eight-sided, as was the mar-
ble-lined pool). In the sixteenth century the cupola was
heightened . . .

JEAN-PAUL COSTE, *Aix-en-Provence and Its Countryside*

M ANY old towns like Aix in the Western world have grown
the way a pearl does, in micromillimeters of skin against
the world, around a germ, an alien seed, an itch, which in most
of them has been a Christian church, at once fortress and prison
and spiritual core.

Aix, however, grew around its baths, which still flow heal-
ingly behind the last of the old walls in the spa that is now run
by the government. Even the Cathedral that later became the

heart of the town was built over a temple bath, which in due
time became its baptistry.

In St. Sauveur, the Cathedral of the Holy Savior, the pool is
empty now in the octagonal room under the high vaulted ceiling, but beside it a cumbersome font still serves the parish, and
from its walls local archeologists are still, discreetly between
Masses, tumbling the bones of believers built into the niches.

Far above the stone ribs of the hushed room a small eye of
open sky in the cupola looks down upon the empty basin that
the first Christians found so conveniently ready for their baptismal rites, after decades of Roman ladies had bathed hopefully
there to give themselves children. Perhaps, it is said, St. Maximin himself, one of Christ's disciples, stood beside that pool . . .

I remember it as about four feet deep, with crumbling steps
down into it, and centuries dry. Once I was standing looking
at it in the shadowy room, thinking of how long it and perhaps even I had been there, when I found myself a near-active
party to a small christening that had suddenly shaped itself
around the modern font.

There I was, and why would I be there for any other reason
than to help make a new member of the parish? The parents
and sponsors smiled at me with a polite preoccupied twitch,
each probably thinking the other side of the family had asked
me to come. I must not startle them, caught as they were in
the hoarse whispers, the cold air, the irrevocability of the
ritual.

I stood facing the fat careless priest, a man I saw often in the
district of the Cathedral and never grew to accept as anything
but obnoxious. His vestments were dirty, and he needed a
shave and almost certainly a bath, whether Roman or Christian.
He held the new child as if it were a distastefully cold omelet
that might stick on his fingers.

The parents and sponsors were mute in their Sunday clothes,
the convenient and almost essential uniform of black which

will do for the next funeral, a vestment of respectability among poor people, who fortify themselves on what other poor people will think of them.

The new believer would most probably lead a long full life, although like many infants of its environment it looked moribund, a blue wax image faintly breathing, its eyes slits of world-weariness.

I prayed for myself that the lout of a priest would not ask me any direct questions about vouching for the little soul's well-being, and then, when the insultingly mechanical drone was plainly drawing toward a final benediction, I made myself disappear.

This is something that takes practice, and by the time I was standing there in St. Sauveur trying not to accept any responsibility for the sickly newborn baby I had become fairly good at it. It is mainly a question of withdrawing to the vanishing point from the consciousness of the people one is with, before one actually leaves. It is invaluable at parties, testimonial dinners, discussions of evacuation routes in California towns, and coffee-breaks held for electioneering congressmen . . .

As I flitted, almost invisible by now, across the baptistry, I nearly walked straight into the roughly paved pit where Roman ladies on vacation had splashed hopefully, where the first Christians had doused themselves, pressed down into the flowing water by the hands of disciples who had once heard the voice of Mary Magdalene praying in her cave.

I wondered as I righted my course around the dim room if anyone had ever fallen in. It would be only a bruise or two, perhaps a cracked bone . . . But why risk it? Why flee? Did I run from looking once more into the cynical eyes of the newest Christian, or did I escape from the more materialistic hazard of having to explain to the dismal young family that I was nobody at all, no cousin's cousin, an uninvited witness to the rites, not even real?

At the wide door into the comparative security of the nave I felt safe again, and the air had a different weight and coldness. I could hear footsteps up toward the choir stalls: chairs were being straightened between Masses on this Sunday morning. In the organ loft, Monsieur Gay flitted mockingly, tenderly, through two octaves of sound that came down to me as pure silver, like hollow clean beads on a string. I could not even hear the priest behind me. It was as if I had been bathed again . . .

ii *AWAY, AWAY . . .*

We hear the wail of the remorseful wind
In their strange penance.
ALEXANDER SMITH, *Unrest and Childhood*

THE SECOND TIME we returned to Aix for more than a few painfully nostalgic days, Anne and Mary and I made a point, with some trouble, of being there during Holy Week so that we could once again see the *reposoirs*.

They took place on Maundy Thursday, the day before Good Friday. It was like a fiesta. People walked gaily from one open church and chapel to another in a kind of jaunty quiet pilgrimage, part relief that Lent was almost over, part plain curiosity to see what the Order of This, the Guild of That would produce.

Chapels that were forever otherwise closed to the lay public were open that day, and in each one an offering of money could be left at the door. In the small convents and monasteries the whole main altar, with, as I remember it, no candle or flame burning, was turned into a wall, a solid wall, of the most beautiful flowers that could be found, which there near the Côte d'Azur meant beautiful indeed. In the larger churches the main altar was dim, and to the left of it, rising from floor to ceiling, sometimes perhaps thirty feet high, was the same solid mass of blossoms, now mixed all in a riotous jumble of spring, now austerely one kind of flower, one color.

It was a miracle that between the late night of Wednesday and the morning of the next day the old women and men could create such stormy pagan beauty, and then even more astounding that by dawn on Good Friday, or perhaps before, every sign of it would be gone, and the statues would be shrouded in black veils, and everything would be waiting for the recital of the Stations of the Cross.

When we saw the *reposoirs* in 1955 we decided that the most beautiful was in the Madeleine. It was, as I remember, mostly white tulips, with some scarlet.

Crowds filed into the great simple church with silent excitement, and gasped at its beauty, and as they left put money into the box to help pay for the flowers, and then went on to the next and the next churches, all over the town, which echoed to the sound of thousands of leisurely feet.

One of the prettiest walls was in the small chapel of a convent of Sisters of Charity behind the façades of the Rue Gaston-de-Saporta, a little below and behind Brondino's bookshop. It was never open to the public except on that Thursday of Holy Week. No nuns were in sight, of course, but a postulant stood by the coin box, pretending not to listen to the size of the sound of each bit of money hitting the rest. A little sign over another alms box said, *For the poor, the sick, and the ashamed.*

The most impressive *reposoir* was in the chapel of the Gray Penitents, or the Bourras, called that in Provençal because they wear sacks over their heads.

They are the last of the three active orders of Penitents in Aix, who devoted themselves, most strongly in the Middle Ages, to the burying of hanged criminals and abandoned victims of the plagues. The brotherhood today is a secret one, made up of businessmen and professionals who celebrate their rites and functions wearing over their regular clothes long tunics made of a gray sacking in much the shape of the Ku Klux Klan costumes, so that on the one time we saw them, silent and nightmarish in their chapel, their secular trousers and shoes showed absurdly beneath their grim disguises. They clanked with brutal-looking rosaries hanging from their waist-belts around their waists.

Their chapel is a plain room, without statues as I remember, but with the whole end an enormous carving, almost life-size, on tortured rocks, of the descent of Christ from the Cross, with the Act of Mercy of the Good Samaritan and perhaps a few others painted behind it. The carving is of gleaming gray-black wood. The altar, which of course was stripped the day we saw it, is in front of the carving and a part of it, so that the figures crouch and swoon and mourn above and behind it.

There were no flowers anywhere. A few of the Bourras stood clattering their rosaries and watching the silent fright-ened people, who filed in and then quickly went away. My children were scared.

And in a way I was too: it was a stern mercy that led those first hooded men to defy custom and disease, in the far days, and I wondered what bones and ashes they might rescue now, so silent behind their sackcloth maskings.

In the vestibule we bought some postcards of the altar, which I lost, and we left money in the coin box, beside which one last thin Penitent stood, perhaps listening to the size of the sound as if he had a real face with a real ear on either side.

We wanted to see all this with our older eyes when we were in Aix again in Holy Week. My sister and her three sons came too, earlier than they had meant, to see the pagan beauty of the flowers, perhaps the medieval fearsomeness of the Bourras. But the town looked the same on Maundy Thursday as it had on

Wednesday or Tuesday, and in St. Sauveur there was not a sign of the blossomed wall, and plainly one could not enter the little convents that are still everywhere behind the façades of Aix.

We went into the Madeleine, and there was nothing to show that once at least a mighty wall of white and scarlet blossoms had stood at the end of the south transept for some short hours, long enough for us to see forever.

I was perhaps a little drunk with being in the place again, and while my family stood gaping at a safe distance, I went up to a tall rounded young priest standing near the door and asked him where the *reposoirs* were.

That was the only time a man of the cloth has ever been discourteous to me, and later I saw this same one be quite rude to elderly women and very irascible with children, in a strangely sneering way. He sniffed, and stared down at me even farther than he needed, and asked in a high petulant voice, "Why would anyone ask that?"

"Father," I said with polite boldness bred of my joy at being home again, "we came back for the *reposoirs,* and I wonder where they are."

He looked me up and down, as the old novels would say, and then remarked in a disdainful way, "Anyone who is a believer knows, and therefore it is plain that Madame is not a believer, that the *reposoirs* have been discontinued in Provence as unfavorable to true Christianity."

I knew at once what he meant about the pagan element in them, but was sorry to detect his puritanical triumph. I thanked him.

"Where, if Madame is a believer, has she been? This is not a new edict," the priest stated suspiciously.

"Away, away," I answered in a half-deliberately fey manner, and I disappeared from his immediate vision and returned to my family and told them that the *reposoirs* had been forbidden.

We went away, away . . . in this case to the Cours Mirabeau,
where we consumed sherbets and vermouth-gins according to
our natures, and as returned amateurs seemed to grow like
water-flowers under the greening buds of the plane trees, in
the flowing tides of that street.

When the violet-man came along, we bought from him, and
held the flowers in lieu of that older vision, ineradicable, of the
walls of flowers, and perhaps of the painful sternness of the
altar of the Bourras.

iii *THE ENDING*

Of a good beginning cometh a good end.

JOHN HEYWOOD, *Proverbes*

THE TWO BEST things for me, in St. Sauveur, were that I was
able to know it full and know it empty, not of people but of
the spirit.

Several times it was almost full when I went to concerts
there, with an orchestra in the transept in front of the choir
stalls, and then a full choir of men and of boys from the
Maîtrise, and everything sacred delicately and firmly shut off.
The organ was alive, with Monsieur Gay there at the console
in his white cap and his wife beside him in a kind of choir robe
to turn the pages, like two gallant old birds high above our
heads, so knowing and so skilled in making near-celestial
sounds.

Twice the Archbishop sat unobtrusively in one of the stalls
to the right, in the big nave, and prelates and priests rustled
beneath him and I sat close by, recognizing his spirit and
looking, invisible and even more so than usual, at the hollows
of his eye sockets.

The music sang out from in front of the dim altar, and I

knew it was a good thing to play it thus in the house of God.

Once I went into the Cathedral and it was a shell, waiting. It was by accident.

We walked up from the Hôtel de Provence on Easter Eve, I think, for no reason that I can remember, along Gaston-de-Saporta and across the Place de l'Archevêché, and there at the entrance to the cloister some priests and acolytes were bending above a bonfire.

It was startling to see. The flames lighted their intense faces. Around them were a few old women, the kind who are always present at such rituals.

I am sorry and a little ashamed to say that I forget now what they were burning. It had something to do with the purification by fire and then water of the vessels perhaps, and probably it was old candles and such-like, or the robes of Judas himself, but at the end a large candle was lighted, I think, and then from it each of us lit a long thin taper given to us by an acolyte or perhaps a lay brother.

Then we walked silently through the passage and through the side of the cloister, where I had been used to watching my children playing handball against the Roman tombs, and into the St. Maximin aisle of the church. From there we went into the nave, and found seats.

It was in one of the most impressive darknesses of my life. There was no sound except for the muted shuffling of our feet and the mouselike whisperings of people telling their beads, ?nd the darkness in that great place was as palpable as flesh. It was oppressive. It pressed in upon my skin like the cold body of someone unloved. There was no help for it, no escape, and so it was not frightening.

I looked toward the dead altar, and out and up, and there was nothing anywhere except from the few feeble tapers that seemed to unlight rather than to light the intense worn hands and faces that nursed them.

A long and to me very pagan ceremony unfolded before the altar and then down into the chancel. It had to do with fire and water and rebirth. I wish that I could remember more of it, but all that stays clear is that it was ageless and real. And then gradually light seemed to come.

Of course it was partly mechanical, electrical. But that did not matter. I watched the magnificent conglomeration, perhaps two thousand years old, come alive, softly, subtly, and then like a mighty blare of trumpets, and seldom have I been so startled in my soul. I had for once known true hollow blackness, and then light. And it seems to me now that there was music too, a great triumphant blast of it from the organ, but perhaps it was only the return of light that I heard.

And then the time that I knew the Cathedral full, not empty, was almost as enriching, for I went to a concert there during the Festival, and listened to even that great place hold as much sound as an egg its meat, or the sea its waters.

It was as full as it could ever be with people too, of course, who had come from many lands to listen.

There was a symphony orchestra. The choir and the middle transept were filled with one large chorus of men and women, and one of boys, with the four soloists for the oratorio. Monsieur Gay was at the organ. The walls hummed with the colors of the Canterbury tapestries; the triptych of the Burning Bush was open and glowing; artful lights made the stones vibrate with subtle colors, as I had often watched them do at sunset with a kind of absorption rather than reflection of the colors outside in the town.

But the thing that was real was the sound. It was awesome, whether from a little flute as single as a pearl, or mighty as Judgment Day from the whole orchestra. Everything was a part of it, and the breath that went into and out of the mortals there, and into and out of the great organ, was in a mystical way the breath of the place itself, very old and ageless. I have

seldom felt myself more identified with anything. It was perhaps as if I were the right grain of sand for me to be, on the
right beach.

Afterwards we were quiet and tired, and that too was in the
right way.

Main Street

Aix is nobility itself. It gives to the least plane tree the grandeur of a cedar. On the Cours Mirabeau, where the song of the fountains mingles with Mozart's music, its good taste comes so naturally that not even the students can disturb it. It was the last city of France to give up its sedan chairs. Since then (the beginning of the nineteenth century) the well-born people of the town have gone on foot, not to economize but instead to show their disdain for money in its weightiest form, that of time.

Marcel Renébon, *La Provence*

i *THE COURS*

Let the street be as wide as the height of the houses.

Leonardo da Vinci

THE Cours Mirabeau is the main street of Aix-en-Provence. It is less than half of a mile long (440 meters) and some hundred and twenty feet wide. It is bordered on either side by a double row of plane trees, growing in front of the straight façades of seventeenth- and eighteenth-century town-houses, most of them with shops or offices on the ground floor now. There are four fountains down the middle of the Cours' length, and . . .

. . . and it is impossible to continue writing of it in this informative vein.

The Cours has teased poets and painters with its ineffable allure for more than three hundred years, but words and lines and colors do not capture the reasons why it is beautiful and not pretty, serene and not soothing, and dignified yet gladsome all the year, even in the stripped austerity of winter.

It is probable that almost every traveler who has ever passed through Aix has been moved in some positive way by the view from one end of the Cours or the other, by the sounds of its fountains in the early hours, by the melodious play of the pure clear sunlight of Provence through its summer cave of leaves. Some of them have tried to tell of their bemused rapture, on canvas and sketch pads and on scratch-pads and even postcards, but they have never been satisfied.

It is a man-made miracle, perhaps indescribable, compounded of stone and water and trees, and to the fortunate it is one of the world's chosen spots for their own sentient growth.

Myself, for too few years I crossed it many times a day, and sat under its trees, and walked up and down it on both sides alone and with my children and now and then with friends, in sunlight and moonlight and rain and fog, and every time it was the first time, and I felt a kind of prickling under my skin and a tightening in my chest and belly and a kind of dazzling in my head and a generally excited stimulated moved sensation, like being in love.

The street was made in 1651, after Marie de Médicis brought from Italy to France the aristocratic pleasure of taking the air in public, either in carriages or on foot or in sedan chairs, instead of walking quietly in one's own gardens. It became at once the center of life in Aix, and so it has remained.

Motor scooters and automobiles have replaced the chairs and open carriages that paraded during the cool of the evenings on the Cours of other days, but the delight of strolling its length at any time, in every season, has never ceased to charm, indeed almost to hypnotize whomever once sets foot on its majestic length and width.

The Cours is wider by some ten feet at its eastern end, for unknown reasons which have never marred the beauty of its perspective. It was built on the location of the ancient ramparts, which in one form or another had shielded the original town for almost two thousand years. Some Aixois say that a river flowed past these ramparts. Others say that the Cours covers the bed of an old canal. Whatever the reason, deep waters and long thirsty roots are why, everyone believes, the double rows of plantains on either side of the street have reached so high and withstood so long the ravages of wind and drought and gradual pollution of the city air.

The first trees were elms, and they too grew handsomely to shade the rich gentry in their carriages and the people of the upper class who strolled beneath their shade. They died in a plague that killed almost every elm tree in Provence, and beginning in 1830 they were quickly replaced by the plane trees which now thrive along the Cours and help make it what has often been called "the most beautiful Main Street in the world."

Perhaps one reason is that it was a deliberate conception of balance, one of those human plans which seemed to be realized most neatly in the seventeenth century, in that part of the world. It was planned from its beginning as a whole, balancing its three dimensions of width, length, and the prescribed height of the buildings which lined it on either side. These laws have always been obeyed except for a few off-set attics above the set height, and the result is one of the most reassuring of all civilized vistas.

ii *ITS FOUNTAINS*

In the hexameter rises the fountain's silvery column,
In the pentameter aye falling in melody back.

Samuel Taylor Coleridge,
The Ovidian Elegiac Metre

THERE ARE STILL four fountains, the length of the Cours, just
as at its beginning.

The one at the west end was first reconstructed in 1728, and
then again in 1778 to allow traffic from Paris and Marseille to
flow near the edge of the city. There were sea horses splashing, with Neptune whipping them, with his face staring up the
length of the Cours, and with jets of water spouting into
the air.

By 1860 it was plain that the Cours must surrender again to
progress and let down its bars to the wagons and stage coaches
which were pushing out the genteel carriages that had for so
long been almost its only traffic. Neptune vanished, and a
monumental waterworks became the center of a wheel of important roads leading out like spokes to other parts of France.
This fountain was named La Rotonde, and unless the mistral
is blowing its spray too far up the Cours, it stops its spectacu-
lar splashings only once a year, when the Canal de Verdon
shuts off its pipes for cleaning.

Compared to the other fountains of Aix, the Rotonde is
melodramatic, overstated, brassy, a trumpet call with flutes.

The first sight of it, when a traveler approaches from Marseille, is exciting. One of them, Emile Henriot of the Académie
Française, wrote it for everybody else in 1920: ". . . since I
love fountains, especially when they sing sweetly, and this one
pleased me so strongly, because of its long sprays of inter-
twined water which sprang from every direction into its pools,

I felt that through it I should salute the whole town of Aix in this one symbol, and I raised my hand to my hat brim."

In daylight La Rotonde tosses out its many plumes and jets of water like the breath of a hundred spirited horses. At night it glows, as do many great modern fountains, with white and colored lights which turn it into a kind of glorified wedding cake, audible if inedible.

It is crowned by three nobly sentimental white stone females representing Justice, Agriculture, and the Arts. The first faces up the Cours, toward the law courts and the prison. The second looks toward Marseille, for rapidly vanishing reasons. The third turns toward Avignon and its older and perhaps even greater culture.

Four jets spout from these figures' pedestal, into a wide basin from which many more mouths send out their waters. Far below an even wider basin catches them, and eight bronze cherubim astride frolicking dolphins send out double streams of water that curve like low rainbows and blow past the rim of the great bowl, sometimes, onto the wide circle of the Rotonde's paving. Big turtles along the edge of the basin spout back at the energetically fat little boys their counterstreams of water, weaving a kind of web, and to hold it all to solid earth enormous lions lie in pairs around the base, at ease but always wary, at the edge of the tent of interwoven crystal.

It is, in truth, a monument to nineteenth-century romanticism, and perhaps it escapes vulgarity simply by being in Aix. Certainly it is curiously satisfying, full of life and joy. It acts as a kind of noisy but melodious introduction to the other fountains of the street, which stretches eastward from it.

At the opposite end, always called the head of the Cours, stands the fine statue of King René, which has lent its serenity since about 1820, when it was sculpted to replace two fountains which had crumbled away or been removed.

As everywhere in Aix, water flows musically below the King's statue into the generous basin, and people fill their

pitchers from its cool jets all day long, or perch on its wide
rim to gaze about them tranquilly.

Traffic flows around the handsome King who made Aix
known throughout Europe as a center of learning and beauty,
and it seems right that he should hold in one hand a fat bunch
of the grapes he helped develop, in his little kingdom, from its
old Greek and Roman plantings.

Westward from René about three hundred feet is Old Mossback, which steams like a theatrically inverted cauldron into
the cold air of winter. It was built in 1737 to stay as it is now,
over one of the fountainheads which first brought gouty
Romans to Aix. Old people still dip their aching hands in its
warmth, and many others drink its waters sparingly to "take
the cure" for various human troubles, for it is credited with
being a purge, a diuretic, an active solution of minerals, a fluid
saturated with actinic rays, and almost every other possible
remedy that one looks for with faith.

It has a faint but harsh smell, and it is one of those strange
fountains of Provence which consist of a great lump of live
stone on which thick lichens grow, with the water flowing up
to the top and then down over the short furry mosses. Often
generations of moss pile one upon another, feeding through all
the rich fur under them to the stone. These monuments can
become grotesque, but Old Mossback is merely comfortable
to look at, like an elderly and benevolent dog, a little steamy
and pungent.

Further down toward the Rotonde is the fountain of St.
Lazarus, which is also thought to be healing and which is now
the most popular on the Cours for drinking-water. People come
for blocks, at noon and before supper, to fill their pitchers
from the graceful curves of its basin, which is one of the most
beautiful examples of Louis XV design in this town of flowing
waters. It is known by everybody as the Nine Canons, instead
of its saint's name, and it is an intrinsic part of many lives in
the Old Town.

And then the Cours ends, after its harmony of light and color and sound and line, in the almost rollicking vigor of the Rotonde.

It is exciting, after the cool green cave of the street in summer, under the leaves, and then in winter the muted rose and yellow shadows on the old façades, to step into the penetrating brightness, never blinding, of its unshaded monument to the three Arts. It is like being a fish, up from the sweet depths to the surface for a different kind of air. Traffic flows around and around the great crossroads, but the sound of all the jets of water rises above it, and seems to drift always eastward, toward the Nine Canons and Old Mossback, to the feet of the tranquil King René with his fruits . . .

iii   *ITS FAÇADES*

To blend in one tangible whole
The manifold features of change . . .
Gamaliel Bradford, *Soul*

THE HOUSES THAT face each other across the double width of the Cours Mirabeau, and then over the tops of the plane trees from their attics, are one of the few remaining entities of the seventeenth and eighteenth centuries in European architecture, unbombed and unburned in spite of the hazards and crimes of progress.

None of them still exists as the elegant town-house it was built to be. The families that flourished in the richest days of Aix, and built these palaces to prove their positions, have long since died out or retreated to their often crumbling country estates.

A few beautiful private apartments are still preserved, and the exquisite iron balconies of most of the houses, and then their staircases inside, are tenderly protected by their care-

Cours Mirabeau

takers and the city and the nation, so that students of all the arts may admire them.

From above the town one can see that many of the old houses now have artists living in their attics, with skylights that gleam like bloodied copper at sunset.

At street level, the tone of the Cours has changed almost completely since it was first built as an aristocratic promenade. For a long time not even a vendor of lemonades was allowed to endanger its gentility. Gradually its Left Bank let a few discreet merchants, all of them convenient purveyors to their social betters, open small shops. By now the Left Bank is an almost unbroken series of stores both great and small and mostly reputable, of open-air cafés for every class of people, of agencies for every need.

Occasionally a noble façade of delicate iron balconies and giant caryatids looms like a great jewel on the two firm straight lines of buildings. There are a few official residences, like the Sub-Prefecture, or like the Hôtel d'Espagnet, now owned by the University of Aix-Marseille which King René fostered, where the president of all the faculties lives and works.

Above the varied offices and shops, puny with silver and crystal and neckties or portentous with learning and crime, and especially on the Left Bank, the gracious old apartments, many of them looking back into gardens and courtyards, are rented to lawyers and doctors and strangers who are willing to fight their endless but beautiful stairways for what they find at the top, and a dwindling but dogged group of local people who still choose that rather than the modern houses of the flourishing new subdivisions that encircle the town like the tentacles of a bewildered octopus.

And it makes a mysterious whole, this generous vital stretch of trees and buildings and live waters. In any language, it cannot rightly be called street, thoroughfare, mall, road or roadway, route, boulevard, highway. It is the Cours.

The Two Havens

Fasten him as a nail in a sure place.

Isaiah, xxii, 23

i *THE 2 Gs*

Club: an assembly of good fellows
meeting under certain conditions.

Samuel Johnson, *Dictionary*

A T the turn of this century, a young Frenchman named Léo
Larguier was stationed in Aix for part of his military
service, and later he wrote a good little book about it called
Sunday with Cézanne, for he knew the old painter as well as
one could, so late and so shortly.

His view of the town, even from the dubious vantage point
of middle age, was a quizzical one:

"We used to go sometimes, in good weather, to sit on the
terrace of the Café Clément, which was at that time the best
and most popular one in Aix, the place frequented by officers,
rich students, and the dandies who were not afraid to lower
themselves by being seen in a public drinking place.

"These last, not too numerous at that, belonged to old Provençal families, and their parents still lived in the rigidly private town-houses which I picture as crowded with beautiful
furniture and dim cluttered group portraits . . .

"There was a piano at the Clément, on a low platform in
front of the door, and the pianist, accompanied by a violin

and a cello, was an exceedingly dark young woman who looked at nobody . . . she seemed like a schoolteacher . . .

"Under the giant plane trees of the Cours Mirabeau, the lazy and the aimless wandered, greeting their acquaintances often and ceremoniously. A few students could be seen on the balcony of their own club, across the street. At the Clément," Larguier added, "people joined their friends, or met them upon leaving, but I don't recall ever seeing a townsman nod to Cézanne. Nobody seemed to recognize him!"

My friend Georges, of Dijon, remembered the Clément from before the First World War. He evidently spent little time in it, having better things to do with his leisure in wild Marseille, where he split his life with the Boys' Lycée Mignet in tame Aix.

Now the Clément is the local showrooms and offices of an important dealer in antiques and paintings, and catty-corner from its noble façade, there at the corner of the Rue Frédéric-Mistral, is the 2 Gs.

I of course could have asked more questions and found out if it was indeed a students' club when Larguier sat looking at it "in good weather" at the Caf' Clem to the strains of the poker-faced female pianist. I seemed to be tongue-tied about such matters. Ghostlike, I listened instead, and sifted out whatever seemed appropriate to me, and applied it as I wished to the actualities of such places as the café where I was to spend many of the pleasantest waking hours of my so-called life.

In Aix, and I presume in every other respectable town of France, both great and small, cafés are known by the company they keep, and in one way or another the towns are known by their cafés. For most of this century Aix has been for itself and its visitors the Deux Garçons, the Café of the Two Waiters. About 1750 it was a chess and checkers club for gentlemen, The Guion, I was told, which they entered through the rear door on the Rue Fabrot to still any rumors of commercialism; and now respectable citizens, students who one day will be the same, and tourists both ordinary and extraordinary make it, still, their club in their various well-behaved ways.

It is two large rooms, elegant in a deliberately faded style.

The larger, which gives now onto the Cours Mirabeau through its door and two big windows, is long, with a looming old zinc bar across its far end, where the waiters fill their orders except for liqueurs and spirits, which are dispensed carefully at the high cashier's desk near the two public telephone booths.

The main part of this room is mirrored, with woodwork painted dimly in gold and black. Oblong tables of grayish marble go along the two sides in front of the leather benches, and then down the middle. People never sit in the middle unless the room is crowded.

There is a large fern in front of this third row of tables, on an obsolete circular radiator, and usually the philoprogenitive café cat is asleep there under its luxuriant leaves.

In the room to the left, which also gives onto the Cours, the elegant old décor is simpler, without any mirrors; and students sit there, as they always have, or rare tourists who do not know that they are intruding on the cabalistic rituals of beer and *Gauloises Bleues*.

Across the whole generous façade of the Deux Garçons stretches a terrace filled with little marble-topped tables, and dozens of green chairs. In summer it is deeply shaded by the double row of towering plane trees of the Left Bank of the Cours. In winter it catches all the thin pure sunlight that falls through their naked branches. In the spring the light is incredibly dappled and of the color of a fine greenish wine from the Moselle. Sometimes in late autumn after a rainy wind there are only a few eccentrics who still sit there, to watch the golden leaves plastered against the shining black pavement of the street.

The only time the 2 Gs, as the students call it, really spills

out to the edge of the wide sidewalk is during the Festival in July, when after a night performance hundreds of people stroll up and down the Cours in the soft air, with no automobiles anywhere. They murmur in a dozen tongues on the café terraces, and drink wine and beer and whiskey and hot chocolate and Coca-Cola and gin, and at the 2 Gs eat little lemon ices from silver cups.

Inside the main room, there is an ornate gaslight in each corner. They are kept in working order, and like everything else there they are well dusted. It is because of a city ordinance: every public gathering place must be prepared to illuminate itself adequately in case of no matter what kind of blackout of electricity. It could be a riot, a strike, an assassination, a prank, one is informed with a shrug. This tacit recognition of any good café's tinderbox subnature is generally ignored, except about twice a year when new students at the School of Arts, Professions, and Engineering serpentine through all the cafés on the Cours, bellowing in doggedly virile camaraderie and only momentarily interrupting the general conversation up and down the street.

Talk is as steady as the fountains themselves, in Aix. It goes on everywhere, sometimes noisy but seldom harsh. Of course there are many people, at least in the cafés like the Deux Garçons, who never speak more than a word or two to the waiters, or sometimes only make one face or lift one finger to get their accustomed *café* with *croissants*, their noontime *pastis*. But in general there is a good play of sound in the two rooms and on the vast dappled terrace, and certainly no need for a piano, especially one with violin and cello!

In the students' side the noise is loudest, of course, but seldom obnoxious, for the waiters can be as firm as any Mother Superior if they see that the other staider clients are displeased.

This is most probably one of the mysterious reasons why the 2 Gs remains through Invasions and Occupations and Liberations and even Insurrections the focal point of public life in Aix . . . along with its never flagging cleanliness, its skilled if basically emotional waiters, its imperturbable cat . . .

It is the first and last café of my visible and invisible life in that town.

I seemed to go there like a homing pigeon, the first day I was in Aix. I walked through dry bright August streets, along the Boulevard du Roi René and the Rue d'Italie from our hotel, with my two bewildered and curious children. I did not know what direction I was taking. We came upon the benign fountain of King René, with the green tunnel of the Cours stretching westward, and it was more like a flashing vision of promise than any I had yet seen.

There was a big café terrace on our right. We sank onto and into it. The little girls drank lemonade and I beer in complete and sudden ease: we were in the right place at the right moment, and we knew it would last.

For more than three years, on and off, this place nurtured various phases of our varied souls. It was a solace and refuge from everything: wind and blasting heat and rain, disasters, anxieties, too much noise or silence. It was protective of us, yet always aloof, able to do without us.

Once I ran from Madame Lanes' apartment at almost midnight to its telephone, to call a doctor for a suddenly sick child. The Rue Frédéric-Mistral was cold, dark, twice as long and quiet as usual. The owner took the coins from my fumbling hands and dialed for me and soothed me.

Often my girls went there for hot chocolate or a cool silver cup of lemon ice when they must wait for me and could not find me, and the waiters welcomed them gently. Often we hid there, singly or together, from things or people we could not cope with for the moment, and even more often we met people there whom we loved dearly, for that day or forever.

The last time we lived in Aix we walked up the Cours for

almost a year, often before winter daylight, to breakfast in the
Deux Garçons' bright warmth, still smelling of hot suds and
wax, before we went our ways to schools and work. Before
and during and after market we would meet there on the terrace, and talk with whoever stopped beside us, and usually
stay longer than we'd meant to, in a kind of daze of well-being
and satisfaction about the rhythm and beauty of the town, the
people, the fountain music.

We knew about Emile's Vespa repair costs, and Léon's ter-
magant wife, and François' prostate trouble. We borrowed
money now and then from the boss, and got advice about
movies, elections, and even the National Lottery, without ever
hearing or even being offered a word of local scandal, of which
there was a great deal that even we strangers knew about.

The cat under the fern on the dead circular radiator became
a friend during the school year we ate breakfast there, and
came, except for an occasional day off for having kittens, to
eat bits of *croissant* which we would put on the very edge of
the table for her to take daintily between her teeth, from
where she waited on one lap or another, and then to eat on the
spotless floor. She had three and sometimes four large litters a
year, and often that heavy plunge from lap to floor worried
us, but unduly; she preferred that pattern no matter what her
bulk.

The most surprising thing about our tacit acceptance as more
than tourists, less than townspeople, was the way the old advo-
cates and judges who were habitués of the 2 Gs when the
Court of Appeals was in session began to nod very discreetly
to us, after a few weeks of inspection over and around their
papers. Inside the café, that is: outside on the terrace they
never recognized us socially.

There was one famous old judge who breakfasted there
every morning, Court or not; he was a heavy wheezing man
with a gray face, who always put five lumps of sugar into the

small cup of *espresso* the waiter set before him, and ate four of the round buns stuck with sugar crystals. Anne and Mary liked him, silently of course, and feared that he might be diabetic and lonely.

His wife had died, they decided. He lived in a fabulously beautiful apartment, early eighteenth-century of course, attended by a devoted but autocratic old woman who had been his wet-nurse. I, on the other hand, thought his wife had run away from him, because he apparently enjoyed belching at sonorous length after his breakfast, as he folded up *Le Temps* and *Figaro* and pushed them clumsily into the pocket of the huge shabby coat the waiter held for him. I was crass, Anne and Mary felt.

One of the strangest moments I can remember in the Deux Garçons was on the fourth day of the Insurrection, in April of 1961.

The café papers did not arrive. *No* papers arrived in Aix, when they always had before.

There was a kind of numbness on the faces of the usual customers in the café. They looked with apathy at the coffee in front of them and ate almost none of the *croissants* which generally were gone by eight o'clock. They sat silently on the benches along the walls under the mirrors. The actuality, the astonishment of the terrible fact that Aix was cut off from Marseille was like stone, a stone going into them instead of oxygen, or perhaps a kind of novocaine or liquid anesthetic that they were absorbing.

Finally a stubby unshaven man hurried in with a pile of papers under his arm, to leave the usual three copies at the cashier's desk; and before he had time to turn around, at least five usually staid habitués sprinted out to go to the tobacco shop up the street.

They brought back *Le Provençal,* and their faces were as innocent and shining as those of a prep-school football team.

They beamed like boys, indeed. They leaned over the shoulders of men they usually snubbed, and held up papers across the room in a recklessly sociable way. The Insurrection was, it seemed, broken . . . over . . . past bloody danger. The terrible four days had ended.

A student waved the front page toward his girl who came through the revolving door. "It's over," he called out, this time without being hushed or scowled at by the usually stiff lawyers and *antiquaires*.

Outside, the Cours had never looked more golden-green, more greenly gold.

The feeling grew in us, increasingly strong, that the café itself seemed to savor our ghostly faithfulness, although it was plain from the beginning that we must leave it sometime for our homeland.

Along with a few old-timers like the judge, and of course the boss and the waiters, most of whom had been there for years in spite of an occasional fugue owing to bad livers, unruly motor bikes, or extramarital furloughs, we sat out all the tides that washed through the old place.

We came to know when the American students would leave and the boys from Eton would arrive for their weeks of "language perfecting." We learned to look over the new customers before the plays at the municipal theater, to see what the artists on tour promised in Paris hairdos and mannerisms. We felt the growing excitement in June about the next month of Festival, and then sat out August happily alone, the only old-timers the waiters recognized in a storm, a mob, of Frenchmen on vacation from every place but Aix while the Aixois were on vacation everywhere but Aix, too. We knew the tension in the students during exams, especially for the dreadful "bac."

Carnaval was fun, with a kind of studied unruliness along the Cours and confetti on the clean floor of the elegant old café.

And the best was the Festival, of course: a high restrained excitement, as if everyone were a little drunk on the music of the long afternoons and the splendid nights.

And we were always there, not inquisitive, but very receptive in an almost invisible way.

ii *THE GLACIER*

> . . . my high-blown pride
> At length broke under me, and now has left me,
> Weary, and old with service . . .
>
> Shakespeare, *King Henry VIII*

FOR ABOUT A THIRD of the time we lived in Aix or near it we ate in our own home, and I cooked, but even then we went oftener than we would have in California to restaurants in and around the town.

There was always a good excuse: we were there *anyway*, in from the country for supplies; we must meet a late bus from Marseille with a friend or two on it; there was an important movie or concert that afternoon; the day was too beautiful for us to do anything but stay as long as possible on the Cours. In almost every case the weather was too beautiful to eat anywhere but at the Glacier.

It was at the other end of the Cours from the Deux Garçons, far back from the wheel of the Rotonde under fine plantains, in a little park called the Place Jeanne d'Arc, which it shared with buses, some handsome old houses, and the Police building. We went to its wide quiet terrace the first day we were in Aix, straight down the long green cave of trees from the café, led by the same blissful instinct that had made us choose that place instead of any of the others along the Cours.

All I remember about our first lunch at the Glacier is that

it was long and lovely. We ate well, and almost surely I drank some white wine from Cassis, and Ange, impeccably suave, observed us with a sudden strong sense of protection and sympathy, from all we could ever guess, so that from the moment he first bowed us into our chairs that dappled August noon we felt an easiness of spirit with him. We never had cause either to use or to abuse it, but it was there, and he knew it as well as we did.

From that day on, the Glacier was our main meeting place after school.

Until the two girls got established at Ste. Catherine we seemed to go there several afternoons a week after Mary and I met Anne at the little door from the school into the alley that turned off the Rue Mignet. All the children tumbling out the door would smile and then whisper to their waiting mothers, and everybody would stare more or less discreetly at us, for until Mary got into classes there too, in a couple more months, Anne was the only American girl who had gone there in the memory of that epoch. It was a daily ordeal which we savored in our own ways, and perhaps it is what added the spice to our almost mechanical promenade toward the Glacier.

Once there, the pattern was firmly set: ham sandwiches for the girls, a Cinzano and soda for me. The sandwiches were perhaps ten inches long, a slender slit loaf of bread spread with sweet butter and curtained limply with ham, and there was a fancy "antiqued" thing of several pots of mustard fitted into holes: pink, hot, cool, brown, yellow. Anne and Mary did not like mustard, but it was amusing, each time without fail, to lift all the lids and choose what one might eat if one wanted to.

Sometimes Anne, *petite voluptueuse*, ordered instead of the ham sandwich a silver bowl of *crème Chantilly*, which the boss was proud of because he actually ordered it fresh from Paris twice a week instead of fabricating it himself. (How? Perhaps with a machine it could be done, and the cunningly right amounts of cream, egg white, vanilla – perhaps glycerin? The idea is nauseous.)

It was fortunate that common sense and Mary's entrance into Ste. Catherine combined to interrupt this gluttonous habit of ours, for gradually I was drinking two vermouths instead of one, and Mary too had switched to *crème Chantilly*, and the daily chit was using much more of my feebly kept allowance than it should.

And suddenly it was winter, and no fun any more to sit alone and shivering on the Glacier terrace: no more babies in their prams and dogs on leashes, no more sweet dusty sunshine, no more tourist buses to unload fifty-eight English people to visit the restrooms and drink tea in precisely twelve minutes and then head for Nice or Lourdes.

When the buses stopped, Ange took the afternoons off, and the woman in the toilets disappeared until Carnaval in February. She interested Anne and Mary because she had a face almost as flat as a Pekingese dog's, with prominent eyes and only two delicate little nostrils to show where her nose should be. She was very kind to them, and probably liked them because they looked at her with such obvious pleasure instead of the aversion she must have become used to, at least occasionally in her life.

When we returned to Aix some five years later, they saw her once on the street, for the Glacier had fallen on thinner times and did not keep anyone ever in the cloakrooms, and she suddenly kissed them both and then disappeared, perhaps forever this time. They were a little embarrassed, not because of her kind flat face, but because they were in their teens.

There were many other changes, of course, and it was plain to us, dedicated to Ange, that they all stemmed from the fact that he was no longer there. The old boss had died, it seemed; yes, that fat meticulous little man had simply dropped dead one day. His wife had too quickly remarried: she was an impossibly stylish and pretty woman, who wore tiny shoes and painted her dog's toenails to match her own, and who sat like a bright bird behind the cashier's desk, checking every tray and, we felt sure, giving every waiter her bright eye.

Then there were complications: contested wills, angry creditors, dishonest legatees. Result: the Glacier changed hands, and although I later came somewhat to admire the new boss, he was certainly a far cry from the old one. He did not, to put it charitably, know the business; for a small town like Besançon or even Montpellier yes, but Aix? Aix was unique, "a town of extreme elegance, of *tone*."

And Ange had been, it seemed, a desperate disciple of everything Aixois, and he had lost . . . too late to take up the first offer of the Vendôme to make him assistant headwaiter, which he had proudly refused . . . too late for him to start his own small restaurant of Aixois "elegance of tone."

He grew careless and bad-tempered. There was a row. *Pom, pan, paou,* as Spirou or Mickey Mouse would say . . . and Ange was flatfooting it in some fly-by-night new joint up on the Cours Sextius . . . and the Glacier, we saw and felt, was subtly shabbier and dirtier, and the service was far from subtly changed into a kind of slapdash who-cares fake of its old impeccable dash and sparkle.

One thing that may have affected it and all of us was the traffic, which roared around the Rotonde now in a flood five times as heavy and noisy as before, and much faster. It changed the air and assaulted our sensibilities.

Another was that the new boss had bowed to the times enough to take on a steady procession of chartered tours, for lunch, tea, dinner. Tired people staggered off the enormous buses like sleepwalkers, and were herded firmly into the back room, a dark unattractive cavern used mostly for piles of coats during Carnaval. They ate fast, and for the most part suspiciously. They fought sullenly for places in the two toilets, which perforce were far from tidy, without our flat-nosed friend to care for them.

Across the street at the Vendôme the more luxurious buses stopped, the ones with built-in plumbing and even little bars, but from what we could see, their passengers were just as tired and sullen, even though they were allowed to eat more slowly and off better plates. They all paid for their meals when they bought their tickets in Paris or Liverpool or Hamburg, it seemed, with the service included, so that the waiters showed small interest in either their wants or their gratitude.

All this gave us a dim view of bus tours, in the face of enthusiastic friends who would be tourists no other way . . .

. . . and we could understand why Ange had quit the Glacier: this hurried and basically tasteless serving was not in his tradition. He was a part of the "old way," his friends told us in quick asides as they dashed past us on the restaurant terrace; he could not endure anything else and would die rather than bow to it.

This was perhaps literally true, for once he "accepted" a very good job at the Deux Garçons, and quit in somewhat less than the two weeks his admirers had bet he would last. He could not, they explained almost proudly, adapt himself to *la limonade*, which was their trade slang for café service: the steady trotting with heavy trays, the tricks of remembering who wanted sherbet and who a vermouth-gin and who a *pastis*, the mind always ready to add up a bill, the hand always there to mop off a table, pick up a package, light a cigaret, empty an ash tray.

In five days Ange lost several pounds from his spare frame. In ten, his face was set in a pale mask of weariness and disgust. Then he was gone, and we saw him only about twice more. He wore rough clothes and carried what looked like a carpenter's kit. He was plainly sorry we had met, and we bowed distantly and refrained from the painful immodesty of asking more about him.

iii *THE MEN*

The sum is six pounds, and be pleased
to remember the Waiters.

English Inn-keeper, 1660

OF COURSE, because of our strangely permanent impermanence and our dependence upon restaurants and cafés, we got to know many other waiters in Aix. Some of the things we knew about them were even intimate, but it is interesting that with not one of them did we intrude upon their lives outside their work. If ever we saw parts of their families, about which we seemed to know something, it was when Anne might say that two of François' girls were in Third and Fourth at the Lycée with her, or we would meet Louis with a dashing Gypsy in Marseille and not nod. Indirectly we would know of Michel's jumping out of a second-floor bedroom window with a furious husband after him; directly we were blandly sympathetic with the hazards of his carrying heavy trays with a broken arm . . .

The nearest we ever came to personal intrusion on the extra-professional lives of our waiter-friends was when one of them got badly smashed on his Vespa. We sent a little note of real distress, through the boss at the Deux Garçons: Emile's back and feet had been hurt, and how could a good waiter surmount that? This one did, of course, for he had five children and a stupendous vanity about his work, and perhaps a month after he came slowly back into the café we received a formal recognition of our message, which none of us had ever referred to in person: "Monsieur Emile Joseph Gagnebin-Lenôtre expresses his sincere recognition of . . ."

Most waiters at the 2 Gs stayed there for several years at a time, for it was the "best" place to work and also one of the most demanding cafés in that part of the country. Sometimes, when they finally left, they bought small cafés of their own, near the markets, the bus terminals, the hospitals: they had made good money in *la limonade*. Others had spent it all and took lesser jobs, often in the new small restaurants that were opening and closing during our last stay in Aix, small pseudo-chic places featuring an open grill for steaks, water flowing down a wall of bad abstractionist tiles, imitation Provençal "specialties." We saw the men grow careless and flabby and sly, as they relaxed after the hard profitable years at the big café.

The few who returned to it could not bend again to its implacable perfection, and it was plain that the ones who had remained made it easy enough for them to quit. They had, in a way, been drummed out of the regiment . . . except for Ange when he tried to come back. As far as we ever could see or know, the men at the Deux Garçons did all they could to ease him into their unflagging pattern of speed and skill, but it was too late: he had been a maître d'hôtel for too long, even in such an unstarred and basically unstable restaurant as the old Glacier. Perhaps by now he is picking up a little work on Sundays at country restaurants where people play *boules* after Mass and then eat enormously. He is almost elderly, but I cannot see him as anything but slim, erect, and autocratic, no matter how shabby his jacket nor how outlandish his customers.

One afternoon, soon after we met him, Anne and Mary and I were sitting on the terrace after a good meal. It must have been a Thursday, because they did not have to go back to school. It seemed too foolish and difficult to leave that dusty golden air.

I ordered another *café-filtre*, and watched the great crazy fountain splashing and spouting in the Rotonde, while the children played a restrained form of hopscotch on the boxed paths of the little garden in the Place Jeanne d'Arc. I saw that a fat child, dressed much as they were in a kind of school uniform of pleated skirt and jacket, had joined them and was solemnly hopping behind them. Then they all sat on a stone bench and talked, in the absorbed way possible only to people their age who do not need written languages.

Ange spoke just over my left shoulder, bowing a little as I could see him sideways. "Madame does not mind the children's playing? I can interrupt it."

At first I thought that he meant the three little girls were being noisy, which they were not, and I started to protect them with a snub, but Ange went on, "They are having a good time. The other little foreigner is learning French too."

He bowed again as if that solved any possible problems, none of which I could imagine, and inside the closed glass part of the Glacier I saw him murmuring into the ears of several people at a big table. Plainly he was mentioning me or my girls, for the others looked out into the little garden and then at me.

I could see through the glass that they had degrees of color in their skins, from a soft non-shade whiter than white to a dark bluish brown. There was one woman with the intangible stamp of a teacher about her, and the other wore stylish clothes as if they were veils upon veils. The rest were five or six men of varying plumposity, in clothes that looked English, at least while they were sitting down.

So I looked again at the fat little girl, who sat by now entwined with my children on the stone bench: she was in a skin of soft ivory, and her eyes were ripe plums laid delicately into her face above the cheekbones. When she laughed they seemed to stretch out, two inches long at least.

Ange came back with the check. I was the only one left on the terrace, and he was the only waiter. He looked very swift and sure, with heavy green and gold epaulets on his apparently impervious white jacket. I asked him if I might stay on, while the children seemed so contented with their little friend. Her family agreed with me, I said, for through the wavy glass wall I could see fresh pots of tea being brought to the big table, and clouds of cigaret smoke blueing the air. There was a lull in the traffic. I could hear the fountain.

Ange brought another cup, and cleared off the cloth under it and flicked the table as he said, "Madame is not a racist."

I could not tell if he asked or stated this surprising sentence. It was very flat. I said as flat a no, without bothering to wonder.

"The little girl is an African princess," he said in an impersonal but urgent way. "She is here with her entourage. They live in Beaulieu on the Coast, until the trouble is over. It is quite different for her than for children from certain other countries. Today she is all right, though."

That was my first real conversation with Ange, and I hear it clearly, but with not the same insistence as his voice the night he would lean toward me, his status for once ruthlessly discarded, and look at me with his stern eyes, and say, "Reflect, Madame. Consider what you do."

The first time, the children told me of it: they loved the little girl, and thought it a waste that she must be royal. The second time, only I could know what Ange said . . .

The Gypsy Way

Steal! To be sure they may; and, egad,
serve your best thoughts as Gypsies do
stolen children: disguise them to make
'em pass for their own.

Richard Brinsley Sheridan, *The Critic*

At the east end of the Cours Mirabeau, running between it
and the Place du Palais de Justice, there is a narrow alley
called the Passage Agard.

One enters it from the Cours, a few feet up from the Deux
Garçons, through an arched doorway and then a dark kind of
tunnel which even when it is crowded with bustling hurrying
people seems to have an echo, like all such tunnels in the world.

Then the Passage widens and is uncovered, with old buildings on either side and a kind of intersection with another
narrow alleyway which has a *pissoir* to the right, very smelly,
and usually the sounds of music from the Conservatory which
looks down on it. Then it is covered again and runs once more
like a wider and more orderly tunnel to the Place, where a
big arch and an iron gate open onto the bright air and the
astonishing monument to Mirabeau.

This whole passage is an artery, or perhaps the cord that
connects a mother to her child, feeding it air and blood. Unlike that cord it can be bypassed, but once its uneven, noisy,
smelly crowded path has been learned, that is inconceivable.

In the early 1960s two or three new shops gave its dingy
walls an unexpected elegance, and probably another few years
will see it completely changed. In some ways I hope for that,

for it could be a delightful surprise to come upon it unexpectedly if one did not know Aix, and to find it bright and welcoming. Meantime I liked its confusion and untidiness, and
its steady flow, during the daytime, of preoccupied hurrying
people.

There were several tiny shops, but nobody ever seemed to
stop long in them. They were dim and for the most part
shabby: a secondhand book dealer, not of good books but of
old paperbacks and comics . . . a little shoeshop with some
dusty handmade "opera pumps" in the window . . . a laundry
where occasionally a beautiful old baptismal robe hung to be
seen, washed and ironed for a new Christian. There was one
foodshop with three or four boxes of fruit outside the door,
a tub of black olives, and in the late spring a wire basket of
snails hanging, very silent yet resentful, like all baskets of snails.

At the Palace end of the Passage, under the building that
housed the Conservatory, there was one blank wall where
posters of all the movies and concerts were plastered. The
other wall had the dim but fascinating windows of Monsieur
Colas, the antique dealer, and of the two elderly sisters who ran
"Artistica," a shop filled with Provençal pottery and glass and
cloth and junk and many other beautiful things.

There was also one small café in the Passage, where occasionally someone played a jukebox, always of Spanish or Italian
dance music. I looked in as I passed: young restless men, perhaps workers in their town clothes, waiting for jobs. It was a
pleasant little pub, but I never went in. I was sure there would
be politeness while I was there, and then the normal sounds
when I left . . . talking, the jukebox again.

The typewriter shop on the Rue Fabrot was remodeled, and
when I was there one day to get my repaired Olivetti I was
pleased by the new windows which opened onto the Passage.
They gave an airy light feeling to the little shop, and made me
hope that eventually the Passage might be modernized in ways

to match the new shoeshop onto which the windows looked. It might be a project somewhat like the one that, over a period of a few years, changed Maiden Lane in San Francisco from a sordid alley to a stylish and even merry passageway between Union Square and the next street down.

There, of course, the general ill repute of the neighborhood had to be combatted, and it took persuasion and daring to get fashionable shops to install themselves. In Aix, however, I was unconscious of any such shabby connotations to the Passage.

I have been in Aix for several years, off and on, but I still do not know if there is any special part of it where prostitutes are lodged. Indeed, I have walked about at night, sometimes through the narrow streets which a few years ago were occupied mostly by the "Arabs," and only once have I seen a girl soliciting openly. That was not long before I left in 1961, and on the corner of perhaps the most stiff-necked and respectable part of the Old Town, Rue Cardinale and Rue du 4 Septembre. I saw her only because a friend was staying at the Roi René and I used to walk her back there at night.

The girl astonished me. She was like a still from an old German movie, one made by Emil Jannings or perhaps about the time of Dietrich's *Blue Angel* . . . thin, young, wearing the traditional tightly belted trench coat, leaning with wary grace and splayed blond hair against the wall under the street light.

Of course I saw tarts now and then, walking two by two on the Cours. They were almost certainly transient: Aix was not good grounds for them. Most were smartly dressed and rather old, perhaps there for a rest and the baths between Lyon and Nice.

But in the light and dark of the Passage Agard, in the life-stream between the big square and the Cours, everyone seemed in too much of a hurry to loiter for paid love.

Undoubtedly in such a town as Aix, where there have for

so long been students and young soldiers, there are girls working for them. The only open reference to them that I can
remember, for I have not read much about the place nor shall
I ever be able to, is in the little book written by Léo Larguier.

He was a soldier at the barracks then, and he explained why
so few of his comrades went into town on Sundays: "One had
to count twenty-five or thirty sous for lunch and as much for
dinner; six sous for an *apéritif,* ten sous for the bottle of beer
one offered in the afternoon to a big dark-haired girl whom
one met in a bar which was usually turned over to the military,
and then two francs to buy the right to follow her to a tiny
room where she was immediately naked on a dirty coverlet."

Of course all this still goes on, but even in a narrow passageway like the Esquiche-Coude or the more vital Agard, there
does not seem to be the slightest sign of a whisper, a dark welcoming doorway, for any price at all.

Indeed, the only sinister thing I know about the Passage is
what my children told me of it and the Gypsy, long after it
had happened, as is part of youthful wisdom.

It of course was a form of soliciting that the Gypsy did, but
of the spirit more than the body. And when it is a question of
real Gypsies, perhaps it is best not to question at all?

They are real, in Aix. There are not many of them left.
But in our own remote way Anne and Mary and I knew them:
the feeling of the pieces of cloth they leave at their shrine at
Les Saintes-Maries de la Mer, the children they have borne
from one scant year to another, the ferocious bravado of them
on the Cours, begging, whining, remaining always haughty.
They go away and then return, in a wave that once known is
always familiar, during the month of April. They gather. It
is for the annual elections of chiefs and suchlike at the end of
May, and for the worshiping and the dancing at Les Saintes-
Maries.

When we first went to Aix, there were wiry, almost stunted

little girls scuttling along the edges of the Cours. The next
April they were bigger, but not much, and with the same sly
mocking manners. Then when we returned we were sitting
at the Deux Garçons again, again pestered by the children but
now complete, completely grown. They were women of
maybe twelve or fourteen years, with the right swing to the
haunches and the bolder gaze. And the next year they were
back, but each with a little baby on her hip or in her arms.
Most of the new ones were towheaded, and there was a boy,
or rather a man of perhaps twenty years, with only one leg,
who swung himself daringly alongside the most boldly begging
girls, and he was without doubt the father of more than a few
of the new Gypsies.

One day I went down a side street and a baby perhaps a
year old stumbled laughingly up a stoop while its mother whispered under her breath to me the familiar "For the love of
God give something to us and bring good luck upon yourself."
The child was covered with sores, maybe impetigo, but was
happy, and most astonishingly blond. I could see his father
laughing too, the bold elated boy with one leg, one crutch,
and several bright birds on his branch.

Neither he nor his covey, though, matched the Gypsy
woman, The Gypsy, who once exerted her own tyranny over
my children, in and at both ends of the umbilical Agard.

She was different from all the others in that she seemed more
beautiful to me, the non-Gypsy. She was taller than most of
the women in Aix, of both our races, and was lithe and slender
in a way that I could understand, although still animal in a
way that I could only recognize with some atavistic resentment and appreciation. She was dirty according to my own
ways, of course, but not so much so as to blur her fine outlines.
She was not dressed in the long swinging skirts that I remembered with a certain excitement from my childhood and the
springtime encampments along the California riverbeds, but

still she was not dressed like us, the non-Gypsy women: her heels were higher, her body was freer, her hair hung with a wilder swing from her small high skull.

She approached us on perhaps the first or second day that we were in Aix, and for almost a year she seemed a part of our daily life there, although I am sure that for weeks at a time we did not see her, while she went on Gypsy errands and pilgrimages.

We were sitting on the terrace of the café. My girls were drinking lemonades and I probably a beer, in the dusty green shade of the Cours on a fine August morning, and there was the Gypsy standing with silent abruptness by my side. She was smiling, in a sidelong sure way we came to know well, partly at us and partly toward the waiters who might chase her off, and partly up and down and all around to see if policemen were looking our way.

"I shall tell your fortunes, all of them," she said.

"No thank you," I said. I felt large and overfed and dull beside her sharp beauty, and I recognized this in myself at once: a kind of intuitive resentment and caution.

"You should let me tell yours at least," she said. "I can see many things about you. I can tell them to you."

"No thank you," I said, feeling even larger and more uncomfortable and wishing a waiter would flap his napkin at her.

The children watched me in a daze of newness. They did not yet speak French. They did not yet know where they were in this world, really, and perforce leaned upon my age and strength with trustfulness and perhaps some despair. I must stay strong and ageless to them, I thought, and I turned my shoulder to the Gypsy and she went away.

Not much later she was back. I felt astonished: I was sure she had been only a fleeting part of the first days in a new town, and not a fixture. The little girls recognized her from far down the Cours, and were disturbed a little because I had already been rude to her.

This time, or perhaps the next, she said, "I know much about you," insistently again. And when I said, "Perhaps. But no thank you," she showed anger for a minute and said sharply, "You have come over many waters, and you will sail on many more," and I laughed.

It was plain that we were Americans, or at least tourists, and so I did indeed laugh, glad to be able to prove her too foolishly obvious for my taste.

She stared boldly at me and then shrugged and walked up the Cours, one step before a waiter motioned to her to go away.

The children said, "You should not have made her angry," and I told them with an impression of futility of how silly she had been to tempt me to a session of fortune-telling by saying anything so banal as that I was a traveler. They looked uneasy.

From then on she never spoke to me, but we always knew when she strolled by. She would look daringly at me, pityingly at the little girls.

Sometimes in other parts of town she saw us and shrugged coldly.

It got so that Anne and Mary would feel she was coming, long before I could sort out her disdainful thin walk from the lesser people. The girls would look pinched, and I would know that somewhere they were seeing her.

Finally they told me that she made The Sign at them, behind my back.

I was astounded, and angry too, but I only told them that she could not possibly hurt them, by Sign or stares or sneers or any other instrument. She must earn her living, I said. She was like the rest of us, made of the same flesh if somewhat more beautifully, raised to eat and drink and sleep like us if somewhat more wildly. But she did not, I said firmly, know secrets or ways that would hurt us, just because I had spurned her foolish suggestion that she did . . . and her hints that she could . . .

Once, I told the children in an attempt at coziness, I had seen her sitting beside a man in an enormous army lorry left over from the Occupation, and she had nodded and smiled at me like any farm-wife . . .

"It could not have been she," they said in a dour flat way.

A little while before we had to leave Aix the first time, about a year after we met the Gypsy, we saw her do a most dramatic thing on the Cours. I have mentioned it two or three times since then, and Anne and Mary have remained silent as if under instructions, but when it happened they were as intense as bees and then hid their faces.

It was a bright twinkly day under the plantain leaves, and we sat as usual on the terrace of the café, I looking up to the head of the Cours at the statue of the Roi René. I saw the Gypsy walking down toward us, a gaunt Samothrace with her clothes fluttering against her and then back. She saw me clearly too, and her smile was more a sneer than ever.

Then it was as if she disappeared: she rolled sideways and onto the pavement and under a car, just like that. A serpent into the grass, she was gone. Two policemen walked by. When they had passed, she slipped in one almost invisible movement out on the other side of the car, and without a shake to her fluid garments or her long dark hair she was upright and scornful once more.

I have never seen anything faster or more pure than that swift casual hiding. I was moved by it, and I remarked to myself how pale the children were. They had already admitted to me that now and then they had seen the Gypsy as they came home from school and that she had made the Sign at them, but after I scoffed they said no more, and in spite of a few things like their obvious blanching at this fantastic roll under the car I was not really conscious of their fear of her.

It was not until years later that they told me about the Passage Agard.

It was when we returned to Aix, and they were almost full-grown. They said, in a reluctant way that meant they felt embarrassed and somewhat hopeless about my belief, that she had tormented them when they were little. She would be just outside the school when they left it at six by the side door that opened onto a little alley. She would stand boldly in the light from a shop, until she was sure that they had seen her, a few seconds, and make the Sign at them, and then go swiftly down across the Place du Palais and wait at the archway to the Passage Agard. By the time they got there, though, she would be gone. And then suddenly at the other end, there she would be.

They could not believe it, that she had run the long way around to be standing there; but although they never saw her go into the Passage, there she would be at the far end, smiling.

From what they told me I pieced together her whole scheme, and I believed it in spite of my wish to disbelieve. It was wrong to think evil of Gypsies because they were Gypsies. But I felt quite sure that this woman had been so rebuffed by me that she teased my children with all the nonchalance and skill and perhaps the detached amusement of a cat teasing two moths or two mice. It was fun for her.

Now and then, that first year, when she came up to me to tell me that she knew my future, she never made a sign that all the time she was tormenting Anne and Mary, and they never once betrayed to me that they saw her almost every day and were literally haunted by her. Perhaps if I had not been fighting my own tiny war of vanity, to keep my vow not to capitulate to her first demand, I would have been more conscious of what the little girls were enduring. I might have said, "Oh yes," just to get rid of her. Then she might have left the children alone. But I kept on resisting her, one woman against another, and she kept on appearing to them by the school and at one end and then the other of the Passage.

Of course they tried not going there, they told me finally. But it did not matter: she would be somewhere else in the town, and since they must go past one end or the other of Agard at least twice a day, no matter how they might avoid actually going through it, they seem to have made a kind of dare and gone right on using it, and seeing her in it, and watching her make the Sign at them . . . and not telling me.

Of course, if they had told me, I am not sure what I would have done. I think now that I would have accosted her, and asked her to leave my girls alone. I would perhaps have said, "Please tell my fortune now." I might even have said, "I am sorry that I laughed at you, for I know that you are a wise powerful Gypsy and that you have second sight and . . ."

As it was, I let this slow haunting go on for several months, and it was not until I saw Anne and Mary turn pale, a very short time before we left Aix in 1955, that I sensed something was wrong. And it was not until we returned in 1960 that I learned a little of what had once been happening to them, and then put together my own reasons for it.

We were sitting once more on the terrace of the Deux Garçons, dazed a little about being there, and suddenly one of the short plain little Gypsies we had known as importunate children was standing by our table. I am sure she recognized us, behind her skillful small whine for charity. I gave her some, and as in the other days she slid away before a waiter could come, and I said fatuously to Anne and Mary, "She has a new baby. She must be about thirteen by now."

It was then that I noticed their still stiff faces.

"What is wrong? Don't tell me you still think Gypsies are magic," I said loftily.

One of them said in a flat way, "That was a dead baby. I looked at it, and it was dead. She is in the power of the Other."

"What other?"

"You know, you know . . . The Gypsy. She must still be here."

"If she is here," one said, "I won't ever go through the Passage again. I swear I won't."

And it was then that they told me her teasing, not all of course but enough. I tried to be calm and wise and tolerant, but I felt sickened by what they revealed, of the months of trying not to see her, of running from her, of facing up to her at one end or the other of the narrow stinking old passageway. Most of all I was moved by their careful hiding of all this from me, the careless mother who had most probably caused it.

I flapped about in my bewilderment, and said something dull and senseless about how time passes and how I was sure it was not a dead baby the girl carried. The children looked in a kindly way at me.

"It was dead, all right," they said. "And it was The Gypsy who killed it and The Gypsy who told her to carry it in that shawl to us to ask for *our* charity. She is here."

They were wrong. The baby was not dead. Before we left again it was a strong blond little boy, and one morning I put two coins in its filthy hand while its mother, great again with child, smiled a radiant and rare smile at me. And although my girls and I looked both openly and sideways, we never saw even a shadow of that woman I had once laughed at. I watched Anne and Mary, and sensed her weight gradually lighten in their spirits, and while I always thought of her when I went into the Passage Agard, and knew that they did too, I felt little more than bewilderment, by then, at the unknown powers, the ancient secrets, of that beautiful woman and the race behind her.

Why did she bother with us? Surely other Christians had mocked or spurned her or even laughed at her approach? What made her use my children, *mine*, to point out our great differences? Or did she? Was it not perhaps an emotional gambit for two little strangers to pin their loneliness upon a shadow beckoning to them, making the Sign?

But what Sign? What did it say? Once I thought I knew. I have never asked. And by now I am not so sure . . .

The Foreigner

I do desire we may be better strangers.

Shakespeare, *As You Like It*

THERE are myriad facets to invisibility, and not all of them reflect comfort or security. Often I have been in pain, in my chosen role of The Stranger. Just as often I have counted on being so, and was not. Learning to be invisible has, of course, some moments worse than others. Perhaps I felt them most fiercely during the first months of my stay in Aix in 1954. I was alone in Europe for the first time in my life really; always before I had been the companion of someone well loved, who knew more than I did about everything, even things like tickets and monies. I had been younger, too, and full of confidence. Now I was single, with two small daughters, and a world war and some private battles had come between the two women of myself, so that I felt fumbling and occasionally even frightened.

Perhaps it was a little like learning to walk again: I must try hard to trust my weakened muscles, my halting tongue, and most of all the dulled wits in my graying head, so that my children would not suspect me and lose confidence. Once I got them into the dubious haven of "family life" with the Wytenhoves, I faced the unfamiliar prospect of long days which were my own responsibility. I went at it doggedly.

I could count on two or three walks across the Old Town to see Anne and Mary as they got out of school at noon, and then in the late afternoon. We would go to the Deux Garçons or the Glacier together for an ice or a sandwich: that would take two hours in almost every day.

Then coffee and reading in bed would use another half-hour or so each morning.

Slow roamings took another two hours or three . . . drifting along the streets to listen to the fountains and ruminate upon the proportions of the rose-yellow façades, three-to-six-to-nine, and the cornices, and the corner Madonnas, and the caryatids turning breasts and backs, male and sometimes female, to my gaze; and the open markets in three squares and occasionally along the narrow streets; and the libraries and museums: all these accustomed me to my invisibility.

Only occasionally did this pattern desert me, for a few moments of sharp loneliness which had nothing to do with my outer life, for I was received everywhere with the dispassionate courtesy of the French people. Friends of friends had sent introductions to me. Ladies of different levels were generous to me and helped me find lodgings and apples and knitting shops. I soon knew where to go for different kinds of books, and early learned the trick of roaming through the dime store, Monoprix, when I knew what something looked like but could not find the word. Paper clips, I learned from a delighted clerk, were called *trombones*, because that is the way they are.

All these warm details of my attempts to be independent of my own self were heartening, but could not ward off forever the flashes of complete aloneness, which I came to watch for as warily as any lost hunter. One danger for me, I soon found, was irritation, exasperation, impatience. I often felt them, not for myself in the main but for the people I was coming to know.

It sometimes seemed unbelievable to me that mature men and women who had withstood all the trials of wars and invasions, imprisonment, grief and hunger could continue to be stupid. Stupid they often were, no matter how tutored or naturally intelligent.

At times there seemed to me to be no order in their actions, but only a fumbling confusion quite separated from what they must surely know instinctively. Such waste of human spirit, I would groan, when I watched Fernande stumbling through ten hours of unthinking labor for what might possibly need one hour, just because that was the way her mother and grandmother had done . . . or Madame Lanes long after midnight, her face drawn with fatigue, secretly darning her white gloves for tea the next day because no lady had ever worn beige gloves or black gloves at four o'clock, in public, in Aix, winter or summer, cold or hot . . . or people hurriedly carrying one small pitcher to the fountain five times before lunch, instead of two small pitchers or even two large ones in one or two trips.

It hurt me to see this senseless extravagance of the strength that even some ten years after the last Occupation was plainly drained in all these sad wearied people. It was not brisk efficiency I wanted for them, but I could not help feeling a kind of cosmic exasperation at their stubborn clinging to patterns which had long since been improved upon. Sometimes it seemed to me that the women I came to know in Aix felt an apparently voluptuous pleasure in exhausting themselves with archaic ceremonies which taxed them almost past remedy.

The meals at Madame Lanes' were a good example of this, with their intolerable changing of plates and silverware and their dutiful chatter. Behind it, I knew of the dismal skullery kitchen with its inadequate dribble of cold water and its diminishing stock of chinaware, and its desperately thin larder. I knew of the frantic scribblings and figurings for each day's market list, and of the hurried scurryings through the town to find beans or even bread a few cents cheaper. I knew that the wine in the fine glasses was watered to its limit. I knew that

the current slavey's eyes were swollen because the cook had
hit her for having an epileptic seizure between the third and
fourth laborious courses.

And always Madame Lanes was imperturbable and gracious,
and did not push us genteelly out of the drawing room until
ten at night, when she would firmly close the door, groan once
or twice, and then sit down to the game table, to attend to her
accounts until time to fall onto the little divan she kept half-
hidden behind the well-polished grand piano (every other bed
in the apartment was rented, to keep up this desperate gentility).

All this impinged upon my spirits in an occasional but
dangerous thrust of world-pain, especially in the first and most
solitary months of my new role of invisibility, and I must go
raging out into the streets and walk with my own ghosts until
we were amiable once more and safely isolated from the confusion of the others.

At first I felt lonely, now and then, because of the language.
I soon got used to French again, although never with the
elasticity of my younger years. Gradually I accustomed myself to the realization that I would never speak the language
as I had always dreamed of doing, and that I must content myself with my blessed capacity to savor it when other people
spoke or wrote it. My conversation was for the most part
devoted to pleasant chitchat with market women and waiters,
but my ears and eyes grew more and more attuned to words,
and often I felt quietly complacent, to keep my solitude in
hand so deftly with a lecture on the radio or a poem from
La Nouvelle Revue.

A side result of this preoccupation with the language was
my keener sensing of my own tongue. I read even the banalities of an American newsweekly with cleared eyes and ears.
I re-read paperbacks like *Brave New World* and Swift's letters
to his domestics with a fresh delight. Harmless drollery like

Cold Comfort Farm became almost unbearably funny to me. I was like a person giddy with a fever, amenable to every drift of meaning. It was a kind of ointment to my creaking spiritual muscles, in those first months of self-inflicted development as a ghost.

As I remember now, I was very conscious for quite a time of being hopelessly and irrevocably an outlander, and more especially an American outlander. This feeling had nothing to do with my own snobbishness. I have never felt any need to apologize for my mannerisms, my beliefs, my accent, or anythings else that betrays my Yankee birthright. Occasionally I have met people of older countries who have seemed patronizing about my less polished reactions than their own, but if they have been ill-bred enough to sneer a little, I have dismissed them as such.

In Aix I came in for a certain amount of the old patronizing surprise that I did not have an "American accent," which I do; that I did not talk through my nose, which I don't; that I knew how to bone a trout on my plate and drink a good wine (or even how to drink at all), which I do. I accepted all this without a quiver: it was based on both curiosity and envy.

What was harder to take calmly, especially on the days when my spiritual skin was abnormally thin, was the hopeless admission that the people I really liked would never accept me as a person of perception and sensitivity perhaps equal to their own. I was forever in their eyes the product of a naïve, undeveloped, and indeed infantile civilization, and therefore I was incapable of appreciating all the things that had shaped them into the complicated and deeply aware supermen of European culture that they firmly felt themselves to be.

It did not matter if I went four times to hear *The Marriage of Figaro* during the Festival: I was an American cultureseeker, doing the stylish thing, and I could not possibly hear in it what a Frenchman would hear. This is of course probable; but what occasionally depressed me was that I was assumed to have a deaf ear because I was a racially untutored American instead of simply another human being.

(Once my ten-year-old Anne came home from the Dominican day school greatly upset because a little girl whose father had been imprisoned when the Yanks occupied Aix said, "Ugh . . . I smell an American." Anne was the only American there, and when she told me of it she said seriously, "I probably do smell a little, because I haven't taken a bath in a tub for quite a while, but I don't smell because I am an American. Dirty American girls smell just like dirty French girls.")

Sometimes at Madame Lanes' I would be hard put to it not to ask to be excused from the table in a silent pet, when she would ask me blandly if I objected to some delicious dish which she had ordered to please one of the other boarders.

"I know you Americans don't care what you eat," she would state, and it was not until I knew her better that I could hear the friendliness in her teasing. "It always amazes me about how little you notice flavor and seasoning. You seem to have no definite tastes . . . only prejudices." And so on.

Then she would detail the gastronomical requirements of her other more demanding and therefore more sensitive and worldly boarders: the Swiss must have cream sauces with their meat; the Swedes would not tolerate garlic, olive oil or even tomatoes; the English wanted mustard always with meat; the Corsicans loathed cream sauce as well as mustard, but could not subsist without garlic, olive oil and tomatoes. Furthermore, Frenchmen from different regions must eat their native dishes and follow their set table-habits. All this was in exciting and glamorous contrast to the sterile monotony of American tastes: we apparently cared nothing at all for the niceties of palate.

And so on.

And so on.

No, I would rage silently. No, we crude Yanks are too polite, too well taught, to demand Boston baked beans or tamales
from a French hostess. And I would smile politely, and curse
the forthright boarders from Stockholm and Ajaccio, and enjoy what was set before me, for it was good.

Gradually I stopped my secret flashes of exasperation at the
table, and knew with an increasing awareness that there were
indeed many areas of perception where I would always remain
innocent, at least more so than a person of an older wearier
race could be. It became a strangely satisfying thing to know,
on the other hand, that there were so many things I could and
did appreciate, for which people like Madame would never
credit me. It helped me to live alone from them, which I had
to do anyway.

My outward blandness with Madame Lanes became increasingly sweetened with a real affection and an understanding of
her veiled mockery, but occasionally in Aix I decided swiftly
to wipe out this or that sneering person from my life and
thoughts. It was as satisfying as discarding a rotten apricot
from a bowl of fresh fruit, or lopping off a dead branch from
a healthy tree. I had no personal feeling about either them or
my ruthlessness; I did not care if they found me, the quiet
perhaps colorless woman, unperceptive and oafish. I did care
that I was thought to be so because I was an American . . . and
when this was made plain in an ill-bred or stupid way, I simply
eliminated the culprit.

Once, for instance, I was introduced through friends in
Dijon to a very important and in some ways charming older
woman. She gave me valuable advice about finding a good
family for my children to stay with . . . things like that.
Finally she asked me to have lunch with her and a few people
who might be interested in helping me with my French, which,
she assured me smoothly, was already past any real need for
improvement.

The apartment above the Place des Prêcheurs was beautiful, one of the long airy waxed places that seem to exist only in old French towns, from Paris to Bordeaux to Strasbourg to Marseille. Tall windows looking into the green boughs, curtains drifting over the polished floors, books everywhere, noble armoires lined with padded Provençal cottons: it was a harmonious simplicity, where only man was vile.

My hostess was a short hearty woman, married late in years to a much older man, a retired colonel who mumbled distantly as he came into the drawing room, where a tiny fire burned in the marble hearth and the windows shook a little now and then from the great organ in the Church of the Madeleine next door, playing for a noon Mass.

There was a fire in the dining room too, made like the other one of the five-inch twigs I was soon to grow used to as the only heat in my room at Madame Lanes'.

There were three other guests, two near-mute assistant teachers from the Lycée who might possibly consent to exchange conversation with me once a week, and a red-headed tall thin Englishwoman with a deliberately throbbing bass voice and department store tweeds, who spoke nothing but schoolgirl French to me and often passed me later on the Cours without nodding, pretending not to see me.

At the table I sat next to the Colonel, who ate steadily. He was very senile, and unbelievably obscene in a quiet way which he knew nobody but I could hear. Now and then he would glance slyly at me through his crumbs and driblets, and murmur an invitation straight from the walls of Pompeii, and then chuckle as he popped a whole chestnut tart into his sagging mouth.

Gradually I came to believe, almost frantically, that my hostess had hated my old friends in Dijon since her first college days with them, and that now she was avenging herself, on me, for their greater worth, their brilliance, their strength

and bounty. I was her victim. It shook me. She shook me.
I could feel my inner head flapping back and forth on its neck
like a rag doll's as she battered me with her merry little
chuckles, her understanding glances.

"Tell me, dear lady," she would shriek down the table at me
with a comradely twinkle, "tell me . . . explain to *all* of us,
how one can dare to call herself a writer on gastronomy in the
United States, where, from everything we hear, gastronomy
does not yet exist? Explain to us, dear self-styled Gastronomer,
to us poor people of this older world . . ." and so on.

And so on.

The other guests smiled or snorted genteelly, according to
their natures, except for the Colonel, who stuffed more
sweets into his toothless face. It seemed the longest meal I had
ever endured, and its rich tedious courses bit like acid inside
me, metamorphosed by anger and ennui.

"And now, dear lady," my hostess would sing out gaily,
"now that we have eaten this little French luncheon, so simple
but so typical of our national *cuisine*, tell us just how you
managed to invent such profitable fiction about one of the
sciences, when even Brillat-Savarin could not! We await your
dictum!"

They would lean forward obediently at her signal, the two
girls stunned with food and fear, the Englishwoman rigid with
snobbish inferiority. The Colonel would belch and finger his
fly under his spotted napkin. I would stiffen my mask and
steady my voice behind it, firm in my ruthless decision: I
would never speak anything but a civil good day to this person
again.

The next day I sent her a huge box, shaped like a coffin
woven of reeds and twigs, filled with the most beautiful
flowers I could find in Aix, fresh from the gardens of Nice.
It was my private funeral piece for her.

All this was good for me. It made me accustom myself to

acceptance of my slow evolution as an invisible thing, a ghost. The art of silent anger strengthened me, and as it changed to tolerance I felt even stronger.

The catharsis of pain, I reassured myself sententiously: it is purifying me with all this anger and exasperation, and it does not make loneliness intolerable, but rather betters it. Or maybe, I occasionally confessed, it simply diverts my attention?

Perhaps it was better not to try to remind myself that to the Aixois I was and would remain, no matter how well they might come to know me, an outlander, a tall, middle-aged well-bred American, just as irrevocably as I might have been a Swede or a German or an Italian, except that unlike older nationals I must face always a basic racial naïveté, rather as a callow young clerk in the diplomatic corps must face himself as such in the company of consul generals and ambassadors. I must remain impassive. Inside, my growing ability to be alone would protect me and keep me from being arrogant.

This certitude has, ever since, been of great comfort to me in thin moments.

17 Rue Cardinale

> . . . the empty perspective of the old
> street, austere and patrician, where a
> delicate little Virgin, high in a corner
> niche in the lacy leaves, bends her head
> to point out to her child the pictur-
> esque needle of the fountain of the
> Four Dolphins, like a musical toy to
> lighten the lazy hours and charm the
> stillness of this discreet and provincial
> neighborhood . . .
>
> Louis Gillet, *Treasures of the*
> *Provincial Museums: Aix*

i

IN most college towns in America there are widows of professors, and even retired female teachers, who hold on to
their emptying family homes by renting suitably discreet lodgings to other people in their own social and intellectual strata.
This is a blessing, sometimes dubious but basically essential, to
almost everyone concerned. Well-run faculty clubs are few,
and most people past thirty feel self-conscious in college
"unions," even in the thin disguise of graduate standing.

As far as I know, though, France has a much better climate
than the United States for people who must find lodgings with
another congenial family. On every social level board and
rooms are offered, usually with discrimination, to people who
inevitably gravitate to their own chosen patterns, whether
they be traveling salesmen or nuclear physicists.

In Albion, Michigan, or Whittier, California, Dr. Doke's relict courageously "takes in" one or two boarders to keep the taxes paid on her empty old house on College Street. In France, almost any empty room in no matter what kind of dwelling, from hovel to mansion, is put to use: it helps pay the taxes, of course, and it salves the instinctive guilt any good Gallic citizen feels about waste of food-space-energy, and waste most of all of what can be called the sense of humanity, or more plainly the basic and instinctive need of people for people.

I have lived with several families in France. More often than not while I was with them I fretted and even raged at the strictures of sharing my meals and my emotions and my most personal physical functions with people almost as strange to me as spiders or nesting egrets. In retrospect I understand that they shaped such strength as may be in me as surely as ever did my inherited genes and my environmental mores. Of course they had these to build on, for I did not meet my first landlady until I was in my early twenties.

She was a born Dijonnaise who lived down the street from the University because she liked to rent rooms to students, not because the house she rented was beautiful or otherwise desirable to them. She *liked* students. She liked to feed them and talk with them and play Chopin for them and occasionally sleep with ones who pleased her enough. She did all this with ferocious amusement. She was a kind of explosion in what had been until my first meeting with her a safe insular well-bred existence.

From then on I was aware.

She has been followed by decades of less robust but equally subtle relationships with French landladies. Now I know that I can live almost anywhere, with almost anyone, and be the better for it. This is a great comfort in contemplating the probabilities of the future . . .

First impressions are perhaps not as important as they are said to be, but they are good preparation for what may happen later, and I know that every landlady I ever met was part of preparing me for Madame Lanes, of Aix.

My mother would understand and accept my feeling that this old lady had almost as much to do with my development as did she, and would not ask for any explanation. It is at once an overt admission that I matured very slowly and a proof that people can grow at any stage in their lives. My mother would be pleased that I could still grow.

I was nearing fifty when I first met Madame Lanes, and well past it when last I saw her. It is improbable that I shall be with her again, for she is old and seven thousand miles away, but I feel serene and sure that if that happened I would be the better for it, and stronger to surmount the admiration, exasperation, impatience, ridicule, and frustration that she has always fermented in me.

The first landlady in my life happened as swiftly and irrevocably as a bullet's flight: I went to the students' office at the University of Dijon, the small elderly secretary gave me a list of boardinghouses, I walked two hundred feet down the first street on the right, rang a doorbell, and became part of a household for two shaking and making years of my life.

It was very different, the last time, in 1954.

I went to Aix for six weeks or at most three months. I stayed well over three years, in two or three periods, and partly it was because of Madame Lanes. I found her in a roundabout way, not at all bulletlike.

In my first interview with her she taught me the French meaning of the word "neurasthenic," which American friends in psychiatric circles frown upon, so that I am careful not to use it anywhere but in Aix.

I had not spoken French for several years when I sat in the autumn sunlight in her drawing room on the top floor of 17

rue Cardinale. I shaped my words carefully, listening to my
rusty accent with dogged resignation.

"I have been told, Madame, that occasionally a room is available in your home," I said.

"Who told you, may I ask?" Her seeming question was
politely direct as a police query: TALK, you!

I told her, and her firm rounded old face was as impassive
as a Hindu postcard of Krishna.

"Why do you not stay in a hotel? There are many pleasant
small hotels in Aix," she said, without any real interest but as
if she were telling me to question myself, not asking me anything for her own information.

I took my first lesson, there in the thinning but still intense
September sunlight, in speaking the kind of French that Madame Lanes expected of anyone who addressed her. It was a
test I met intensely and even passionately whenever I saw her
during the next seven or eight years, and even this long since,
my accent in dreams is better when I am dreaming of her.

"Madame," I said, "I am very well installed in the Hôtel de
France, where I was sent by Monsieur Bressan, the concierge
of the Roi René . . ."

"I know him well," she interrupted. "A good man. A very
reliable courageous man."

"He seems so. He saw that I did not like to keep my children in a hotel . . ."

"It is not the life for children. It is also expensive."

"Yes, Madame. So we went to the Hôtel de France until I
got the children into Madame Wytenhove's . . ."

"Yes, I know her. Her sister-in-law's mother occasionally
comes to my Afternoons. Your children will be subjected to a
fairly good accent, vaguely Alsatian but better than Aixois in
the correct sense of the word. Madame Wytenhove has had
a sad experience; her husband died of cancer. Unfortunately
her children speak like Spaniards after living in Spain while

their father was an engineer there, but basically they are fairly well bred."

I felt desperate about my own way of shaping the half-forgotten sounds. "I do not like living alone in a hotel," I plowed on. "It is too impersonal. I miss my children. I hate the sound of the Vespas revving up in the garage on the Place des Augustins. I have no place to be except in bed. I hate to eat alone in restaurants. I feel unreal when I walk down the Cours at night from a movie where I have gone because otherwise I would have to go to bed."

All this suddenly sounded very voluble but logical and necessary to me, and my accent was forgotten in a relieving gush of words I had not used for too many years.

Madame looked dispassionately at me. We were sitting across from each other at a beautiful small chess table piled with her account books, bills, and correspondence, which I soon learned was cleared every night for cards or games. I do not know where she put all the papers, but they were out again in the morning.

"Madame," she said as coolly as any medical diagnostician but more frankly, "you are neurasthenic. Your surroundings are making you so."

I protested, for the English connotation of the word was not at all the way I thought I was. I thought I was bored and lonely but not at all neurasthenic in the dictionary sense: worried, disturbed in digestion and circulation, emotionally torn, tortured by feelings of inferiority.

"Oh no, Madame," I said. "I am very stable. I am very healthy."

"You are not mentally ill," she said. "You are simply moping. I have a small room, cold, ill heated, formerly for a maid, during the time when Madame de Sévigné's daughter used this as her town-house. I will show it to you. It is now occupied. But until it is free you may lunch and dine here."

I followed her across the tiles of the drawing room floor, and down the long dim corridor that split her apartment into halves, one sunny and spacious and elegant, the other small, with low ceilings and cramped dim space, made for servants and filled with people like me who lived there more happily, perhaps, than any varlets had.

ii

TEN YEARS AFTER the Liberation, French people were still steadying themselves. I became increasingly conscious of this the first time I lived in Aix. Anecdotes, some half-laughing and some apologetically tragic, came willy-nilly into almost every conversation, and little marble plaques saying things like *To the memory of six martyrs shot down by the invaders* still looked very new on the street walls. People were defeatist, and basically exhausted.

When I returned, some six years later, there was a feeling of comparative easiness of spirit, in spite of the mounting anxiety about the Algerian problem. Women who had seemed really harried to the point of masked hysteria in 1954, no matter what their social level, were relaxed and younger-looking.

This was true of Madame Lanes. She was on guard when I first knew her, wary but conscious of the fact that she had survived the Occupation (which was really three: German, then Italian, then American) and had escaped trouble in spite of being a staunch worker in the Underground for all its duration.

She was remote and hard. She fought jauntily a daily battle against poverty and rising prices and inefficient servants and inconscient boarders. She was like a tired aging professional dancer who would not dare stumble.

When I saw her next, in 1959, she was younger. A year later she was younger still.

Part of this, I think, was because her daughter Henriette had moved permanently to Paris. Most of it was because she had accepted the new stresses of postwar existence and recovered a little from the strains of war itself. She moved somewhat more slowly, for she may have been well into her seventies, and she used a graceful little silver-headed cane on the streets, but she still supervised the marketing and paid her calls on other ladies on their Afternoons, and went with composure and no apparent shortness of breath up the beautiful stone stairs with their wrought iron balustrades that rose from the street level of the Rue Cardinale to her top-floor apartment.

Generations of boarders had flowed in and out since first I met her, and instead of the cool acceptance, the remote calculation which I had first sensed in her, she seemed, the second time round, to feel a deep enjoyment in them. She was warm, and I could remember, with no regret and with real delight that she had changed, my early despair at ever having her like *me*, Mary Frances, the person who was me-Mary-Frances.

Often during that first stay there I would write home about this unaffrontable detachment. I would talk with my few friends in Aix about how I wanted Madame to accept me as another woman, and not as one more outlander who paid for her food and lodging and took as her due the dispassionate courtesy of the household which was forced to welcome her. Perhaps it is because I too was having to adapt my former ideas of the world to new necessities that I was oversensitive to this attitude of Madame Lanes and her like.

I knew that she approved of me as a person of some breeding, but there was always present an overt amazement that any American could really know how to hold a teacup, how to tell the difference between sixteenth- and seventeenth-century sideboards, how to say *Si* instead of *Oui* at the right places.

I would fight hard not to show my helpless hopeless rage when Madame would introduce me as the only American she had ever known who did not talk through her nose.

"Of course you must have taken many difficult lessons in voice placement," she would say blandly, and when I was fool enough to deny this and to say that both my parents were from Iowa but that I had never heard them speak with nasal voices, she would smile faintly and with heavy-handed tact change the subject. I would go to my room in a fury, and swear to leave the next morning.

This tumultuous resentment of my status lasted as long as I stayed with Madame. I never really accepted the plain truth that I myself could hold no interest, no appeal, for the cool gracious old lady. It was a kind of rebuff which perhaps Americans, very warm generous naïve people, are especially attuned to.

Spiritually we are fresh children, unable to realize that other peoples are infinitely older and wearier than we. We do not yet know much world-pain, except vicariously. Europeans who grow bored or exasperated with our enthusiasm are not feeling superior to us, any more than a group of "senior citizens" feel superior as they watch teen-agers rock-and-roll or do the twist. There may perhaps be a little muscular envy in the oldsters, but there is also tolerance and understanding which the young people are as yet incapable of recognizing.

Et cetera.

Et cetera.

This is the way I talked to myself, in an almost ceaseless monologue while I lived with Madame Lanes. It was good for me. Many things I should long since have known, about both outer and inner worlds, grew clearer to me as I learned that no matter how long I lived nor how many other lives I might be able to cram into my one span, I would never be as old as one of the children in the streets of Aix. I was the product of a young race of newcomers to a virgin land and must accept every aspect of my racial adolescence.

It was soon plain that I would stand a better chance of this with Madame Lanes than with any other of the people of her education and breeding who accepted boarders like me. They were more violently cynical and exhausted than she about the changes in their ways of living and the wounds of Occupation.

Some of them were openly resentful of my ambiguous state. I was too old to be a student, yet obviously not qualified to be a scholar or professor. I called myself a writer, but what did I write, and for whom, and even why? I was obviously middle-aged and yet the mother of two young girls whom I did not even live with. Neither fish nor fowl . . . and in spite of my appearance of respectability I was still an American, which basically meant that I must have been raised on De Mille spectacles, football and comic books.

iii

MADAME LANES, in spite of her deliberate detachment from her boarders as people and her overt acceptance of us as financial necessities, was unswervingly courteous and thoughtful. She remained unruffled through the maddest domestic upheavals, which occurred more frequently in her house than in any other place I have ever lived. She remained in full control of herself, a real lady, even at midnight with a maddened serving-girl whooping through the hall and down the corridor with her brain wild with nightmares of what the invaders had taught her. There was never any feeling of hidden frenzy in the old lady.

This was not true of other women I met, that first time in Aix.

Now and then, when I went back to Aix in 1959 to live again, I saw some of the people to whom I had been introduced just ten years after the Liberation, and I thanked God that I had made myself stay with Madame Lanes. She emerged from my memories as an unruffled monument of dignity and wisdom, whereas much that I had first felt about her fellow-landladies was plainer than ever on their ravaged proud old faces.

One, a Madame Perblantier, was their archetype. Her name was given to me by the head of the Girls' High School, a friend of an old friend from Dijon. Madame Perblantier would take two or three guests into her home. I should arrange an interview with her. I did.

Then I fled her, deep in sadness and depression about what had happened to a countless number of good French women.

She lived on the Avenue Ste. Victoire in a big house, nondescript from the outside, flush with the bleak street, very much like Spain. Inside, all the living rooms, the bedrooms, and the dining room faced toward the southwest onto a beautiful garden that descended gently to the edge of a little tributary of the Torse.

Inside, the house sparkled with that particular waxen clutter of the upper French bourgeoisie: varnished cabinets filled with Sèvres teacups; fans spread out in crystal cases; embroidered footstools from faraway military campaigns; a few minor etchings in recognizable styles from the eighteenth century, speckled in their heavy frames. There were flowers. The sunlight poured in through the beautiful windows, and stripped Madame's face like a scalpel, seeing viciously into the essence of her, the skin within the skin.

She was, like most of the other women of her class, used to a much easier life and was now accepting bitterly, bravely,

Fontaine d'Albertas

with muted noisiness, the new ways. Probably she was raised as the child of a high official of landed if discreetly small gentry. She had inherited or been given as dowry this large elegant undistinguished house, with fireplaces and back-stairs and all the other necessities of well-run domestic slavery; and now the rooms were almost empty of family, thanks to death and taxes, and there were no more slaves.

In a kind of insane denial of reality the women like her (many of them saddled with senile husbands or horribly mutilated sons or unfortunate grandchildren kept as much as possible out of sight), these exhausted women, in background very much like my own aunts and their friends, tried to keep their homes running for "paying guests." They tried, and doggedly, to pretend that it was really intimates they were sharing their homes with, and kept them bathed in an utterly false atmosphere of well-being and charm and interesting meals.

Madame Perblantier invited me to come to dinner, for a kind of mutual and of course unmentioned inspection: perhaps I would *do?* I arrived (Madame Lanes had approved my invitation in a discreetly noncommittal way in which I could sense a tinge of professional curiosity) bolstered by an armful of flowers which were accepted almost absentmindedly, as if of course anyone would have known enough to bring them.

The evening was ghastly, because Madame, like all the other women of this level whom I had met in Aix, was incredibly stubborn and brave and wasteful.

The dinner was in its way as elaborately presented as was every meal at Madame Lanes': plates changed from four to six times, with the gold fruit knife laid this way and not that way over the steel cheese knife and the pearl-handled fruit fork, even if it took some three hours, twice a day, for the retarded or deformed little maid-of-the-moment to stumble around behind us and then finally serve the beautiful artfully mended bowl of grapes and pears . . .

After the endless ritual of coffee, Madame Perblantier sat like a death's-head, her eyes frantic and her speech witty and stimulating, and she and I knew, but nobody else seemed to, that she had been up since before daylight dusting the countless opulent gimcracks and waxing the beautiful tiled floors; and that she had gone halfway across town to the open-air markets and carried home heavy baskets of carefully chosen and delicious fruits and vegetables, and flowers for the sparkling rooms; and that she had supervised the laundry and had done part of the cooking and all the planning.

She was dying, literally dying of fatigue, I thought . . . and years later she would still be dying of it, although much less plainly as the strain of the war faded.

Her pettish elderly husband, sneering with thinly veiled ferocity at something she twittered about Montaigne or Voltaire to the young American engineer . . . the two English girls tittering over their cigarets behind the Directoire writing table . . . the old poodle going desperately into the corner and making a mess on the tiles because always before that there had been a *valet de chambre* to trot him out before bedtime and now Madame was simply too bone-weary to do it (and dared not ask it of her embittered feeble old husband, who had never been himself since his legs had been broken in several places during an "interrogation" in the War) . . . the sound of the slavey's feet shuffling heavily between dining room and kitchen with piles of dirty dishes, down the long corridor toward the last-century sink . . . the beautiful flowers: there we all sat in the luster of this insane bright shell, and I felt a child's fear and dismay.

I was caught with a blind woman, fighting with courage and stupidity to hold on to shadows.

I returned with eagerness to the imperturbable remoteness of Madame Lanes and her pattern, which suddenly seemed less mad to me, although still criminally wasteful.

Instinct perhaps guided me, for surely when I saw her, years later, she had survived it with enrichment and was younger in spirit than before. She permitted herself to smile with a real gaiety, and to make mischievous but gently amusing comments which before had been only malicious.

iv

JUST AS THE waste of human energy in the upper-class landladies of Aix depressed me, so did their deliberate self-dramatization exasperate me. It made me feel like a bland phlegmatic "Northerner," I suppose, a cow caught in a flock of darting swallows. It seemed ineffectual, and actively stupid, to make such mountains and caverns out of trivia: screams, shrieks, vituperation, tears, passionate embraces of reconciliation were the daily music at Madame Lanes', over a broken cup, a few sous' cheating on the coal bill, a letter that did or did not arrive when expected.

Through all this hullabaloo Madame herself was the storm center, impassive and impregnable, and as I found myself growing fond of her in spite of her detachment toward me, I decided that she deliberately collected about her a group of near-maniacs which she used as tools: they would scream in substitution for her, and haggle in her place, and strike people she would like to punish with her own whip.

I also came to believe that one reason she kept me at a safe distance was that on the surface at least I too had been schooled to maintain something of her own calm and detachment.

All the time I lived there on the Rue Cardinale I floated on a hysterical flood of personal clashes which involved the boarders, the servants, the tradespeople, Madame's one child Henriette, and even the cats, who were perhaps the only creatures in the apartment with whom Madame permitted herself to be openly tender.

They slept with her on the couch in the salon, which she made up at night into her bed after we had all decorously left her: that way she could rent one more room. Sometimes I would hear her singing and murmuring to them when she thought she was alone, as she attended to her accounts on the card table by the windows.

They were very handsome big cats, always lazy except when Minet would yowl for a night or two of freedom. This always excited Henriette and the maids, who obviously felt more desirable in an atavistic way at the direct approach to sex of the tom. He would pace in front of the wide windows that opened onto the garden far below, and then, practiced as he was, he would station himself by the carved wooden door to the apartment and at the right moment evade every effort to catch or chase him, and streak down the great stone staircase and into the staid street. In a few days he would return, thin and weary, and revert to his cushions and his voluptuous naps.

This blatant maleness, a never-ending titillation to the younger females of the house, interested neither Madame nor Louloute the other cat, and they seemed oddly free and happy when Minet was on the tiles.

Often Louloute would care for Minet after one of his escapades, and wash him gently and play with him as if he were a kitten. He accepted this as his due, plainly.

Once he returned with a bronchitic cough, and everything in the apartment, conversation, bickering, dishwashing, would stop while he wheezed and hacked. Another time was the most dramatic, for all of us: Minet came home drenched and shivering, and that same night developed pneumonia. A doctor was called: for three weeks the tomcat must be confined to quarters, not just the apartment but one small cupboard that led off the seventeenth-century boudoir of Henriette's room.

It was straight melodrama, played to the hilt of course.

It involved elaborate and increasingly smelly arrangements about his functions, all of which had to be attended to several times a day with infinite labor, since the cupboard was at the farthest end of the hall from the front door, and the front door was perhaps sixty broad steps up from the street, and the street was where all the rubbish was left for the city scavenger service.

The little maid-of-all-work stumped up and down the staircase with her face set and her arms loaded with carefully folded newspapers. I held my breath as I passed Henriette's toilette to my room. Conversation at meals hinged largely upon Minet's temperature, his chest rattle, and his appetite. The three weeks seemed longer than usual.

But everyone was relieved to find that the big tom's illness acted as a kind of release for Henriette's neurotic world-anger; she became for that time as serene as a young mother with a puling infant.

v

THE HEAD OF the Lanes' household, after Madame herself, was Fernande, a tall, firmly stout woman of perhaps twenty-eight, who looked much older. She had a big stern face and a pasty skin that periodically turned bilious and yellow.

Her position was strange, as only that house could make it: she was the servant in charge of everything, and yet she was accomplice, personal maid, almost-governess to Henriette and almost-confidante of Madame. She was dictatorial about the continuous changing of charwomen, laundresses, and slaveys, and for the most part she was embarrassingly, mockingly servile with the boarders.

She and Henriette were violently jealous of their somewhat

similar dependence on Madame's tranquillity, and had dreadful rows, screaming and cursing each other behind ineffectually
closed doors. Madame would speak nonchalantly of nothings,
with not a wrinkle on her round noble little face, while the
wild yells pierced the clear air of Aix. At the next meal both
ferocious unhappy women would be bland and released, for
a time at least, from their helpless rage.

A good custom in the Lanes' house was that breakfasts were
always served in our bedrooms. This made it simpler for Fernande, even though it meant ten or twelve trips for her down
the long corridor with trays, and I always thought that it gave
Madame a fairer chance to turn her narrow little bed back
into an elegant couch again, in the salon.

Now and then Fernande would talk with me, as she knelt
in front of my minuscule tile stove to start a morning fire with
the five-inch kindling it would hold. Once she was open, and
with no real bitterness, but only resignation.

That was when she told me how she never went to church
any more, because of the day of Cease Fire, when everyone
flowed helplessly into the chapels and cathedrals of France to
thank God, and she cursed Him instead.

"It was all a lie," she said without obvious emotion, "and
now I am damned with all the rest of us. But I am not damned
for being a hypocrite."

And that morning she told me that she had once had a real
gift for music, and that she had been considered very advanced
in piano when her town was invaded, early in the war. Her
family was killed, but she was kept on in what must have been
her well-appointed home by the commander of the invaders,
who chose it because of the fine concert piano in the salon.
He heard that Fernande missed her music, so with what she
called "relish" he permitted her to sit for hours to listen to
him play. Orders were given that if she even touched her

piano she would be shot, but as one music-lover to another the officer let her silently enjoy his own technique.

I came to know Fernande as a person so far beyond normal despair that she was magnificent. She did not even walk through the town like other people; she strode with a kind of cosmic disgust from marketplace to meatshop to wine merchant, a fierce frown on her dark-browed face, and her firm breasts high. She got a certain amount of money each day from her mistress for all provisions for the table, and if she could buy what was ordered for less than her allotment she was allowed to keep it. She marketed honestly, and we always ate well, although with an insidious monotony after the first interest wore off.

Fernande had a good taste for style and often made Henriette's clothes when she made her own. She also saw to it, in a tactful way, that Madame on her Afternoons or on her formal calls to other old ladies' Afternoons was neatly turned out, in a way unique to places like Aix and perhaps Paris where such rituals are still followed.

Madame's was every third Thursday, and on those days Fernande was the perfect domestic, plainly reveling in her characterization. She was deft, silent, attentive, almost invisible in her correct black and white uniform, which was somewhat like seeing the Cyrene Venus in livery but not at all ridiculous. The little cakes were delicious. The tea, one of Madame's self-indulgences, was of the finest in all Europe or even China.

And usually the supper that followed an Afternoon was pure hell, with sulks, screams, and general bad temper from Henriette, Fernande, Minet, Louloute, and a few of the boarders. Madame remained aloof, a pleased little smile on her lips to remember that the old Countess de Chabot had taken two sandwiches, and that little Lucie de Troubillers was finally engaged to an elderly diplomat from Istanbul . . .

Now and then Fernande would cry out that she could not stand her life any longer, and that she would kill herself unless Madame let her run away. These were tense moments, no matter how often they arrived. Madame would become pale and stern. Henriette would hide in her room and clutch at passersby in the corridor, to whisper about how evil and dangerous Fernande could be in one of her crises, which were decorously referred to as "liver spells," but obviously came at monthly intervals and involved violent headaches, nausea, and tantrums. They grew very dull, in a noisy way, but I always felt ashamed of my ennui in the face of such overt fury, and stolid and undemonstrative and therefore unfeeling.

One time Fernande got so far in one of her threatened escapes as to dress for the street, which was very correctly in hat, gloves, high-heeled shoes. (She always looked more like a young astute madam than a respectable whore.) She was leaving. The household held its breath.

We all heard her come down the narrow stairs from her tiny room in the attic-above-the-attic, which she once showed me and which she had painted to match a postcard of Vincent van Gogh's room in Arles. We heard her go firmly down the corridor to the toilet, and then come back and stop at the salon, where Madame was waiting for her, at her accounts.

Henriette sent the maid-of-the-moment slipping into my room. The trembling little halfwit held a big stylish handbag under her apron. She motioned me to be silent, and without a by-your-leave hid it under some papers on my desk.

I felt like a hypnotized hen, too dazed to protest, and when the door opened after a perfunctory knock which I did not even bother to answer, and Fernande stood stonily inside the room, I sat numbly watching the little maid pretend to dust the top of a table with her apron, and observing that Fernande was puffed out like a maddened turkey hen, with a face as yellow-white as frozen butter. She was handsome.

"Where have you hidden my purse, you filthy sneak?" she asked the maid in a menacingly quiet way.

I felt that she was very dangerous, and was glad my girls were at school, for I did not think their presence would have stopped this, even though she showed them more affection than anything else. She was always gentle with them.

The little slavey lied too volubly, and Fernande turned to me and said flatly, "Perhaps you will help me. I must flee this. I am desperate. I will stop at nothing. If these beasts keep me from taking what is mine, my own money, my wages, I shall kill myself. Here. Now."

It is perhaps as well that I have forgotten what I said, but I know it was ambiguous and basically weak: something about not knowing enough of the true situation to permit myself to be involved in it . . .

Fernande shrugged, looked once at the maid as if she were a slug under a board, and went out. I gave the purse to the maid, for Madame Lanes.

By suppertime that night she was back in her black serving-dress, and she had cooked an omelet with fresh chopped mushrooms which was superlative, along with the rest of the evening ritual of soup and salad and a delicate pudding. I noticed a kind of awed constraint in Henriette and her mother. The little servant trembled more than usual as she changed the plates endlessly.

The next day Madame said, almost in an aside to me when I paid my monthly bill, that the household was quite used to Fernande's crises. They were the result of the Occupation, she said. They were frightening but unimportant, she said. Fernande was a courageous soul if one came to know her . . . "And I cannot go on alone," she added almost absentmindedly.

vi

IT IS UNDERSTANDABLE that a woman fiercely enough disillusioned to curse God, as was Fernande, would find the human
beings she must work with beneath her contempt. This complicated the extraordinary difficulties Madame Lanes faced in
trying to find domestic help in Aix in 1954.

Many people had died. Many more were maimed in one
way or another. The children born during the war years were
not yet old enough to go into service. Worst of all from an
employer's point of view, the few adolescents whose families
were willing to have them go into service as they had done
for decades were handicapped by malnutrition and worse, and
were unfit for anything demanding normal wits and muscles.
Many of them were Displaced Persons, who had been shipped
here and there to labor camps all over Europe, and who perhaps mercifully hardly remembered who they were or what
language they had first mumbled.

The procession of these human castoffs was steady, in the
beautiful enormous apartment on the Rue Cardinale.

Sometimes a maid would last for two or three days. Then
the orders of Madame about what plate to pick up and from
which side, or the ill temper and loud mocking of Henriette,
or the patent disgust of a boarder over a ruined dress or jacket
would send her with hysterics to the kitchen, and she would
vanish into her own swampland of country misery again.

Once there was a feeble old Polish woman. She spoke almost
no French. She crawled slowly up and down the great staircase, carrying buckets of ashes to the trash cans on the street
and loads of coke and kindling up from the cellars on the
ground floor. I had to set my teeth to pass her, but if I had
tried to help her she would have cowered against the wall in
a hideous fear of my motives or my madness. She did not

stay long. She was too feeble even to help dry the glasses
without dropping them.

There were many Spanish refugees in Aix then, and one of
them, Marie-Claude, lasted long enough for me to remember
her as a person instead of a sick symbol.

She was sturdy and almost gay, and she and Fernande alter-
nated laughter and passionate hatred in their relationship, for
they must sleep together in the van Gogh attic, and eat together in the dark dank kitchen, and in general cope in the
most primitive way with all the exigencies of living in an
ancient house with several other people, archaic plumbing, and
gigantesque rooms heated by drafty marble fireplaces or tiny
porcelain stoves, which were set up like teapots every late
autumn, after everyone was either in bed with severe colds
or wrapped in all available shawls, sweaters, laprobes, and
tippets. (For dinner, Madame often wore a finger-length cape
of thick, long monkey fur which her husband had given her
in Monaco in 1913.)

Marie-Claude was cursed with eyes so near blind that finally
they were her undoing. She stumbled willingly about the
apartment, knocking over little tables and leaving a thick film
of dust and crumbs, which fortunately Madame herself was
a little too nearsighted to notice. Fernande stormed after her,
on the bad days, and yelled jokingly at her on the others, and
between the two of them there seemed a general air of fellow-
endurance, until on one of her days off the little Spanish maid
ran her bicycle straight into a large truck, perhaps seeing it
as an inviting continuation of the highway she felt fairly sure
she was on, and a car in trying to avoid the zigzag truck hit
it and then her, so that she was badly crushed. We felt sad.
Her weak eyes were blamed on the hardships of her refugee
childhood, and the motorists were dismissed as men whose
driving undoubtedly had been influenced by the liberating
Yanks and Tommies in '45.

There was one very strong coarse woman who for a time gave at least her physical makeup to the ménage, although Fernande shuddered often and volubly over her foul language. She was completely of the streets, not necessarily in her morals, which were undoubtedly as blunt and sturdy as she was herself, but in her skill at survival.

Every city evolves such people in its most evil districts. They are built in a special way, with bodies like brick walls, cruel eyes and mouths, stunted bowed arms and legs. They are as tenacious of life as it is possible to be in this world, and after plagues, famines, and wars they reappear from the holes in which they have managed to exist. They are not loyal or sincere, the way cats are not that. They are capable of unthinking devotion and tenderness, though. And unlike the more sensitive and highly organized people, they seem almost incapable of being hurt in their spirits. If they have not bred out their own spiritual nerves, they have at least developed through the centuries of travail a thick skin to protect them from weakness and above all from fear.

Louise was one of this breed.

I had never lived so closely with her kind, and I was glad to, for she was not at all unpleasing. Her manners were not uncouth with me, any more than a dog's would be, or a parrot's. Once she asked me if she might take my mending home, and I agreed gladly, but she would not let me pay her.

Like many charwomen in the world, she lived alone in a mean room in one of the ghettoes that every old town hides. Perhaps Aix could admit to more than its share of these sores, many of them sprawling behind some of the world's most elegant and beautiful façades, and I knew the quarter where Louise slept. It was miserable, with litter in the doorway and from far down its dank hall a sickening whiff that drifted out almost as tangible as sulphur gas into the street.

Louise admitted to being sixty-five, Fernande announced

mockingly, the morning there was nobody to help her serve the trays. Where was she? On her way to Spain with a man . . .

Fernande read the note harshly: "Cheerio, old girl . . . I'm off on a *voyage d'amour* . . . he's young and handsome . . . see you in Barcelona? Yoicks."

Madame reached automatically for her list of domestic last resorts, and said mildly, "Perhaps a proof that while there is life there is hope."

Fernande shrugged bitterly and closed the salon door without a sound behind her, but slammed the one into the kitchen with the report of a cannon.

The maid I remember most sadly in this procession of bedraggled broken women was the first I met there. Her name was Marie-Claire, and she walked with the shuffle of an old, weakened, exhausted person, although she could not yet have been twenty. Some of her teeth were gone.

Mostly she was unconscious of the world, so that she had to be told several times to pick up a dropped fork, or close a door. She used to exasperate Henriette to the explosion point, but Madame never allowed her daughter to scream at the little maid as she did at her own mother, and often Henriette would leap up from the table and run down to her room, sobbing frantically. The little maid never blinked at these outbursts, but they left the rest of us less interested in the amenities of the table, which were observed to their limits by anyone in Madame's presence.

One night, perhaps a few weeks after I had moved into my little *chambre de bonne* in the beautiful old house, I was propelled out of deep sleep and bed itself, and was into the dim hall before I knew that a most terrible scream had sent me there. It still seemed to writhe down toward me.

The two American girls who were staying for six weeks on their way to the Smith College course at the Sorbonne

came stumbling to their door. One was weeping and chatter-
ing with shock.

There was another long dreadful scream. It came from up
in the attic, where Fernande must share her bright décor with
the current slavey, and already I was so imbued with the sinister spirit of the big woman that a logical sequence of unutter-
able crimes, crises, attacks flicked through my mind as I stood
waiting.

The door to the salon opened, and Madame was there, calm
in a gray woolen dressing gown and the kind of lacy head-
gear I had not seen since my grandmother died in 1922. I
think it was called a boudoir cap.

There was a great crashing of heavy feet on the wooden
stairs to the maids' room, and Marie-Claire ran out into the
long tiled corridor. She was almost unrecognizable. Her eyes
were alive and blazing, her hair stood out wildly instead of
lying dull and flat, and she moved as fast as a hunted animal
down to where Madame stood. She threw herself on the floor
there, sobbing, "Save me, help me," and a long babble without
words except for the way they sounded in the air.

Both American girls were crying helplessly.

Madame frowned a little. "Tell them to calm themselves,"
she said to me. "Get up, Marie-Claire. Stop that noise. Fernande, come down at once."

Fernande was halfway down the stairs, pulling her hair up
with pins. She seemed as forbidding as ever, but not upset.
She looked at Madame with a bored shrug.

"Here we go again. This is the last time, you understand?"
she said, and gently picked up the half-conscious girl and carried her as firmly as any strong man could, up into her garish
room.

Madame sighed. "We must retire. Thank you for being
patient. That poor soul was cruelly tampered with when she
was a child during the Occupation, and she stopped growing.

Now and then she comes alive, and remembers, and it is terrible. Good night."

In spite of myself I reached out my hand to her arm. Perhaps it was because I was still hearing the first scream and then the second, and I too was shocked. Madame Lanes moved away from me with almost imperceptible reproof, and I turned from her with a polite good night and went along to my room, feeling chastened, reduced to clumsy childhood at my ripe age.

Marie-Claire was sent back to her farm: Madame respected her family as one sorely tried by the state of their daughter, but she knew that no patience from her could make the poor thing into even a slavey, and we started the long stream of nitwits, sick old whores, and dipsomaniacs again . . .

All this intimacy with the raw wounds of war was doubly intense with me, perhaps, because I was alone, and middle-aged, and scarred from my own battles since last I had lived in France. At times I felt myself almost disintegrating with the force of the incredible vitality of the people I was with. They were wasteful and mistaken and hysterically overt, and buffeted as I was by all the noise of their will to survive, I could not but admit, in my loneliest hours, that I was more alive with them than I was anyplace else in my known world. I was apart. I was accepted only as an inoffensive and boringly polite paying guest. But the people who blandly took what they needed from me, which was openly nothing but money, were teaching me extraordinary things about myself and my place in this new knowledge. I learned much from the warped malnourished drudges of Madame's household, that year.

vii

THE PHYSICAL CLIMATE of the Lanes' apartment was almost as erratic as the emotional, with dramatic fevers and chills from everyone and at unexpected times.

One night Minet the tom would let out a gurgle from his suppertime position on the dining room sideboard, and flip off onto the floor. Henriette would scream and rush to pick him up. Fernande would dash from the kitchen across the corridor and cry out, "No no, do not touch him, I implore you . . . He is plainly mad! He will bite you."

Madame would look in a mild way over her shoulder and say, "Leave him alone, both of you. He has perhaps a small stomachache. Fernande, you may serve the caramel custard."

Minet would lie on the floor, while Henriette gobbled viciously at her pudding, her eyes red with tears and anger. We all knew that after dinner she would slip out of the house to the Deux Garçons, the nearest public telephone, and call her vet. While she was thus secretly away, Madame would just as secretly carry Minet into her couch, give him half an aspirin . . .

Henriette herself was, inevitably, a mass of neurotic symptoms. They were of course unknown and inexplicable to any of the countless doctors she had consulted in her forty-odd years of world-sickness. They involved mysteries as yet unplumbed, at least by the medicos, and her fear of psychiatric help was almost frantic.

She had monumental hiccups now and then, which called for deep sedation. She had fits of dreadful weeping. She had dolorous shooting sensations in this or that part of her basically very strong body. All of these attacks were as close to the rest of us as this morning's coffee, and as inescapable, and her medical pattern added a kind of rhythm to our lives.

So did Fernande's periodic "liver crises." They usually meant that for at least one day we made short shrift in the dining room. This was basically agreeable: Henriette became helpful and almost pleasant, and Madame seemed to be less graciously remote.

The laborious and genteel clatter of changing plates and silverware diminished, and we lingered over two or three courses instead of five or six, which would be normal in the twentieth century, even in Aix, but which in the eighteenth-century manner still clung to on the Rue Cardinale was quaintly country-style.

Now and then Madame herself succumbed to human ills, and they always seemed especially poignant to me, for except in dire trouble she insisted upon continuing the serene pattern of her secretly frenzied efforts to keep the family head above water. She would walk slowly to the table at noon, her face suddenly small and vulnerable under her carefully combed white hair, and the conversation would lag a little in her general apathy, but when she finally walked away we would know that she most probably would be there again in the evening, ignoring boldly the fact that Dr. Vidal had told her to keep to her bed.

Once she had to stay there, with a bad pleurisy. For the first and only time the salon was openly admitted to be her bedroom, since there was no other place in the big apartment to put her. I wanted to offer her my room, and finally did so, but I was snubbed with exquisite tact for such presumption: it was a family problem, not to be shared with an outsider.

Any such illness was complicated by Madame's insistence that the household try to function as it would have done fifty or a hundred years before, with five servants or even ten. It was insane. But it served to bring all of Fernande's ferocious courage into full splendor, and we ate in muted satiety while in the beautiful room next to the long airy dining room with the crests over the doors and mantelpiece Madame lay wheezing as quietly as possible.

Once she had a bad attack of sciatica. She hobbled gamely about, but gave up her trips to market. My room was next to the bathroom, and one day I heard her sitting there in a steam tent made of old towels, trying to warm her poor aged muscles, and she was groaning without restraint, although I had seen her a half-hour earlier looking almost as always, if somewhat preoccupied.

It is very hard to listen to an old woman groan, especially when such is not her custom. I had to fight my instinctive feeling that I was in some way her daughter and that I must try to help her. I stood impotently in my little room. Finally I went down the corridor and knocked at Henriette's door.

"Please excuse me," I said, "but Madame is in the bathroom and she seems to be in considerable pain."

Henriette looked coldly at me. "Please do not worry yourself," she said. "She is quite all right. She is simply making a little scene."

I went out for a dogged fast walk through the streets, and stood listening to several fountains to get the sounds of the old woman, and even more so of the young one, out of my head.

One time Henry Montgomery and I, two boarders for the time being, met a decrepit old nanny trying to push an empty perambulator up to the first landing of the house, where the Countess de Chabot was entertaining a niece with a recent baby.

Henry insisted in the firm simple way of most Anglo-Saxon men that he and I help carry the pram on up. The old woman cringed and scuttled ahead, and for several weeks we were somewhat testily teased by Madame about this breach of etiquette: a man of a certain class, and Henry was unmistakably of the top level in his own country, does not assist in any way a man or woman of a lower class than his own.

This was a flat statement. Henry had betrayed his background. I on the other hand as a relatively uncouth American could not be blamed for my breach of breeding and manners, but I might perhaps have learned a lesson . . .

"But she was very old," Henry said flatly.

Madame's reply I can still hear. "I shall never forget one time I was about to cross the Cours Mirabeau. I felt very faint. I leaned against a tree. A kindly woman, very ordinary, came up to me and helped me across the street. It was most good of her, but it was rude."

We said, "But Madame . . . did you need her? Could you have crossed alone?"

"Yes, I did need help, and I could not possibly have crossed without collapsing, but she was not at all of my station, and it was basically forward and pushing of her to offer to help me. I would have preferred to fall where I was, unassisted by such a person."

Henry could appreciate this in his own inverted Scandinavian way, but I was, and I remain, somewhat baffled and very repelled by it. It was a conditioned reflex in the fine old lady, which was as natural to her as her need of a fish fork for fish and a game fork for game.

One more question we asked, before each in his own way pushed the matter into partial limbo: "Would you not have helped this woman if she had felt ill, just as we helped the old servant with her pram?"

"Never," Madame said simply, and we tackled the scallop of veal.

Letters from Madame between my two stays in Aix told of a series of ghastly operations, collapses, and maladies which afflicted Henriette in Paris, but never mentioned her own state

of health, and when I saw her again in 1959 she did indeed
look younger and less withdrawn.

She was perhaps encouraged by the fact that she of all her
old friends was the one who had fought through the strange
profession, come so late in life to her, of being a landlady.
They, she told me mockingly, lived in their moldy shawls,
playing bezique and bridge and tattling over their teacups. She
alone supervised her household, her table, and her social life,
and she did it with a late but appealing jauntiness.

Fernande was gone, in a cosmic huff. She finally ran away,
convinced that Henriette had become the mistress of a man in
Corsica for whom Fernande cooked during one of her summer
vacations. If it was not that, it was something equally fantastic, Madame shrugged.

Life, she added, had been a dream of tranquillity since the
big ferocious tyrant had disappeared, and now things pro-
gressed in seraphic perfection under the thumb of a sallow
cricket of a woman, well-spoken and as sharp-eyed as a ferret,
who "lived out."

It was she who hired the continuing but somewhat more
palatable flow of maids-of-the-moment, and attended to the
meals and the accounts. She coddled Madame. She put up
with no nonsense from the boarders. One had the feeling that
if it was her prescribed time of day to leave the apartment
and return to her own home she would step neatly over any
number of bleeding bodies and be deaf to no matter what cries
for help, but that up until that moment she would do all she
could to be a devoted and well-paid savior. I did not like her
at all, and do not recall her name, but I felt thankful that at
the end of Madame Lanes' troubled life she had fallen into the
deft hands of this assistant.

I was glad for the look of relaxation in my friend's smooth
old face, for by now I could freely call her friend. At last
she had accepted me, perhaps for one of the rare times in her

life, as a loyal and affectionate admirer in spite of my lack of ancestral permanency.

"Madame is originally from Ireland," she would say defensively, when I was the only American among her world-exhausted friends. "Her culture is obviously inherited."

At first this enraged me, but by the last time I saw Madame I was as unaffected by it as an ant by a fleeting shadow. I forgave her. She had accepted me for myself, in spite of any such linguistic protests.

We lunched together in a beautiful old converted château, the day before my last departure. She told me with laughing cynicism of how it had been declared a Historical Monument in order to reduce the taxes, and refurbished by a retired chef and his rich wife in order to profit by the armies of hungry tourists who wanted real French cooking in the proper Crane-fixtured setting. Meanwhile we ate slowly and delightedly, and drank with appreciative moderation, and savored the long reward of our relationship.

Never had there been any display of affection between us, beyond a cursory peck on each cheek, but no more did I feel pushed away, held at cautious distance because of my newness. At last with this adamant old woman I was me, Mary Frances . . .

She took my arm as we walked down the long stairway of the château-restaurant, and when she next wrote to me, in far California, she began, "Dear and faithful friend . . ."

Oath to Asclepius

> . . . some patients, though conscious that their
> condition is perilous, recover their health
> simply through their contentment with the
> goodness of the physician.
>
> Hippocrates, *Precepts*

i *THE PURE ONE*

> A well-trained sensible family doctor
> is one of the most valuable assets in a
> community, worth today, as in Homer's
> time, many another man.
>
> Sir William Osler, *Aequanimitas*

S OME doctors are fine writers, and what they write is often
read, even centuries later. Some doctors, on the other
hand, are very fine doctors, and how they are so is usually
written about by the other people.

Few write much more than aweful praise. It is considered
a breach of human decency, really, to criticize or mock anything as essential as our healers, and the few good authors and
artists who have dared bare the other side of the coin are
classed forever as satirists, caricaturists, and worse.

It is of course easier to lampoon than to praise if one has
the needed amount of scorn and hate in one's pen or ink-
bottle. Even for me, it would be. That is why I think it a
test of my powers to remember and to consider, over and past
my moments of horror and fright, the few real God-sent

healers I have known. They are as rare as hen's teeth, as are real God-sent men of God.

It is a curious thing that although I have lived more of my life in the United States than anywhere else, I have met only two or at most two and one-half real healers in my own country. I have of course met many doctors, mostly men who helped my parents and friends, and in spite of my need for them and my helpless desire to trust them, they have seldom come up to my inner standards. In the same way, I have met only two people who were true men of God, during my life in America.

In other countries I have known one woman of God, in Lugano, and I have sensed the Godly presence, as strong as wild thyme or a lion's roar, of an archbishop in Provence. I sat near him once, and once I watched impatiently as he swept up the aisle toward the altar of St. Sauveur, letting old women kiss his great ring. Then, even though I did not like him, I knew I was in the presence of a spiritual healer.

In the same way, for many years in Aix I had to recognize, at times grudgingly, that Dr. Vidal was, according to every severity of my preconceptions, the realest doctor of my life. This I resented having to do, for it displaced one other man, in California, who had saved my own and many other lives, and who had taught me in every way to know what both life and death could mean. I did not want to divide my allegiance, but it was impossible to ignore the purity of Vidal.

Much of what I know and sense about him is legendary, a myth, a dream, as is true of everything that has ever happened to people like me, the wanderers in space and time. His enemies, if ever they should read my own word-picture of him, would sneer and smile with pleasure at my ignorant betrayal. His friends would contradict much that I myself know, knowing their own versions more firmly.

The doctor, if ever he bothered to read my report on his

right to be called a healer, which in his case may be synonymous with man of God, would shrug and dismiss it as unessential.

I met him once in the hall at Madame Lanes' early in the
1950's. He had been called to look at a young Swede, Henry
Montgomery, who felt worse than peculiar after a month in
Spain.

Being passionately Nordic, Henry had detested the olive oil
and garlic and hot peppers and strange fishy sauces of his
travels, and once free of them had collapsed with a kind of
nausea of relief, especially after he realized that Madame Lanes,
in deference to his country and his own high position in it,
would do her best to serve him the boiled pale potatoes and the
poached livid fish and the bland puddings of Stockholm. He
ran a fever, and tossed in his Louis Quinze bed, convinced that
he had contracted dysentery, or typhoid, or Malta fever, or
perhaps all three.

I went down the long corridor from my room. At the dim
end, a tall strong young man came out of the Swede's room.
He was dressed like an English country doctor, in gray slacks
and a carelessly shaggy tweed jacket, which is to say that he
looked utterly different from the professional men of Aix, who
wore tight dark clothes, usually black, and hats always.

This man's hair was pale brown, and cut like an English
schoolboy's, with a lock over his forehead. ("He is," Madame
said tenderly, later, "a true Northerner, like myself.")

He spoke in a quiet resonant voice, looked keenly at me with
large steady pale blue eyes, also so different from the dark hot
gaze of the Aixois, and ran in an almost jaunty way down the
wide stone stairs, the three deep floors of them with beautiful
ironwork balustrades. I listened to the great carved doors bang
behind him.

After I had asked politely for the diagnosis (and repose, a
bland diet, aspirin for restlessness), I got Madame Lanes to tell

me that Dr. Vidal was the best man she had ever known: so young, so strong, so sympathetic, so wise, so brave.

He had been a great hero of the Resistance, one of the youngest doctors to be able to practice, both in and out of the prisons he was held in. He had escaped a few times, to work underground, always as a surgeon and healer. He had been closest friend with the priest who became Archbishop, the youngest man ever to be named so by the Pope, and they still were like men born from the same father, even to their structure.

This I knew. The two times I came close to the man of God I saw Vidal in him, and when I talked later through the years with Vidal I saw the Archbishop; they might have been one man except that I think the priest had dark eyes. Both of them, though, looked with the same piercing quiet look at everything around them, with a kind of sensitive inner trust that has been rare in my life.

The second time I saw Dr. Vidal was about a year later. My two small daughters now lived with me, in the room where our bilious Swedish friend had lain in his final protest against Spanish gastronomy.

The younger girl, Mary, subjected to a regime of everything destructive to a human liver, especially a reputedly damaged one, had gone into a strange dream. It was increasingly hard to rouse her. She lay quietly, a remote half-smile on her face. At first I thought she was merely tired. Gradually I became painfully uneasy, and at last I ran through the town, to the Place de l'Archevêché where the children had lived for a few months, and asked my friend who had sheltered them to find me a doctor.

I remember being surprised that without hesitation she called Dr. Vidal, for she and Madame Lanes moved on different social planes, and in old towns like Aix they are as clear-cut as layers of bricks in a wall: lawyers and doctors and dentists and even hairdressers go always among the same groups in their various ministrations.

Vidal came within an hour or so, as I sat near Mary's bed. She lay without motion, and her breathing was faint and her face looked very remote and beautiful. I was taking nail polish off my hands, and repainting them, because I was inwardly frantic and must identify myself with inanity.

Vidal opened the door quietly. He was the same tall strong man, with deep eyes that regarded calmly whatever they chose. He sniffed. Then he came surely to the bed, and said in his resonant quiet voice, "Madame, do you recognize the smell of acetone?"

"Yes," I said, thinking he was talking of the strong hint of polish remover in the air. I felt clumsy: I should not have been doing such a vain silly thing while my child lay half-conscious and I sat waiting.

I started to apologize, but he went on firmly, "There is the unmistakable odor of an acetonic crisis in the air. The skin exudes it. The urine is undoubtedly heavy with it. We shall make tests at once. It could be diabetic but is more probably a slowing of the liver functions."

This was of course a hair-raising coincidence, but in spite of the open bottle of nail-polish remover I never questioned Dr. Vidal's judgment, and his treatment convinced me that he had known the odor under the odor, the body smell unmasked by the artificial one. It was slow and quiet, and as right to me as had always been the other doctor's I most admired: careful simple diet, almost no medication, rest, much lemon juice and pure water.

The little girl responded like any healthy trusting animal, and from then on she has known, as have I, how to avoid rich pastries, eggs, milk, ripe cheeses. Vidal also taught her how to recognize danger signals, and said in his almost hypnotically firm quiet way, "You must learn how to be rude politely, and say no."

Several months later Mary and Anne and I were living at Le Tholonet, and it came time to ready ourselves for the long journey back to California on an Italian freighter. Various shots and tests were necessary, and I was pleased to have an excuse to be with Dr. Vidal again: he satisfied me in a good but still subtle way, just as the Archbishop had done, the night I sat near him in St. Sauveur during a concert of Campra.

While Vidal was writing instructions for yellow fever shots, a small medicine kit for the ship, things like that, I permitted myself to enjoy him. I liked the way he sat easily, as all tall men do, at his desk. I liked his detached tenderness, his gift of making me feel reassured and yet held gently off from him, not held off as a female or even a person, but as an object of his care, toward which he must remain ever impersonal and clear-minded.

His offices were on the second floor of a tall noble town-house on the Cours Mirabeau. He lived there too, like most French doctors, with his wife and a growing family of handsome children.

Madame Lanes, who literally worshiped him, dismissed his wife by saying that although she was charming she was "very simple." In Madame's language, that meant that Madame Vidal made no effort to be social and worldly, but was content to devote herself to her family. Over a period of several years I often looked at this "simple" person as she answered the door-bell when the idiotic little maid-of-all-work was busy else-where, and I found her tall, attractive, well dressed, and full of the same courteous detachment as her husband. I would have liked to know her more, but accepted the fact that I never could.

The waiting room at the head of the long corridor which was the family's apartment was furnished with discretion: Pro-

vençal cloth for the curtains and upholstery, gauzy curtains to
mask the big window giving down onto the Cours, a few prints
of *santons*, a rubber plant in a copper pot. The magazines were
tattered and few. Most people who came into the room were
really ill or in pain, and most of them looked poor.

Dr. Vidal's office, behind a door heavily curtained with a
Provençal quilt like an old-fashioned American bedspread, was
even narrower than the waiting room. His plain handsome desk
was by the twin to the other window. They had balconies on
them where in the eighteenth century the visiting grandees
saluted the crowds below.

Toward the back of the office, on the corridor side, was a
kind of cubicle. I never went into it, but assume it had some
sort of table for people to be examined on. There was a low
divan in the office, covered with green Provençal tissue. There
was no sign of any medical paraphernalia except for a shabby
stethoscope on the tidy desk-top. There were no framed di-
plomas on the walls.

Vidal looked up dispassionately at me with his steady eyes.
"How do you like living with the peasants at Le Tholonet?"
he asked me.

I told him we were happy there, living more simply than we
ever had and perhaps than we ever would again. He asked me
what we ate. I told him some of the intricacies of getting food
for our meals, and he smiled with his eyes but no more. Then
he asked if we ate any cheeses, especially the local ones rather
like our cottage cheese but made with farm milk from cows
and goats and sheep, and I said that now and then the shepherdess made us a *brousse*.

This is a delicate kind of bonny-clabber made from fresh
ewe's milk left to "set," and sweetened and faintly spiced with
nutmeg and perhaps ginger. It is as light and fresh as brook
water, and leaves one feeling light and fresh too.

Dr. Vidal frowned a little, and shrugged. "How long do

you plan to be on this small ship through the Panama Canal, with no adequate medical facilities aboard?" he asked idly.

I told him about six or seven weeks.

"You are very foolish to risk getting Malta fever, then," he went on in the same remote way. He looked up from the directions he had been writing about yellow fever shots and urinalyses and so on. "I would surmise, Madame," he said in a way which from that moment on became part of our family-lingo, "that such a probability is *counterindicated*."

That was all.

Perhaps I murmured agreement. Anything counterindicated to my hopes to help shepherd my two girls, two younger nephews, their mother and a sixteen-year-old French friend through the ordeal of life on a freighter did seem worth a fair warning.

I thought firmly about it, as I made plans to go in to Marseille with the children for the horrid yellow fever shots. I even read about Malta or undulant fever, which sounded damnably unpleasant, at sea or anywhere.

Then I looked at the five children, who had lived from sixteen to six years with plenty of freshly made cheeses and milks in their diets, and for the last few months the rare treat of the delicious *brousses*, and I decided that the die had been cast, and that we would not offend the shepherdess at this point.

She brought us one last bowl, the day we left, and her best plates because ours were packed. Never had it tasted better, nor had I felt more philosophical.

There was a long pause in my active relationship with Vidal because of distance, but I talked about him with my other important doctor, the American, and told him of the way Vidal would recommend fasting, bed-rest and (not a good book, as Dr. Lister once wrote) floods of hot herb teas . . . thyme, verbena, mint, sassafras. We agreed that such was an increasingly rare treatment.

At the end of the 1950s I went back to Europe with Anne and Mary. We stayed in Lugano about nine months, while they learned how to exist in Italian. We had a good life, when I could see them at Sant'Anna, which at first was seldom, and I coughed steadily all the time I was there. In the fine lake air I felt as if I were mildewing. It became a problem that remained unsolved by a series of doctors to whom I was referred by Swiss friends. I grew quietly despairing, but kept telling myself that a real illness was counterindicated.

A few months before we were to leave Lugano we came to the irrevocable decision that since we were already some seven thousand miles from home, we should stay a year longer and return to Aix, where we seemed to have left large parts of our human significance. As soon as we were sure of this, I began to think, most often against my sensible protests, my reason, my logic, that if I could last until I saw Dr. Vidal I would be well again.

I had spent several months in the hands of highly recommended and earnest specialists who swabbed, irrigated, sprayed, probed, and generally tortured me with a hundred medications, and who somewhat obviously considered me a neurotic, lonely, well-heeled tourist. I continued to cough like a sick cow, and to sweat and shiver at perfectly spaced intervals.

Let me get back to Aix, I prayed. Let me lie in a meadow, and drink herb teas, and know that Dr. Vidal's quiet voice will reassure me that all these humiliating pills and probes are silly.

This came about, by Providence. I did lie in the meadow in the penetrating Provençal sun, and I did drink teas brewed from herbs picked that morning by my children, and I even lay in baths redolent of branches of fresh thyme. I did find once more the serene dispassion of Vidal, and his deep calm eyes, and his fine voice, and the sureness of movement in his long frame.

The only change was that he had become a pill-man: he

prescribed intricate schedules of a dozen different kinds of capsules, troches, dragées, and pastilles. He was very firm about the rhythm of taking them. Gone were the simple teas and infusions. He was still loyal to his fasting and resting. Otherwise he had joined the pharmaceutical cabala.

I felt disillusioned but loyal, up to the same point where I had accepted his smelling the acetone and suspecting the *brousse*. I let the hot sun and the meadow smells soothe me, and I put the pills down the toilet drain, except for very rarely, when I knew he had prescribed a tranquilizer and I felt a fleeting need to dull the razor's edge.

During those first few months, sunny, coughless, and serene, I observed with astonishment the new intake of drugstore products by the general population.

The pharmacies were, as they always had been in France, almost like little outpatient hospitals; the owners were, as always, highly trained. They prescribed skillfully for aches and pains, and bandaged sudden cuts, and revived fainting old ladies and pregnant passersby. But most of them had streamlined their stores, and they did less free prescribing than straight prescription work, with not even a mortar and pestle in sight, and a stern list of what nostrums, placebos, and quackeries had been dispensed from hour to hour . . . to whom . . . why . . . on what physician's say-so.

I read, idly but with an increasing chill, that the daily, not the weekly-monthly-annual but the DAILY, consumption of pills in France was over 400 tons. I think it was 470, but must allow for time as well as natural shock.

Perhaps it was time that made me more tolerant of all this. Perhaps I felt that the air of Provence would protect me. When I needed Dr. Vidal to tell me that one of my children was losing too much weight and looking gray around the gills I trusted him, so wise and kind and remote, to tell me that she needed to stop trying to do three years of Latin in six months and go

lie on a rock on Porquerolles. I also trusted Nature and myself
to carry on from there, and I threw most of her pills down the
toilet drain again, for if I had tossed them into a rock pool the
fish might have turned up their tails, and I did not want that
to happen to them or to my girls . . .

The Aixois are very sensitive to things like the mistral, the
cold mean dusty wind that blows down the Rhone Valley at
odd moments. Indeed, if a crime can be proved to have been
committed during the mistral it is wiped off the slate, such is
the pernicious influence of this blustering devil. It is because it
comes from the north? In other countries people, usually
women, often complain about how a north wind makes them
nervous or peaked . . . Well, Vidal was prescribing what
Madame Lanes laughingly, affectionately called mistral drops!

Another thing the Aixois dislike intensely is drafts, although
most French people have somewhat the same aversion to any
fresh moving air. Anglo-Saxons notice this most keenly, especially in hotel dining rooms, buses, and, in the old days when
there was no so-called air-conditioning, in train compartments.
For every staunch British believer in fresh-air-and-be-damned-
to-the-cinders, there were a good half-dozen desperate Frenchmen who would have slammed down the windows in the face
of Queen Elizabeth herself, I or II. In Aix there are special
medicines against drafts — "draft-draughts"!

One more thing is a prime subject of commiseration and
medication, there: rheumatism. There is a great deal of it.

People have been going to the thermal places in Aix for more
than two thousand years, and the hot and warm and cool
waters have soothed and even cured Greeks and Romans and
Gauls and Saracens and Celts and in other words some two
millennia of aching crickety tourists. They arrive. They bathe
and rest. They leave beatific.

Meanwhile the Aixois themselves, forced to remain, are basically and incurably rheumatic. They ache. They hobble.

They creak. It is a locational hazard. They do not have time to dip themselves in the healing waters of the place, nor lie in the sun around the steaming glittering pools, nor take the Roman-esque massages and rubbings that go on all about them.

Often the simpler citizens take a pitcher to Old Mossback and let the steaming water spout into it, and then at home they cautiously sip a little of the water, to cure gout or swollen joints or plain misery.

Mostly they hobble about, especially in January and February.

I know, because I did.

I was amazed. I remembered how Madame Lanes had an occasional *crise de rhumatisme*. I looked about me. I admitted, now and then, that I could barely climb the five flights of stairs to my room, and that often I had to stop for a minute on the Cours and discreetly try to joggle my right hip into a firmer and less excruciating focus on the path ahead.

Finally I went to Dr. Vidal, in his tranquil austere rooms above the Cours. I could hear some of his children roughing it up a bit with the current nitwit maid. There were only a few patients in the discreetly Provençal waiting room, sitting like sick wilted birds on their chairs, all puffy with miserable feathers.

Two nights before, Dr. Vidal had been ambushed in a corridor of the Opera house by a hired band of ruffians from Marseille, during a political meeting in which he got up on the stage and denounced something that was very clear to me at the time but has now fled my mind. He was against something that most of the conservatives were for. Or perhaps he was for something all the radicals were against. I think it was the former, for although he was the most conformist of people in his behavior, albeit completely un-Provençal and of the "Northern" type, he seemed to like to express his social impatience by very overt behavior in politics. It was always surprising that people like Madame Lanes loved this rebellious streak in him, and deplored it voluptuously.

I had read about Vidal's latest entanglement with the Marseillais toughs with some dismay: he had been hospitalized, and I hated to think of it, for I plainly had a personal attachment to him, even if as distant as his own recognition of me.

Finally the last of the sick people pulled up the heavy quilt over his office door, and disappeared in a muffled murmur from behind it, and I could hobble in.

The room was very dim. He sat with his face toward the cubicle and the door into the corridor, firmly away from the light. Even then I could see that one eye was still swollen almost shut and surrounded by cruel smears of brown empurplement, and that his lower lip and his chin were nearly immobile with plastic bandages and stitches in the skin. He was a schoolboy mess.

For the first time in almost a decade of knowing him, I permitted myself something besides the banalities of bowel movements, temperatures, and other such data.

"I am very glad to see that you are still around," I said, looking at him as firmly as he always looked at me.

He almost smiled, and for an instant was one human to another, perhaps even one man to one woman. Then he withdrew again. "Yes, I was fortunate this time," he said formally. "And I see that you have become one of the Aix citizens at last: you are suffering from rheumatism."

His prescriptions involved my going twice a week to a beautiful convent, for most doctors in that part of France never give injections except at accidents. The treatment, which involved my bending over, bare up to the waist, before a kneeling nun armed with an enormous hypodermic, may not have been as efficacious as the passage of time and the return of spring, but during it I learned a lot about how the water flowing everywhere under Aix, but especially down the ancient canal on which the Cours Mirabeau is built, has affected the aches and pains of the citizens.

"Even the doctor himself," Sister Marie-Angeleine told me debonairly after we had become intimate, which of necessity was almost at once, "has to bow to an occasional injection."

When I had to go away again from Provence I thought with an actual pang, amongst many others perhaps even more severe, of whatever mysterious thing it was that Dr. Vidal had always given me, a kind of courage in the face of my own skepticism, indeed a jauntiness of spirit quite ill adjusted to his outward manners. I knew him to be brave, from hearsay and from my one sight of him after the beating. What I could not understand was how, and even why, he made me feel brave too.

I decided that I must thank him in some way for this. I composed a note. I even mailed it. Of course he never replied, for I did not put my American address on it, and one thing I like about him is that most probably he has never thought of it again, except perhaps when he goes to his confessor, who I was told is the Archbishop.

ii *THE UNKNOWN*

> The art of medicine consists of amusing the patient while Nature cures the disease.
>
> Voltaire

THERE WAS ONE doctor we saw for only a few minutes, whom I shall always remember for his strong charm over my girl Anne, in the Military Hospital in Marseille.

I reviewed the whole adventure exactly four days after it happened, when I sat feeling miserable about the mimeographed sheet of instructions which an officer had thrust at me. Perhaps if I had never read it I would have blamed my sensations on the weather, or a touch of liver. As it was, it acted like a delayed evil spell, and I huddled and shook where I sat.

Courbature, the sheet said I could expect between the fourth and seventh days, and *courbature* I definitely felt, if it meant aching bones. If it meant "bent over," I was. I was at least ninety-six years old.

It also said that I could expect *céphalée*.

This is a word not commonly used, in daily conversation at least, by the respectable middle-class people with whom my girls and I had been living in Aix, and I could only assume that its resemblance to "syphilis" was accidental, since it seemed improbable that even in a French military hospital a yellow fever shot would cover V.D. It probably had some connection with words like hydrocephalic. Perhaps it was merely a medical term for headache, which suddenly I had.

Neither *courbature* nor *céphalée* was in my paperback dictionary, but the third thing that the sleazy directions said I could expect was easy: *fièvre* . . . "light fever yielding easily to a dose of aspirin." I got out the little tin box, still holding almost its original dozen after a year in the traveling first-aid kit. Bent aching back and headache were already my lot, and with fever next on the witch's spell sheet, I would be prepared . . .

The whole business had been surprising, Anne and Mary and I agreed. A year before, we had come through the Canal to France without a thought of yellow fever. Now, doing the voyage in reverse, with perhaps a few more ports of call on the list, relatives in America were shouting sternly at us, and even the travel agent in Marseille said a firm "Of course" instead of his usual Belgian "Poof!" A little grimly I got the project under way.

By then we were living in Le Tholonet, northeast of Aix, and without either car or telephone except at the Relai de Cézanne.

I had a vague idea we should have urinalyses made, at least for the children: they had both caught the school-bug of sore throats a few weeks before, and analyses were made almost automatically for everything in that part of the country. Dr. Vidal agreed somewhat vaguely by telephone that it was "indicated," and I got the two little bottles onto the weekly market bus from the village and into the chemist's at Aix.

He said he would telephone the results to the doctor, who would in turn leave a message at the bar in the Relai. "No albumin" was the word when I walked down two days later for bread and cheese at the grocery which was the other half of the bar, so I engaged a taxi for seven the next morning, Friday.

It was a fine day, too fine to give a thought to the slight ordeal ahead: I hate things like vaccinations, but I knew this would be a little scratch with a quill on our upper arms, and then forgotten: "Absolutely no reaction," friends had assured me, and I said nothing at all to the children.

The salt air came in soft early summer puffs over the rolling hills as we neared Marseille. There was dark rain behind the city as we went down into it, and Notre Dame de le Garde was blurred on the far height.

Fernand, a dry skinny friend and one of the world's best drivers, drunk or sober, got us expertly to the enormous hulk of the hospital. He used to run a bar near it, and he knew an infinity of shortcuts. He parked deftly between the hospital and another bar run by a brother-in-law, and we agreed to meet him there in a half-hour.

At the gate a handsome officer with drooping eyelids and silvery hair asked for my certifications. I looked blank, or dull, or however it is that foreigners look to French people who are speaking clear correct plain words. He shrugged, and said firmly and loudly, "Urine . . . papers . . . *urine*." Anne looked embarrassed, and Mary tittered. He handed me a smudgy mimeographed sheet which I stuck in my handbag to read later. I had no papers at all, I told him. He smiled wearily and told us to go in anyway, to hurry up the line that was forming behind us.

The forecourt was packed with military ambulances on the ready. There was a long tunnel-like passage smelling of lye. Then we were in a great leafy pleasant square, with discreet signs pointing this way and that. Thin men in baggy pyjama suits walked in a gingerly fashion from bench to bench under the trees, and very short fat elderly women in white trotted briskly along the covered arcades at the sides, mostly carrying trays of tubes.

We got up to a third-floor room in a creaking stretcher-elevator marked *Forbidden to be operated by the gravely ill*. A boy in pyjamas and with no hair ran it for us. "Some tropical disease maybe," I murmured to Mary, who was plainly thrilled by this note in her mental book on how to become a doctor. Anne was discreetly withdrawn.

We were almost the first people in the ugly windowless waiting room, which had enough benches for perhaps twenty people along its walls. As it was to happen, we were also almost the last to leave it, and meanwhile it must have held four or five hundred of us.

Before it got too full, a very chubby woman in an old white tent formerly called a Mother Hubbard by American missionaries pounded gaily into the room. "All got your certifications?" she shouted in a smiley voice.

Instead of saying "No," which I did not yet realize I should have stated-screamed-even-wept everywhere from the very first, I said that the children had been "analyzed" three days before. She looked disturbed, and a sleepy young woman next to me on the bench said that albumin could form in twenty-four hours, and the fat attendant banged into the next room marked *Head Doctor for Dermatology and Anti-Amarile Vac-*

cinations and came out cheerily to say that it would be all
right anyway.

For a couple of hours we sat, while the room got so full that
we could not possibly have stood up to offer our seats to older
tireder people. There were a lot of soldiers' wives, with many
babies both inward and outward. There were a lot of colored
men in uniform. There were a lot of teachers and nuns and
so on, all going deep into Africa, Dakar, Djibouti . . . Everyone was polite, withdrawn, bored.

Gradually, from the murmurs, I understood that I too must
have an analysis made. I pushed out into the hall and through
the patient mob there to a room where a harried nurse agreed
with me. In fact, she looked completely astonished at my
stupidity, but forgiving. I pushed back to my pale children
in the corner of the stifling room, advised them to stand in the
hall where there was a little air, and said I would be back
almost right away.

When I finally found the laboratory on the ground floor and
across the leafy courtyard, the same fat merry woman in a
Mother Hubbard was there to hand me an expertly designed
little flask and point to the left. "Hah *hah*," she said as if she
were glad to have one more routine task to do . . . which she
did, of course, with the help of a tired mild young pharmacist,
who flitted patiently up and down the rows of numbered tubes
colored subtle numberless yellows. Fifteen minutes later I was
handed a little paper saying *Albumin — None,* and I worked
my long way back to the waiting room.

This time the elevator was run by a man in pyjamas with
one arm in a big cast with dried blood on it, but he had a lot
of curly hair on his head.

Anne and Mary looked smaller and paler, behind a solid wall
of Moroccans, and I asserted myself and got them out into the
almost equally crowded but less stifling hall, where they had
been too polite to shove themselves at my first suggestion.

Once more and very gradually, from tired women and exasperated men, I learned that I should have signed up and paid, and then presented my certifications. I got into the necessary room somehow, and twenty minutes later came out feeling embarrassed and fatalistically frustrated: it would be impossible to vaccinate the two children unless they too had their correct new papers stating *Albumin — None.* The nurse in charge, with several shades of red, black and blonde hair and large beautiful eyes, looked patiently at me and shook her head. "This is over, closed up, at twelve noon, you know," she said with a kind of sadness about me.

I got the children down and across to the laboratory. The air in the big courtyard felt fine. The fat gay woman said, "Hah," and then, "Hah *hah,*" when she saw us. Anne and Mary were somewhat taken aback by the straightforward arrangements for procuring the necessary specimens. Nothing happened. The young pharmacist suggested running some water, loudly, which the attendant did with great amusement. Anne seemed desiccated with distaste and embarrassment, and even Mary could fill none of the basic requirements. I said firmly we would try again later, and was reminded with a reassuring guffaw that things closed at noon.

We straggled across the street to tell Fernand we were late and would be later.

It was hot in his brother-in-law's little bar. A woman from the hospital waiting room who by now seemed an old acquaintance was nursing her baby at the back table, and drinking a beer. Her husband, who had begun to turn purple in the hospital, looked almost normal behind a milky *pastis.* I would have liked one . . . or two. But I asked for a small blackish vermouth, and Fernand joined me, peering longingly at the *pastis* down the room. And I got the girls to drink almost two lemonades apiece, fast, before we hurried back across the street.

Everything proceeded smoothly; the fat woman congratulated them with a reassuring bellow of approval laughter at my strategy, and went right on hah hah HAH in a comfortable way as we trotted off toward the third floor waiting room with the correctly marked little slips.

The elevator was now run by a man in pyjamas and a large white turban. "Head injury," Mary diagnosed professionally. "Mohammedan," Anne said firmly, and I knew she was relieved to have everything behind her but the little scratch with the quill.

The crowd had perhaps thinned a bit, and this time I could pay the forty-five cents required for each of us and get through the long joking interview with the rainbow-haired woman and her young assistant, who were apparently very bored by hours of ordinary French people of all colors and who found three Americans as refreshing and delightfully heady as champagne. Even the children cheered up completely at the fun the young assistant had, a boy with an accent as thick as garlic mayonnaise, pretending to stumble over the names Anne and Mary, as if they were some new Yankee invention. It was entertaining, but the hands of the clock went on around toward noon. It seemed to me that if I had to face Fernand with the news that we must return on the next Tuesday or Friday and start all over again with the analyses and the waiting, in order to be able to flash our international vaccination cards at some bored official in Trinidad or La-Union-Cutoco who had never asked us for them before, I would need much more than one of his brother-in-law's *pastis* to keep me from a good public cry. My face was stiff from the joking, the cheerfulness . . .

It was four minutes to twelve when our names were called, along with three blue-black soldiers and two young nuns, and I heard fifty or so unfortunates stump glumly down the stairs as the lock turned in the waiting room door.

The office was bright and efficient, and so was the nurse, who must have swabbed alcohol on several hundred forearms that morning. I myself felt smudged, shiny-nosed, and rumpled. The doctor reassured me by looking somewhat worn too, but unruffled, and he sent off the mysterious strength and calm that some men manage to do in his profession.

It was as well that he did, for Anne, who had once been brutalized with some penicillin shots by a "country doctor" who was the antithesis of our sentimental picture of such men, gave one look at the large tray of hypodermic needles and turned gray-green.

I was glad I had not deliberately lied to her about "a scratch with a quill." I prayed.

The nurse said, "Now don't be afraid, honey, because this . . ."

The doctor interrupted in a voice that was magnetically right for Anne, full of charm and sex and security. "*This* young lady is not bothered. I can *feel* it. We'll do her first . . ."

Anne looked fleetingly at me, and I knew she would not fly out the window in panic: we both recognized a fine man when we saw one. Then she smiled feebly with her large brown eyes straight into the tired smiling blue ones of the doctor, as he plunged a big needle into her skinny little arm, casually fastened a syringe to it, and pumped what looked like a half-cup of anti-amarile serum into her.

Later she was almost prostrated to realize that she had actually allowed anyone to give her an injection, something she had apparently vowed to prevent with her very life, if need be; but for time enough to get her out of the hospital and even back to Le Tholonet she seemed in a trance of happiness at having shared a moment of such intimacy with that wonderful man . . .

At exactly eight minutes past twelve we clattered down the suddenly echoing stairs, behind the hurrying black soldiers and well in front of the shy nuns. The leafy courtyard was empty.

Most of the ambulances were gone, and there was no handsome patient officer at the gate.

Across the street in the bar, when we pushed through the bead curtain, Fernand stood patiently in front of a *pastis* with the man whose face had once that morning turned purple and was now almost the same color again. At the back table the mother was still nursing her baby, with three other women who had not been able to make the noon deadline. Everyone tried to cheer up the few others who had been turned away, and congratulated the ones like us. Fernand stood the girls to a round of lemon soda. The air stung with the fine Marseillais perfume of licorice from the milky glasses and I felt so cheerful that one was plenty . . .

Lunch tasted better than usual, on the Vieux Port: there was something triumphal about us. Our favorite waiter dipped and dashed for us in a frenzy of silver platters and suggestions. Anne touched her arm softly now and then, and her eyes were starry.

And driving gracefully along the auto route and then the bumpier prettier route toward Aix, Fernand manipulated his car like a good horse and we chatted lazily, winily, about the new television towers far to the right on the Ridge of the Stars, the modern church steeple to the left with an angel something like Brancusi's *Bird in Flight*, the smell of the salt marshes of the Camargue as compared with the smell of the salty fjords around Cassis. In back, the two little girls sang a round, "White Sands and Gray Sands." Life was all right, indeed, and I felt like laughing hah HAH with the fat woman, behind her rows of yellow flasks with everything including death in them.

It was not for four days that I remembered to sort out the rubbish in my handbag. And there was the smudgy sheet the droop-lidded beau at the hospital gates had thrust at me. I read it with cool interest, still buoyed by the general well-being we had felt since that almost dim morning. It was clearly written, in spite of a few merely guessable words like *anti-paludique*, and I skimmed along casually through Precautions to take . . . Before presenting oneself at the vaccination-seance . . . Preceding the vaccination . . . After . . .

It was there I halted: ". . . it is useless to change one's diet, but dietary excesses and undue fatigue are strongly advised against, since a post-vaccination state can arise between the fourth and seventh days which it is best not to aggravate . . . *courbature, céphalée*, and a light fever yielding easily to a dose of aspirin . . ."

I counted back . . . four days! I thought of the delicious long luncheon on the Vieux Port. I thought of the afternoon spent climbing from bottom to top of all available parts of Notre Dame de la Garde. I thought of the two helpless little girls, pumped full of yellow fever serum and now out in the June mizzle with the shepherdess of Le Tholonet. My vision suddenly seemed less clear and my head was heavy. My back ached as if I were twice my years. That would make me more than senile, with a curved lumped spine: *courbature*! I felt sickish. I decided bravely not to mention all this to the children, but to watch them closely for the signs.

Outside, a little later, the early summer storm blew over. A friend drove up in her old Army truck. Creakingly I agreed to pile into it with all our children for a picnic: I would be silent about my misery, which disappeared almost at once. While we were gone, the mimeographed sheet must have blown off the table and into the meadow, for I never saw it again. I felt that my abrupt short reaction to it was normal, which is always a comfort, and as far as I could tell, the children never learned the words *céphalée, courbature*, even *fièvre*, although Anne perhaps learned a little bit more about *amour*.

iii *WHITE IS BLACK IS WHITE*

Evil and good are God's right hand
and left.
                  Philip James Bailey, *Festus*

IN THE OTHER TOWN, Dijon, there was long ago a doctor who,
in the human sense, was definitely counterindicated. His name
was Blanc, and he lived in a new part of the town in a villa
with heavy lace curtains of a pale coffee color.

My landlady had sent me to him when I was about to go off
for a long vacation at Christmas and was nagged by a pain
which was plainly from an outraged appendix. I thought of
how unpleasant it would be to fall howling to the floor in a
hotel in Nuremberg, but then when I went into the villa I
thought how unpleasant it was to be there too. I seemed to be
alone with the youngish, tallish, blondish man in a black coat.
The light through the curtains was sickly. Upstairs I could
hear a piano playing a faint approximation of Chopin.

The doctor made some notes about my name and suchlike.
I wrapped myself in my innate innocence. He changed into
a white coat, unlike most European doctors. Later, when he
had examined me and confirmed my own diagnosis, he leaned
too easily against the table where I lay half-exposed, and I
knew even in my innocence that he would like to continue
another kind of examination of my helplessness. I arose, no
doubt with frigid dignity, paid him, and went away in a confused state of amazement and outrage.

When my landlady asked if all had gone well I was courteous. I stopped eating as much as I wanted of her delicious
sauces and puddings, and in Nuremberg I forgot to worry at
all about being caught by pain and gluttony, and sat gobbling
bratwurstglöckleinen and drinking beer to keep warm, where

perhaps Dürer had sat gobbling and drinking with the same hungry insouciance. But in the ghost-life I have led in Dijon since that far year and day, I have felt a certain regret that my one doctor there was such an unprincipled horny one. The only good thing about him was that when I met a second Blanc, I could exorcise that nasty one.

He was a young allergist Vidal sent me to. He was a shadowy man, with a feeling of dedication about him but in some indescribable way without Vidal's purity. He was most probably more intelligent, which was doubtless an asset in his ambitious path but quite unessential to Vidal's: a matter of training versus instinct, perhaps.

His offices were on the second floor of a moderately noble town-house on the Rue Eméric-David. He lived in Marseille, I think. The rooms were not shabby but were ugly and undistinguished. Most of his patients were very poor, and since he specialized in infections of the chest, there were many Algerians, who at that time were a menace to public health because of the tuberculous state they had fallen into in their French ghettoes.

I got to know several people there, well enough to salute reservedly. Most of them had alarming wheezes and coughs. There was a woman in a grubby overall who summoned us. I disliked her because she was very polite to me and barely civil to the Algerians.

They were of course something of a problem logistically in the small stuffy waiting room across the hall from Blanc's offices, because if one of them had an appointment, seven or eight came to keep him company and give him strength, like the Gypsies. They sat on the floor, and leaned against the walls, and overflowed silently into the cold ugly hallway. They were used to being shunned and did not seem to notice the surly woman's manner as much as I did.

Dr. Blanc was very efficient. He was the only Frenchman

I ever knew who used the archaic form of "Sit down," so that from him, in his detached light voice, it became "Pray have the goodness to be seated": *Assoyez-vous*. I liked it, and looked forward to it as a kind of sop, of solace for the long coughing, wheezing periods in the waiting room, where I seemed always to be the only well person there and perhaps in the whole world.

He used some rather elaborate equipment on me now and then, to see what clouds he could detect in my chest; but mainly his treatment consisted of an almost undetectable prick of a needle dipped in a Pasteur vaccine: he was riding his favorite horse, and fighting fire with fire.

Rarely, I could get him to talk. Usually he seemed on the edge of an exhausted collapse. Always he was detached, like Vidal but in a more personal way, somehow. Once when I knew that I must soon go away, I told him that I should always be glad to welcome him in California. There was a flash of first amazement and then warm pleasure behind his thin worn face, and then he was back in his prime role again, the detached young scientist struggling along in a provincial town.

When I left, he went to a lot of trouble to get names and sources and suchlike, so that when I got to my home I could continue with almost no break his treatment, which he believed was all-important to my future as a person and a writer. (Like many doctors, he was in awe of people who did anything with their thoughts.)

His past treatment and future prescriptions were reduced to scornful shreds by my American doctors, but I shall always be thankful that I met him, to lay the ghost of that other Blanc in the other town and to know that there are young men who seem to have *something* of Vidal's purity. They are not counterindicated in this world . . .

The Sound of the Place

... and the song of multiple fountains,
which one discovers with enchantment
in the fresh silent shade of the courtyards and gardens, where dolphins and
bearded gods blow water into their
deep beautiful basins.

Martial and Braive, *Aix-en-Provence*

A ix has been called "the city of fountains and music," and
the two are synonymous in it.

Summers, during the Festival, the whole town quivers to the
sounds, in the open air of cloisters and courtyards, of violins
and flutes and voices, and above them rises always the indescribable soft steady music from at least fourteen public fountains and uncounted murmuring basins hidden in gardens and
inner courts.

Late at night the year around, and even during the midday
hours in summer when all else sleeps, a person seeking it can
hear water flowing and falling somewhere nearby, and then
walk on a little to the magic radius of another and yet another
fountain, rather as in the Tivoli in Copenhagen one can stroll
from orchestra to orchestra without ever hearing the various
sounds conflict and snarl.

Each quarter in Aix has its main public fountain, to which it
is unquestioningly loyal. It is always the clearest, purest, most
beneficent water to its users, in this or that particular source,
which springs up through the subterrain as if through a miraculous filter, here warm and fumy, there icy-sweet.

When I lived on the Rue Cardinale I was caught between

two loyalties, for at the east end of the old quiet street spouted the wall fountain in front of the church of St. John of Malta, perhaps a hundred feet from my attic room, and further to the west there stood the beautiful basin and statue of the Four Dolphins.

St. John's basin is simple, a half-round with one jet of cold water pouring down into it, and a broad rim to hold the pitchers and buckets that are filled from it.

The Four Dolphins is its antithesis in elegance, and is in perfect balance with the small square of fine town-houses that frame it. Its sound steals always down the four streets that stem out from it, and in summer generous chestnut trees bend toward it. Four of the merriest dolphins ever carved by man spout into the graceful basin under its stone needle, topped by a stone pine cone, and it seems unlikely that anyone can pass by this exquisite whole without feeling reassured in some firm way.

The most beautiful private fountain in Aix, perhaps, is the one half-hidden in the garden of the Hôtel d'Espagnet, one of the prizes of all the great town-houses there. Now the official residence of the rector of the University, its garden, simplified by time and negligence to a few straggly beds of begonias and a graveled driveway for official cars, still bows to a monumental wall fountain of four diminishing shells, with water flowing down over them from the myth-figure at the summit, to the final low wide-lipped basin, with a most magical sound. I walked past this fountain hundreds of times, and when the wide shabby wooden doors were open, I went into the garden, and when they were closed I stood outside, long enough to wash other lesser sounds from my heart.

The doors were shameful, probably built temporarily a hundred years before, perhaps to replace forged iron gates that once stood there. A revolution, a war, a need for metal . . . I could never find out.

For a time I tried to interest the Rector in giving new ones to the city. I talked with Monsieur Colas the antiques-man, and he with enthusiasm enlisted the help of architects and a master iron-worker. But the University could not afford to help with the costs. And the costs would come to about a million francs. And the Algerian situation was precarious. And I did not know where I could find a million francs, even from lovers of Aix, who know the intense proprietary passion for it that has always been felt for real beauty. And then I had to leave. And the same scuffed barn-doors still mask the beauty of the noble wall fountain from people who should gaze at it through a beautiful Provençal grille, but the sound comes through always, and over, and around . . .

There are other fine fountains in Aix, simple and grandiose, amusing, lovely, even a little sad. Every street leads finally to one. They are made for man and often for beasts too, with generous stone troughs for muzzles and sturdy iron bars placed under the spouting water for pitchers and jugs, and often they are called for some loved native: Dumas, Marcel Provence, Cézanne . . .

Some are flat against the walls. Others stand free to the air in small squares and marketplaces. Almost always they are deeply shaded in the summers. Almost never do they cease their play of sound, and when once a year they must be silent for a day while the great canal is cleaned, everything around them seems uneasy and waiting.

Of them all, perhaps I feel most deeply about the Four Dolphins and the four-shelled one in the garden of the old town-house. It is impossible to say why, except that I have known them, in day and night, for much longer than any one person could ever be in Aix.

The University

In 1196 Alfonso of Aragon founded the chairs of Law and Theology in Aix. In 1409 Louis II of Anjou added the schools of Medicine and The Arts, eager to train and perfect competent administrators. His son René, born that same year and destined to reign until his death in 1480 as a painter, musician, poet, and romantic writer as well as king, became the protector of letters and arts, and built Aix into one of the great cultural centers of Europe. By 1957 its students made up one-third of its total population, and increasing numbers of foreigners who enrolled in its schools of Law and Letters, its normal schools, and its National School of Arts and Professions strengthened the ties between it and other hubs of learning.

Jean-Paul Coste, *Aix-en-Provence and Its Countryside*

S OMEWHERE, I read once that Aix had more bookstores and shops for students' supplies than any other town in France. It is easy to believe. It was easy to believe, when we were there, that people fed on the printed word as in other places they feed on meat and bread . . . except of course that there were plenty of places for eating food too.

On the Cours Mirabeau were a fat handful of stores, ranging from tobacco shops where a hundred different newspapers and periodicals were sold, to venerable monuments, warren-deep and with their high walls lined with carefully catalogued books, where any scholar in the world would find his own contentment.

On many of the squares, not one of which met the requirements in the true sense of being a space enclosed by four walls

of equal length, at least one bookstore supplied its own devotees with everything from Petrarch to Mickey Mouse.

One of the best, and perhaps the oldest in the town, was
on the Place de la Madeleine, up the street from the Palace
of Justice. Its floors went up and down, in many little rooms
of what had once been a house. Its owner, who looked like
an Italian tenor, short and rounded but with a sharp eye, would
discuss seriously the merits of Latin dictionaries or prize novels,
and knew a great deal about the history of French poetry. He
sometimes appeared bored with people who were not students
of any of his main subjects; and while he seemed always to
be polite, it was for the girls from the Lycée across the Place,
or the young men from the engineering school at Arts et
Métier, or the professors from the Law School, or even the
stuttering newcomers from the American University School
that he laid out his real skill and kindliness.

He was typical of every book dealer in the town: they
seemed to feel a kind of protective pride in the students who
consulted them and bought their books. Some of them sold
nothing but second-to-tenth-hand textbooks, and the others
were apparently eager to pass along young men and women
who could not afford the cleaner copies. Many of them specialized in books of a certain period, both new and old. A
few, like the big stores on the Cours, sold nothing but new
books. More than half of them, I would say, sold old and
new prints and reproductions too, and there were several small
galleries connected with them, upstairs or in the cellar, where
good and bad artists gave shows of their canvases.

And besides the food for thought in this student town there
were good places for them to eat for their stomachs' sake, and
drink the wine advised for that.

Since the opening of the cafeteria in the New Faculties,
which moved from the Rue Gaston-de-Saporta in 1950, most
of the resident students for Law and Letters ate there: it was

inexpensive; the food furnished in part by the government was simple and good; in spite of the fantastic overcrowding and noise it was amusing.

Then there were dozens, perhaps hundreds, of families who fed anywhere from two to twenty students, more or less well, and there were many hole-in-the-wall restaurants, often of short life, where students could eat well-prepared cheap food with their friends.

Both feeding and housing were a serious problem when I was last in Aix, because of the hordes of new students, but except during the dull years of the nineteenth century this must always have been so, for the town seemed to generate a kind of fever for learning, a fever for life, in almost everyone who came there.

As in any university town there were levels of endeavor, just as there were levels of behavior, appearance, ambition. The young officers did not mingle with the young engineers and architects. The future lawyers and teachers held off from all of them and even from each other. They all had their own rituals, which often brought life on the Cours to a patient standstill while two hundred graduating architects would serpentine in and out of the cafés braying happily, or groups of visiting German students solemnly serenaded the fountains.

There were favorite cafés where those with enough money could go, and of course the one or two that had long held favor on the Cours were always filled with a predictably changing crowd. There were seasonal currents, too, which soon became familiar: in Lent, for instance, there would always be dozens of fresh-faced lanky boys from England, wrapped in their long scarves. One boy we knew from Eton who lived in Aix almost a year said peevishly that he was thrown constantly, during the long vac, with everybody he had spent years avoiding at home . . .

Every autumn about sixty girls from Smith College spent six weeks in Aix, to get used to French life before their year at the Sorbonne. They lived two to a family, with people who were able to provide adequate bathing facilities, not easy in that seventeeth-century shabbiness, for what seemed a very generous fee. The girls were for the most part serious and attractive, even though they complained bitterly each October that French boys never lit their cigarets for them . . .

The American University School, as I think it was called, grew firmly while I was there. Several of my friends worked for it, in one way or another, and the reports I got from them were interesting. They said, for instance, that the boys were much softer and more spoiled than the girls, who seemed to adapt themselves quickly and with real enthusiasm to the lives they led with French families. The boys would languish, away from Mother's Cooking, and would often do childish things like going to Spain without their passports.

There were several Fulbright students there, both times I lived in Aix. They seemed to have very little wish to identify themselves with the life of the town, and small talent for it when they showed any at all. They lived apart from the ordinary students because of their comparative financial ease, and most of them were married to boot. They rented apartments as much like the ones at home as possible, and seemed to be made remote by the knowledge that they were birds of passage.

One Fulbright wife I knew grew openly depressed when her husband, after several months of eating in Aix restaurants and at the student cafeteria, requested that she learn how to make a decent soup without packaged "mixes." "What's the use?" she said despairingly. "I can't ever do it at home, so why learn here?"

"Oh yes you can," I said flatly. "There are bones at home, and carrots, and cabbage . . . things like that."

"But nobody does it, and I haven't time, and anyway he wouldn't eat it . . ."

It was a cultural quarrel, or perhaps only a gastronomical impasse!

In the early 1960s the New Faculties, with their dining rooms and lounges, were trying to assimilate all this into a vague approximation of an American campus imposed upon a European university cosmos, but the heart of the student life in Aix continued to be the Cours, whether or not the constant tides of young men and women had the inclination or the money to sit on the café terraces.

There was a never-ceasing flow, as in a streambed, of their intense living, their passionate interchange of thought and words. They would drift up and down the beautiful street, three or ten abreast, and salute one another with the local male handshake, a quick touching and thrust downward. They would exchange cigarets often. They would discuss politics of course, and the next examinations, and the New Wave films, and they would whisper scathing wittisms of Brondino or one of their other teachers and then go along shaking with knowledgeable laughter.

From the café terraces the foreign students would look casually at them, lost in their own intensities, their own poetry of the way they were living in the most perfect of student towns.

One of these young people, a Frenchman named Albert Aynaud, wrote many years after he had lived in Aix of the way of it: " . . . this hovel lost at the end of a nameless alley had lived in my memory as one of the most splendid places I have ever known, so much did the fervor of its host and the exaltation of his visitors ennoble it. We literally grew drunk with poetry there, and the lines listened to by their tireless devotees sometimes rolled on until dawn broke. Young poets (later to become the pride of France) brought their efforts there, and to a hundred other such garrets, and would murmur a marvelous sonnet, for example, which would in the next few days be recited, pale with admiration, the length of the leafy shadows of the Cours."

The Man and the Words

Ah! what avails the classic bent
And what the cultured word,
Against the undoctored incident
That actually occurred?

Rudyard Kipling,
The Benefactors

ON my invisible map of Aix, the Rue Gaston-de-Saporta has two lines of sad and bloody ink in its printing that should make it a distressing street for me, but that do not keep me from walking often there with gratification. They are both connected with the old Law School, and one is for a man and both are for words.

Brondino is the man. He is indelibly alive for me, although the last time I saw him he was dying, and later I read that he had indeed snuffed out, like the final inch of a very slender candle. For weeks before that, his bookshop was locked, with a quickly dusty card stuck in the door saying *Closed because of illness,* and the reprints of pictures which he used to clip on cords strung across his small window were curling and losing their colors in the dampness and the rare sun of the dark narrow street.

That last time, he was climbing painfully out of a taxi to go into his shop, with of course a pile of framed reproductions on the sidewalk and under both his arms. I helped him with them, and he told me that he had been very ill and had submitted to all kinds of tests, which proved at least that his heart was a strong one.

He spoke somewhat hysterically of a miraculous cure that he was being given by a radical young doctor who was despised and feared by the established physicians of that most radically conforming of all towns, Aix. From there he went on to a poster of an exhibit he had sponsored several years before, when his choice of a Picasso sketch of bathers was banned by the City Fathers as lewd. And that reminded him of another case of provincial stupidity, and another, and all the time he was weaving with weakness against his table.

I left as soon as I could. In one direction or another it was Brondino's usual pattern, impossible to alter or arrest: a half-hour of agreeing and listening, mute in his feverish flow of scorn and erudition . . . I had an appointment I must keep, and I never saw him again.

The time before that, the next to the last one, I was walking down the Cours past the open-fronted flower shop on the Place Forbin, and there stood my poor little twisted friend leaning against the wall.

He was shocking to see, and I knew that although he actually looked much the same as always, he was in deep pain this time, so that his normally green-gray pallor and the normal suffering in his large sunken eyes were suddenly shocking. It seemed improbable that he would recognize me, so intense was the expression of agony in him; but he took his hand away from the wall when I spoke, and I shook it gently in the inescapable habit of the Midi.

I could not help asking him if he was all right, although the words were fatuous and almost insulting.

He replied with only a little less than his customary flow of impeccable angry French, but this time he was furious not at the government nor the art critics nor the publishers but at his own mortality. His breathing was shallow, and grew lesser with his railing at the pain he was being subjected to, which he considered a personal affront; and after I made sure that he would not let me help him and that he preferred to walk at his own creeping speed to the taxistand, I left him as fast as I could, to save for him some of the air for his diseased and martyred lungs.

I went to the shop a few more times, but it was always closed. I could tell by the occasional new reprints in the dirty window that he was still there occasionally. And I could tell from the withdrawal of my children when I mentioned getting Christmas presents there that they dreaded to see this little tortured man who had for so long been good to them.

When we first came to Aix, and they lived in the old Archbishop's Palace on the shady square to one side of the Rue Gaston-de-Saporta, perhaps the first or second shop they noticed in their neighborhood was Brondino's. They stopped always in front of his window, to look at reprints they recognized, or new ones they loved or hated, and he noticed them too with his lost feverish eyes.

One day we went in together and it was as if we had been there before, and when he saw that Anne and Mary knew how to open portfolios and let the pictures stand up or fall forward with hardly a touch, he was as delighted as an innocent child himself, and invited them to come whenever they wished, alone or together or even with me. They accepted gravely, and the invitation always stood and was often used.

When we went away the first time we had an agreement with him to send me posters whenever really good ones came along, for by then he knew my tastes. Of course he never did. I in turn knew him well enough not to expect him to. I never wrote to him, but often, especially when I looked at my favorite of all I had bought from him, the one Marc Chagall did for the town of Vence, I thought poignantly of him and of the murky legends I had half-heard, half-deduced, when I was in Aix.

He was, everyone agreed, eccentric, perhaps mad . . . not

dangerous, but often foolhardy, and as often ridiculous to the
straitlaced Tories like Madame Lanes. They shunned him for
a radical and perhaps even a Communist, and deplored what
was felt to be his strange attraction for the young law students,
the foreigners, the struggling artists, the intellectual mavericks
of this rigid cultural hub.

Here is what I remember of his history, one person's vision,
distorted, untrue, prejudiced, but which for unknown reasons
I heard with my inner ear and saved from all things I did hear
straight and not listen to:

He was a professor in the School of Law, and after the Liberation he was put on trial, having been accused of revolution-
ary activities or at least tendencies toward them. He was re-
vered by many students, largely the hotheads and idealists and
most vociferous and of course least acceptable in the stiff aca-
demic society of Aix. Because of the inexplicable esteem in
which he seemed to be held, he was informed that he would
be let free, but free from what I do not know except imprisonment itself, if he would take an oath that he believed in Divine
Justice.

He shrugged.

In some embarrassment the Court then said, "Well, perhaps
in Human Justice?"

At that he sneered openly, or laughed, or even spat. I do
not know any truth at all about this except my own inner
recognition of some such admirable follies.

He was allowed to go free, but never again as a teacher of
Justice as it is meant in the governmental parlance. So he set
himself up, almost next to the old Law School, and for several years sold books of every kind to the loyal and fascinated
students.

Gradually he let his obsession for modern art take over most
of his ponderously crowded little shop: he had a hundred
theories, all passionate of course, about exposing children in

schools, and their parents in bars and cafés, to the best of all
paintings well but inexpensively reprinted, and he bought piles
of good reproductions, so that this unbelievable clutter swelled
upward and outward until going into his place was like being
a pin pushed into a ripe fruit: it seemed as if a sweet juice of
papers and prints and dusty books would spout out into the
street through the door.

Almost always other people were there when we were . . .
brave pins. They were elderly decisive nuns buying replicas
of all his *Last Suppers* from Da Vinci to Dali, or bearded
young *cinéastes* discussing Italian camera techniques, or, rarely,
people like Picasso or Poulenc or Tailleux shaking Brondino's
hand in a strangely conspiratorial way . . .

From his taxi drivers and other mutual acquaintances and
our own eyes it became plain that at times he was more exalted
than at others, and whether it was because of medication or
alcohol or plain neurotic exhaustion none seemed to know.
I myself would guess that now and then he deliberately over-
dosed himself with any of a possible dozen modern tranquil-
izers or mood-changers, from the way he acted, but I doubt
that he drank much at all, for I have known people of his
same feebly articulated build who reacted much as I think he
would have done to alcohol: unrewardingly. However that
may be, his absences from the shop became more frequent
after we returned to Aix in 1960, and he forgot even more
things that he had promised to remember . . . packages to be
mailed, books to be ordered, prints to be laid aside.

Once, for instance, in early January of that year, Donald
Friede uncovered a ripe pretty prize in Brondino's place, a
clean and complete run of a series of satirical lithographs by
a German artist whose name I forget. He snapped at them
like a happy carp, paid for them, and got Brondino's firm
word that they would be in New York within three weeks.

Then, that April, when the children and I returned to Aix

from Lugano, Donald asked me to remind Brondino that the prints had not yet arrived. It was our first view of the change in him, the one that seemed to make Anne and Mary unwilling, like most young animals sensing the touch of Death's finger, to return to the overcrowded excitement of his fat portfolios and all the quick conversation and the purchase of another print, a new Dufy, a forgotten poster . . .

He promised to send the lithographs to New York at once, and to my embarrassment climbed dangerously up over half-opened cartons of old papers and new books to show me that they were indeed there on a high dirty shelf, wrapped, ready to mail. I should have taken them and sent them. Instead, fearing to offend him, I left him a new copy of the address.

But several months passed, with occasional weary reminders to me from America and from me to Brondino when I could pin him down. Then in November the prints did arrive, in perfect shape, and were even more valuable than Donald had at first suspected. This pleased him because he liked them and had concluded a good bargain, and me because I felt quite sure that Brondino had known all along their real value and had not really cared about either selling or sending them.

Not long before we left Aix the first time, he had said that his only child, a remote handsome girl I had seen once or twice, was applying for a Fulbright to America. I told him that I would be glad to help if I could, but I felt that my suggestion was not of any importance to him and perhaps even a little unwelcome. Then, when we returned, five years later, I asked him about it and he became very sardonic, in a contained quiet way which was more disturbing than his usual furious blast of sarcasm. She had been turned down because of his reputation, he inferred bitterly. There was nothing more for me to say except ask where she was . . . teaching Greek and Latin in a small provincial high school . . .

I felt a curious satisfaction in him, behind his love and disappointment for his daughter. It was as if he had finally, conclusively, proved himself the scabrous and even destructive rebel he had always fought to be.

And then he was not at the shop for many weeks.

Since one final day when I stood looking passively at the dead flies under the fading pictures on the sagging piece of cord in his window I had not walked up the Rue Gaston-de-Saporta. I had had enough of it for a while. Or was I like my children, averse to feeling Death's finger? This kind of anesthesia was short-lived, of course. There was too much more there on my map, especially in the Place de l'Archevêché nearby, that was traced in less murky colors than his own . . .

Brondino died on April Fools' Day, 1961. I read many notices and heard much talk of him, largely good now that it was too late. On his door a black-bordered notice said that he had died suddenly, but I knew better. And I agreed with what one of the editors of *La Semaine à Aix* wrote:

"Our visitors to the next Festival of Music . . . how many musicians and amateurs, how many critics and writers, how many famous soloists frequented the literary meeting place led by Brondino . . . will be as lost as we are, robbed of an interpreter who was always for them the best guide to our regional painters and writers, just as Aix itself is robbed bruskly of a devoted and faithful lover and we are of a friend."

I can never think again of him without hearing in the back of my head the word *justice*, and then back of it, the dark bloody spot on my map, the word *assassin* as I am told it was said once, over and over, in a whisper that became a kind of scream, echoing now always in its syllables for me, in a classroom filled with young men, studying law in the old building past Brondino's and perhaps still in his shadow.

They were all between twenty-three or -four, a little past the Occupation which they had lived through as boys, and they were perforce hard and old for their ages. They were taking an advanced course in jurisprudence from a professor whose domestic concupiscence was even more noted than his legal knowledge. I do not know how these things become public property, but it was said openly, and apparently believed, that after the birth of his twelfth child he had been told that another confinement would kill his wife.

Nevertheless she conceived again, delivered the child, and died at once of an exhausted heart.

And as the professor returned to his class after her funeral, and stood to face the silent room of young-old men looking at him, a slow whisper began to beat into the air, never more than a whisper but endless, like a drumbeat, or like a cuckoo in a dream . . . "the snakelike sound of hissing," one great American criminal lawyer said of it, "which of all massed human noises is the most frightening."

"Assassin, assassin," the students whispered. "*Assssassssin, assssssassssin . . .*"

I do not know anything more about this day: how the man left the room, or if he paled or covered his ears. I was told that within a few months he married a young strong woman with eight children.

And willy-nilly the word is always a nightmare scream of whispering to me as I pass the old Law School in my ghostly wanderings, and Brondino's self-crucified face is a part of the meaning of Justice itself, but the Rue Gaston-de-Saporta is still a good street for me, because of the way it bends, and the places it leads to, and all the other inks it is printed with.

A Familiar

Angels may be familiar; those
Who err each other must respect.

Coventry Patmore,
Thoughts. V: "Courtesy"

ONE interesting and perhaps dangerous thing about the
manufacture of inner maps is that sometimes they become two, as has happened with the one I made a long time
ago for Dijon. My real one is there as plain as any ink, with
all the streets named correctly and existent because they exist
for *me*, but still conforming to the maps sold in bookstores.
Then there is another one by now, which is printed only in
my dream life and which, although it differs somewhat from
the other, is immediately recognizable, so that even when I
am awake I can remember its various aspects and when I sleep,
and by chance go into it, I know immediately and always
where I am.

These dreams of Dijon happen rarely, and I always savor
them in a part of my consciousness which I keep deliberately
awake, the better to enjoy the rare visit.

So far my map of Aix is completely conscious, and I have
never to my knowledge used it or a facsimile of it for dream
wanderings and revisitations. If I am fortunate, perhaps a few
years from now when I am asleep in a place far from it, I
can return and recognize it, even changed as is already the
second one of Dijon.

Something of this recurring familiarity can happen, and just
about as rarely, with people. One face, or one tone of voice,

or the sound of one footstep and no other will recur like a chord in a long piece of music, always the same, even though sometimes heard a few seconds after it has merged with the other notes. It will sound without apparent reason, and linger on the inner ear or eye like the black image of the sun, perhaps, after an unmeant upward glance.

There are at least two of these faces in my life, as real as the maps that can be bought, or the inner maps I have printed for myself, shifting and merging like the one of Dijon that has made of itself a new but still recognizable plan followed only in dreams.

I saw one of these familiars in Aix, and several times, on the Cours Mirabeau. It gave me a strange and at first an almost frightened feeling, although I could not rightly say how or why: that town is a logical place in Europe for such people to come to.

It was the stylized, mawkishly handsome, almost pretty face of a boy about twenty — the kind that schoolgirls draw in their English Poetry notebooks when they are studying Byron and Shelley — with large slightly protruding dark eyes in hollow sockets, the small curling lips of a Greek hermaphrodite by Praxiteles, and abundant dark hair that framed it too luxuriantly and made it oversmall for the tall willowy body and the long white neck.

The boy moved with self-assurance, but also very consciously, and on the Cours or in the Deux Garçons his casual grace was painfully stiff and cautious to my old eye. To Anne he was beautiful, without stricture, and I could see that Mary too was drawn by his small perfect head at least. He wore an invisible cloak lined with cloth of silver.

Once we watched him for several minutes. He was waiting for someone, or pretending to, and he sat gracefully, very long of body but not fidgeting, at the little front table under the big fern in the middle of the café, where nobody ever sits unless he is a stranger. The friend never came, and finally he got up in a calm, rather disdainful way and went out onto the Cours.

Two or three other times I passed him, either strolling with a much younger less pretty boy, or leaning in an amused way against one of the big plantains that make the green vault of the Cours. His eyes always flickered over and past me, and it seemed to me that his lack of recognition was as exaggerated as was his whole appearance: too remote, too tall, too beautiful, with the head too small.

I felt a definite relief when several days went by and we did not see him. That was during the Festival, when everything is almost too much so. I had to admit to a slight obsession about him, for the first time I saw him was almost a nightmare in my life, and he carried the feeling with him, perhaps not to anyone else in Aix . . .

Sometime about a year before, perhaps in November for it was very cold, I had risked shaking Thomas Cook to its venerable foundations by being sold a ticket on a nonexistent train by one of its representatives in Switzerland. When I mentioned it in the station in Lucerne, the regular ticket seller was jubilant, and almost prayed me to make a fuss: it was plain he hated Cook's guts. I sympathized with his feeling of triumphant inferiority, but of course did nothing about it except wait for almost six hours in the great station for a train that did exist and that did run at a real hour, not imaginary, on the direct track between Lucerne and Lugano.

I had been in Lucerne a short time before with my children, and I recognized my sentimentality when I decided against walking across the bridge and getting a bed in the Hôtel Fédéral where we had stayed: I felt that it would be almost unbearable to lie there alone, with no living soul to know where I was or why. I contemplated telephoning or wiring to my landlady in Lugano, but it was past ten at night by the time the delighted government ticket seller and I had located a train that existed, and I feared to disturb my elderly friend.

It was the first time I had ever been stranded in a big station, even with people I knew, and there I was, completely alone, as if invisible except for the ticket-man, who dismissed me from his world as soon as he had told me that a train would leave at two minutes to four in the morning. I could feel his bitter regret, as I thanked him and disappeared: the chance of his lifetime to get even with Cook ruined by a foolish woman . . .

I considered leaving my suitcase in the checkroom and going out onto the wide terrace at the mouth of the river, where it flowed from the many-fingered Lake of the Four Cantons. I could go only a few steps to my right, past the beautiful bronze horses and into the new Kursaal: there was always some kind of exhibit on . . . or I could go to a late movie, or even the last half of a play or opera.

I recognized a core of old evil panic solidifying with this unexpected solitude, and in self-protection I deliberately turned my back on it, somewhat as I had done at the ticket seller's chance to shatter Cook's impregnability, and decided to spend all the time inside the station. It would be an experience in my life, most probably unique. I would continue my invisibility, perforce, until I got on the predawn train for Lugano. It was not childish, but instead wise of me, I said, to carry the little valise along instead of checking it. Inside it were the only identifications with my other existence: a hairbrush, lipstick, clean stockings, things like that.

First I went to the restroom, which I had visited on a few other trips. It was large and bustling, with pay toilets, and in the daytime a big rough-spoken but cheerful woman in a white pinafore to attend to things like towels and tidiness. At night, I found, a small frail old man was there.

He came out slowly from a little cubicle which I saw without real surprise had a kind of cot in it instead of a toilet and lavatory. I was afraid to permit myself to be depressed by this, and instead noticed that the air was fresh, indeed more so than out on the station platform.

He got me a towel and bowed me into one of the pay cubicles with a mirror and a chair, and then disappeared. I spent more time than I needed in the safe little locked space, and then felt ashamed of myself. I was not acting maturely enough to survive, at this rate, the creeping hours.

I went into the first-class buffet-restaurant from the corridor entrance of the station, instead of going out onto the very cold platform again. It was crowded. It was always crowded, for Lucerne was a focal place, and yet there seemed to be several groups of habitués, old men forever playing intricate Swiss card games on thick pieces of green carpeting unfolded on their tables. I found the last empty place, and put my suitcase on one of its two chairs.

The waitress took a long time to come. I studied the menu with resignation, and decided on a fairly expensive *plat du jour* which I knew would strengthen my aversion toward Lucerne dishes but at the same time strengthen me. I ordered a vermouth-gin with only the usual amount of difficulty, and when it came it was just what I wanted, except that as always in that part of Switzerland it was about the right size for a three-year-old midget on a spree. I would have liked to order at least two more, but although I had to laugh at myself I was afraid that the maid, already somewhat alarmed by my ordering such a potion . . . a woman alone . . . would report me to the police who must be somewhere handy in the enormous station.

After that I asked for, like a correct Swiss matron instead of a foreign sporting-lady, a small carafe of the Valais red, which helped me, when it finally arrived, to swallow the hideous *plat du jour*, which was exactly as I had expected, a real *Luzernerplatte* of old veal covered with a rich creamy sauce and piled heavily on a mound of pure glue called a *risotto*, with the rice grains almost homogeneous.

It was easy to eat some of this very slowly, and push it downward with my completely inadequate supply of the coarse cleansing wine. I would gladly have ordered another little carafe of it, but once more my prudish timidity denied the impulse, and I knew I had time ahead for more absorption.

I drank a coffee as slowly as I could, while I paid the bill. People were waiting for my little table, and I took my suitcase, the proof of my self-reality, and went out onto the platform.

Even with the ticket seller and the old man in the toilets and then the shy gluey supper I had covered only about a third of my wait.

I walked up and down resolutely a few times, with people laughing and pushing toward ski trains along the cold platform and around the lunch cart. I went with them to the edge of the crowd, and suddenly the woman who ran the little wagon looked straight at me and nodded and smiled, and I remembered that only two or three weeks before, my girls had amused her in a quiet moment by conversing at some length with her about the different kinds of hot sausages she sold. Her flash of recognition, of me there without them, was almost dangerous, and I hurried dazedly away, suddenly fearful and defenseless.

I stumbled into the small first-class waiting room, and sat on a bench along the wall, pulling myself roughly, angrily into cool focus again. There were less than four hours to wait, now, and I would do so with grace, I prayed.

It was the first time in my life I had ever spent more than a minute or two in such a room, and I knew very quickly that it would be a real test, for the air was almost tangible with human waste and pain and plain horror. My old panic was as heavy as a rod of black iron in my spirit, and I kicked at it with deliberate scorn for fear of anything softer in my actions.

I suppose all waiting rooms in big stations at night are much like that one in Lucerne in the winter of 1959 or '60: bright light and the occasional passing of a policeman outside the large windows onto the platform; the old man coughing blood into a rag behind his trembling newspaper; the occasional fidgety prim young women too correctly bred to sit alone anywhere but there while they waited for late trains; the drunken young man who might or might not vomit on the floor under his rumpled head that he rocked slowly between his hands as he bent in a kind of cramp, with his elbows on his knees; the whore so short and square that she was almost a dwarf, and so overpainted and underclothed that she was a caricature of a whore.

I looked at and through all these companions, determined not to feel despair for them or for myself, and just as I was about to leave or die, the boy I saw later in Aix came into the warm bright room with a girl.

He was extraordinary to look at. I soon felt that he was impervious to any stares, as if he moved in a kind of envelope of crystal, so I watched him easily. He saw me and knew what I was doing, but his large beautiful eyes flicked a half-smiling look over and past me, as if I were a natural part of the world outside his own.

At first I thought he was painted, but no, his skin was as pale and hairless as stone, except on his bright rosy cheekbones; and his lips, fully modeled like the small almost pouting mouths of ancient Greek boys or Flemish cherubim, were moist and coral-colored. His dark eyes flashed and rolled in their noble sockets, and his extremely fine silky hair fell over his high white forehead and down almost to his collar, in soft black tendrils.

He was very tall, and wore high-heeled black leather boots which obviously had lifts inside them, so that he must have stood almost seven feet high. He wore very tight Italian-style brown velvet trousers with a line of black silk braid going down the sides, and a vast and tightly belted black leather trench coat, with the collar turned up to frame, as it were, the unusually small beautiful face on the long neck. His hands were gauntleted in black kid.

All his movements were floating and affectedly graceful, but apparently not rehearsed. He tossed his head and flashed his eyes and shrugged, as I watched him across the bright terrible room, as if he were on a stage just the size of himself, fitted in every curve to his body and yet still a stage, on which he pranced and simpered with constant self-attention. When he bent with exaggerated coquetry over his little companion, his eyes still flashed about him as if he were weighing the applause that roared and pressed up to him from the mighty audience beyond his footlights, and I felt that if ever he kissed anyone or took a human body onto the stage beside him, his magnificent eyes would still roll and weigh and accept.

Once he picked up in his black-gloved hands the bare paw of the tiny woman beside him, and kissed each fingertip as if he were turning it with the faint touch of his full perfect lips into a pearl or a moth.

She looked up at him with love and satisfaction on her small pert face. She was older than he, perhaps about twenty-five, and smartly dressed in the clothes that are pictured in popular magazines for women: high heels, pretty legs, a coat of thick green wool with a fur collar. She could be a doctor's secretary or a salesgirl in a middle-class shop, except for the man she was with: he was so fantastic in his beauty, his manners, his clothes, that he made her almost as unbelievable.

He knew that I was fascinated by him, and although he seemed to see me no more than he saw anything or anybody,

I felt that he was acting *toward* me and that he was passionately interested in his acting.

His silent miming with the girl became more active. He pretended to embrace her and then to chide her waggishly, to comfort her, to wipe away a tear on her dry cheek, to forgive her . . . she smiled and wriggled.

Once some young men outside peered in, and when they saw this freakish figure they rapped on the window and nudged one another and called something jeering and most probably lewd, in dialect. He heard it, but was impervious there in his crystal skin, on his immense stage the size of his body, and he went on acting toward the girl and, more and more plainly, toward me.

I felt that I must break away, at once at once, or lose all the careful control of myself and go out into shreds of horror. I walked as fast as I could toward the door onto the platform, and it seemed quite normal that in one lithe jump he was there to open it for me, with a disdainful remote non-look on his too small but exquisite face.

The air was as cold as Death, and I welcomed it and sucked it into my lungs, which seemed almost to have stopped moving for a few minutes.

There was no one at the lunch wagon, and I saw that the sausage-woman had high boots on her thick legs, and that she was beating her hands up and down her crossed arms, and stamping, the way people do in Russian movies. I half-smiled at her, so that if I had mistaken her first look of recognition she could ignore me, which she did.

I went into the third-class buffet. It was about one o'clock. The place was pleasantly crowded, mostly with men from the tracks and engines. There was a lot of rough warm noise, and laughing and shouting, for they all knew each other and were full of jokes. It was as if working in the night drew them closer together and made everything doubly important. It was their club.

It was hard to get the big breezy waitress to catch my eye, for she knew everyone but me. I wanted to get up and leave, but by then was involved politely, for I had sat down first at a table that was tacitly reserved, it seemed, for some trainmen due any minute for their regular steins of beer. I could barely follow the dialect of the man at the next table who told me this, but he was kindly, and when he picked up my suitcase and put it down beside still another table, I followed him meekly, feeling stupid and confused.

I asked for a coffee and brandy.

I did not want to drink it quickly, from shyness, for there was still a lot of time left; but in spite of myself I emptied the small cup and tiny glass fast, paid the waitress between her quips with the men at the big tables around me, and went out onto the platform again with my suitcase. I was beginning to feel a part of the place, like the trainmen and the little street-walker in the waiting room and the woman at the lunch wagon.

This time when I passed her I did not half-smile, for fear of her blankness again, but she unexpectedly beamed at me, still beating her wool-thickened arms around her shoulders and stamping her booted feet. She spoke cheerily to me in dialect, things like how cold it was and where was I from and oh what a mess to take a train that did not exist.

I hesitated about buying a roll and a sausage: I knew I could not even bite into them, and I feared that she might see me drop them into a dustbin. I lingered to the fatuous point, and then said good night to her.

The platform was impossibly cold for me, and I went back through the main hall of the enormous station, which seemed to look and sound and smell exactly as it would at three in the afternoon or at eight in the morning, and down the long corridor to the toilets.

The old man crept slowly from his improvised cot in the first cubicle by the door, and brought me another clean towel and let me into a pay booth. I wondered how many people had relieved themselves and put water on their faces since I was last there, and at the same time I wished that he had remembered me. His face was too small and gray for any kind of smile, at least in that place.

I could have bought the sausage after all, and brought it to him . . . but probably he had no teeth . . .

The first-class buffet was dark. I felt a kind of relief, but it was plain that I must stay off the icy platform; and between the third-class buffet which ran all day and night because of the trainmen and served as a kind of club, and the glassed-in bright warm room marked *First Class*, I finally chose the latter. I could not drink anything more, and with the trainmen I had not been as invisible as in the other place . . .

I felt that it was dangerous for me to ask myself any questions about the people; to observe them with compassion and detachment was my job for another hour or so. Then I would leave them forever.

There was still one decorous girl, sitting upright but with her head tilted in cautious sleep against the wall, her purse straps wound inextricably around and through her clasped hands, and her ankles firmly crossed.

The sick old man had gone.

Soon after I returned to this bright hell, the drunken young one lunged to his feet, both hands pressed desperately against his mouth, and ran by some miracle to and through the door, somewhere to rid himself of his painkiller and perhaps his pain too.

Then the shabby little whore stood up slowly, pretending that she had been there to meet someone by the way she looked at her watch and sketched a frown. She smoothed her clothes over her grotesque squat body. Her dirty white shoes were sizes too big for her and clacked on the marble floor as she simpered desolately out of the room, out of my life as far as I yet know.

A few men lay snoring on newspapers along the benches, but the truth was, finally, that I was alone with the unbelievable boy and his girl.

It was a test, I said to myself . . . a test of what . . . a test of my strength, my courage . . . but against what? I felt that if I could last through the next hour with them, I would know that I was brave. I was not yet sure if they were evil, but this was the chance to find out if I was good.

Nothing happened that was visible in the big room, until I stood up in a kind of disbelief and walked out to the track where my train was due in three minutes; and when I left I was not sure of anything except that I had grown a little inwardly.

The boy had been conscious of me all the time, and his gestures were almost daringly coquettish, not toward me but toward himself, with his girl as a receptive but unimportant audience.

He tossed his beautiful head so that the silky hair, so long and dark, fell this way and that over the startling white and rose of his face. His black-gloved hands moved lightly, flittingly, through the air and over the shoulders and arms of his companion, and occasionally he stood up with the lithe swaying of a cobra about to open its hood, and arranged the belt of his long voluminous trench coat. His feet in their highheeled boots were tiny and elegant. He studied them now and then with a pleased smile on his small soft mouth.

There seemed to be an understanding between us that my study of him was far from displeasing, and that I was neither impressed nor repelled by his increased show of mannerisms. That is, we were in our own ways enjoying one another.

From the way he acted, I decided for a time that he was a

female impersonator, really a very effeminate man who usually wore men's covering but who for a change, this night, was doubly masquerading in a completely feminine form of it. Then what of the girl? I watched her, speculating: perhaps she was a small solid pretty little man? Or was she a woman in love with another woman whom she had dressed in this travesty of manhood?

It became very complicated, plainly, and as soon as I felt sure of one surmise a gesture or look would weaken it. Once the girl opened her large stylish handbag and powdered her nose. With exaggerated tenderness the boy took her mirror and studied himself lovingly for several minutes, pursing his lips, arching his perfect black brows. Then they laughed silently together, with their heads touching, in a secret way, as if they were indeed playing some enormous joke. But on whom? What had they escaped from?

Perhaps he was a dancer, although he looked too frail and lightly built, and too tall for anything but perhaps miming.

She could easily be something in the theater, something healthy and fresh and dependable, a standby in a chorus line or perhaps a check girl in a respectable music hall. But she watched every move of her companion, every flutter of his white lids over his great flashing flickering eyes, with plain worship.

It seemed clear to me that no matter what he wanted her to do, she would do it without question and with unfailing passion. At the same time, although he seemed always to dictate her smiles and gestures, there was something protective about her. I wondered if she were shielding him from the world, so that perhaps after all he was not alone in his crystal self-sized stage, but had enlarged it to hold her, invisibly and blissfully his audience.

They never seemed to look at the time on the wall clock. Neither of them had a suitcase. Perhaps they had been more sensible than I, and had checked them. And they did not eat anything. Where were they going? What would they do when they got there?

The boy looked at me as I left. He was as blank and vivid as a cheaply colored postcard. He murmured something to the girl, and they laughed silently inside the crystal, but I knew it was not really about me.

Reflecting upon this extraordinary being helped me stay awake until I got to Lugano in time for breakfast, and afterwards when people asked me about my trip, I told them of the nonexistent train, and when they asked me what I did while I was waiting for a real one, I boasted about the hours I had spent alone in the big station, but I never mentioned the boy.

And a few months later, when I was running through the underground passage in Lucerne that leads to the train platforms, with my children, after a little vacation, I did not say anything when I saw him again. I hurried past him, but I know he saw me.

He was drifting, not walking, and he was alone. His very thin long body seemed supernaturally tall in the high-heeled boots, and his small beautiful head above the tight pants and the bulky black coat was like a perfect wax model, not quite life-size, floating through the clanging gritty tunnel.

When one of the children asked me curiously what was the matter, I said nothing: I must have looked startled, or amazed, or perhaps a little frightened. I do not remember now, but I know that when I saw him again, many months later on the Cours in Aix, I felt some of all that . . . and also an astonishing resentment, or perhaps horror, when both girls noticed him and exclaimed innocently about his beauty.

It is true that if he had been dressed as when I first saw him, they would have noticed his eccentricity first, being young. But he seemed, in what to my almost possessive eye was a supercilious way, to have tuned down everything for Aix. His hair was a little less Byronic; his coloring was muted by a pair of stylish dark glasses that hid the bright flash of his eyes and dulled the pink and white wax of his skin. His clothes were dandified to the extreme, but in Aix, especially during the Festival, there are fops and fairies everywhere.

I observed somewhat irritably, after three or four times of hearing the children remark upon him, that I thought his head was too small. They dismissed me with a smile: I was too old to know one end of a man from the other . . .

I wondered with a dread that I told myself was foolish if he would be there again the next winter, perhaps going to the University, or merely floating from the Deux Garçons to the Opera House to the Casino as some people seem to do indefinitely in Aix. But he disappeared.

And I hope very much, indeed I pray, that I never see him again. I cannot say why. I have tried to be clear about it, when I discuss it with myself, but I am really at a loss about him. I am not at all scared, as far as I know consciously, by sexual or physical anomalies, and I have always respected the right to be ambiguous in deed or thought. So why does this extraordinarily pretty and mysterious human being stay in my mind's eye, and why do I hope so deeply that I may never more see his face?

I reflect on all this now and then, and it did not surprise me, a little while ago, to recall that I very probably knew him when I was about nine years old. This seems to simplify things, for I was not bothered by him then, when he was called Lloyd Richardson Renfrew and went to school with me in Whittier for a few months.

His name is a part of my invisible book of inaudible sounds, and I can say it without thinking, every now and then, a string of remembered vocables without significance or necessity. They fade and swell again, with no warning, no invocation, and I think most people have them somewhere within. I am walking along the street, or lying await for sleep, or washing my hands, and suddenly my inside voice is saying rhythmically, "Es-ca-mi-llo-Escamillo-Escamillo," for no reason that I know. Or *"vomiteusement chocolateux."* Or "Lloyd Richardson Renfrew" . . .

Undoubtedly this name is scratched deeply into my subconscious sound track because the boy was always called Lloydrichardson at school, which is the only place I ever saw him. I think we must have been told by the teacher never never *never* to forget this exotic sound, almost like a title among the Bills and Harrys we knew. And he did seem like a prince or a count perhaps, so different from the rest of us: taller, with skin softer and whiter than a girl's, and long pale hands which he drew often across his large eyes and under the thick dark silky curls that seemed to float down his neck and above his wide high forehead. His cheeks were not pink, but exquisitely rose-colored, and his lips were like those of a prince in *The Blue Fairy Book*.

As I remember him, it would have seemed quite normal for him to stand aloof on the dusty playground in a dark velvet cape lined with silver, with gleaming buckles on his tiny pointed shoes. As it was, he did indeed wear clothes different from ours: dark and immaculate, always a jacket and a very white shirt.

Nobody ever played with him on the Boys' Side, at recess, and although he stood close to the fence of the Girls' Side, he never spoke to us unless we said nicely, "Lloydrichardson. Hello, Lloydrichardson." Then he would turn his eyes toward us, and smile dazzlingly and bow a little, as if we were applauding him. Sometimes we saw him shrug and make small graceful gestures with his hands, and we believed that he was saying poetry to himself.

He went away, and much later my mother told me somewhat ambiguously that his mother had been a peculiar lonely

rich woman who had always longed to have a daughter, not a
son.

And that and his name are all I know about him . . . except
that now it seems to me that probably I met him after so many
years, that long night in Lucerne, and then on the Cours. Yes,
yes, of course it was he . . . exactly the same tall slender lost
beauty, the same airy walk and gestures . . . Lloydrichardson!
He has not grown old as fast as I, that is all. I would know him
now, even in the dream-streets of Dijon.

The Unwritten Books

... not the book returneth, but its
ghost!

Andrew Lang, from *"Colletet"*

W HEN I first went to live in Aix, I felt that I wanted
to read everything anyone had written about it and
Provence.

I soon knew that this was a greedy impossibility: time was
against me, some two thousand years of it, long since caught
up with my half-century. In much the same way I came to
recognize that every book I must ignore had been written because of many of my own reactions to the compelling town.

"Oh no!" my old friend Georges from Dijon cried out when
he saw a writing-look in my eyes as we walked down the Rue
Cardinale toward the fountain of the Quatre Dauphins. "Not
you too! Not another tiny poetical masterpiece on the trees,
the flowing waters, the many-hued effluvia of Aix!"

And thus I closed my reading eyes, so that now I do not
know what has been written, really, since the commanders of
Caius Sextius Calvinus confirmed his directives to found, in
123 B.C., a military post near the abundant waters, part steaming
and part chill, of Aquae Sextiae. Except for guidebooks, to
verify some such detail as that one, I am innocent of conscious
research, and must follow my inner map to know what street
I am on, and even why.

One result of my possible frustration as a writer about the

shape and the shadow of this town is that I can think of several
books about it that I would like to put into proper form.

The one on Balzac's view of Aix would, of course, demand
a fair amount of research, at least quasi-erudite: even I knew
that this fecund and romantic scribe had mentioned our town
quite often and lovingly, but where? And why? It was too
complicated for my limited patience . . .

I asked one or two people like Monsieur Colas the antique
dealer about it. They got a delighted smile in their eyes, a
kind of sly cautious sparkle.

"Have you said anything about this project?" they murmured as if discussing an indiscretion. "Does anyone know of
this?"

When I assured them that it was simply a passing wish of
mine to see some of Balzac's impressions of Aix collected in a
little book which would interest some of the visitors, they
almost pushed me out of their shops, with a last whispered
warning never to mention it to *anyone*. I assumed that later
one or another of them would then whisper a few juicy hints
to a friend of a friend: the pipeline, it is called there with
various significances . . .

Such a book could be entertaining, I still think . . . unless it
became the sterile thesis of some pedagogic *docteur ès lettres*.

Another booklet which I approached with a kind of cautious
languor, mainly as an excuse to visit the Musée Granet often,
would also make a minor "item" for art collectors and gallery
hounds. Egocentrically, I felt better qualified to attempt it
than the one about the fat novelist, for it would be a kind of
gastronomical tour of the fine town museum.

I went so far as to make a tentative list of the canvases that
I, self-styled culinary *raconteuse*, would point out to my occasional reader.

There was the whole history of man's need for food in that
beautiful old priory of the Knights of Malta, waiting for me to

unravel a silver thread from one to the next. It would begin
with the exquisite little Virgin suckling her child, I thought. It
would wind through the simplicity of country feasts to fatuous
wanton *soupers en ville*, and it would pick up the crumbs of
poverty and lonely old age. There would be still lifes of many
schools, and magnificent flowery "studies" of grapes and dead
birds. It would be amusing.

Of course I never wrote it, for want of my own hunger to
do anything but look and wonder.

And why was there not a little book, well edited of course,
a kind of anthology of everything good that could be gleaned
from other writers, poets, essayists, statesmen, diarists, even
worldly gossips, about the fountains of Aix? No visitor could
be there one hour or a dozen years without knowing their
harmony, their undying sound. Why not ease man's restlessness by letting him read what more vocal men had sung?

Perhaps Monsieur Colas would feel this too was a valuable
idea, to be guarded with jealous care from the ambitious, the
unscrupulous scholar . . .

Probably the luckiest creative carelessness on my part, professionally, was my almost compulsive shunning of what could
have been a very amusing and lucrative job of gastronomical
reportage.

Every year, oddly enough during Lent, there is a series of
luxurious dinners given weekly at the Casino, which is a gov-
ernment-subsidied institution throughout France and which in
Aix is called the Vendôme. Good and sometimes famous chefs
are installed for one week in its kitchens, according to a pattern which changes each year. The last time I was in Aix the
specialties were, with not too startling originality, of several
great regions of France. Once before the chefs had all brought
with them their best menus from well-known station restaurants like Dijon and Toulon.

The year I was asked by a magazine to write a series of

"portraits" which probably would have sold at a fairly fat price, the Vendôme had ensnared an impressive list of "*mères*" to prepare their most famous dishes for their respective seven days behind the pots and pipkins, and then produce one gastronomical blast in culmination.

There were of course several *mères* from Lyon, of one- to three-star renown. There was perforce one, *the* one, from Mont-Saint-Michel. A few other culinary centers produced their motherly quotas, and the redoubtable ladies brought off their Lenten tours de force with skill and poise, as far as anyone could judge by their series of expert menus.

I met a few of them, and found them brisk poised businesswomen, with decidedly less poundage and fewer gray hairs than their titles would lead one to expect. In more than one case I felt that the charming person I talked to could more possibly be a well-tutored granddaughter than the old omelet queen or fish-dumpling dowager whose name she bore. It reminded me a little of the letter of introduction I was asked to present to "one of Cézanne's most promising pupils," who turned out to have been a suckling babe when the old master died in 1906 . . .

The director of the Vendôme invited me to be his guest at any of the weekly orgies he planned for Lent, that year. He asked me to bring an escort. He asked me to write something nice about his ventures, present, past, and proposed.

All this seemed entertaining to me. I tossed a coin for Normandy or Périgord, and the truffles won. I asked Félix, less than half my age but the most available male, to escort me. We discussed clothes seriously: he would wear his new brocade cummerbund to the gala dinner. I outlined on invisible paper a series of interviews with all the famous *mères*.

Then the director of the Vendôme let it drop, too casually, that as guest of honor I would naturally be mistress of ceremonies and in full charge of the public address system, the

giving of prizes and cotillion favors, and the general gay witty
ton of the evening. I must, he said in a brotherly way, do
everything but sing for my supper.

My throat closed as fast as a clam; my brain washed white.
Of course my psychogenic nose dive was abrupt and complete. Félix put away his cummerbund, I spent the night of
Mère Poularde's dinner in bed with a hot toddy, and the
director of the Vendôme never again bowed over my hand
when I crept in to his cozy bar to meet visiting firemen.

Most irrevocably of all, the invisible pages I had written
about all the non-gray, non-old *mères* of France turned to ash
in my head. It was a beautiful chance, forever gone, to write
an unimportant, pleasant, and perhaps profitable little book
about a unique gastronomical congress. Ah well and ho hum.

The other important near-miss in my literary approach to
Aix was impelled less by my professional curiosity than by an
aesthetic one. It itched at me enough to make me scratch my
way through two interviews with a formidable tiny woman
who ruled one of the great pastry shops of the town.

She was about half my size, which always affects my accent:
it becomes lumpish and awkward, much as I myself do when I
must be with Oriental women. Great white cow, I am with
them; great Saxon oaf I am with some of the birdlike females
of Provence.

There were at least three other pastry shops as good as hers,
in a town perhaps more noted for them than any other in a
country dedicated to the gastric hazards of almond paste, chest-
nuts soaked in sweet liqueurs, and chocolate in all its richest
and most redolent forms. There were, in fact, two other
famous stores on the same side of the Cours Mirabeau. Like
hers, they served tea in the afternoon, in discreet side rooms
where English and Swedish people hummed over the trays of
goodies. And like hers, they seemed to follow a rigid pattern
of production which from my first months in Aix interested

me to the point where I grew brave enough to ask the woman about it.

By the time I did so, she recognized me as an inoffensive and fairly good customer: her cookies and wafers and cakes were plainly made of ingredients I approved of for my children, in spite of my responsibility to their livers, and the shop always smelled right, not confused and stuffy but delicately layered: fresh eggs, fresh sweet butter, grated nutmeg, vanilla beans, old kirsch, newly ground almonds . . .

Once my older daughter designed and ordered a birthday cake there for her sister. Madame looked openly shocked by the picture, and called the head chef. He came in with his hands rolled in his apron and a cigaret on his lower lip, which he dropped and stamped into the waxed floor when he saw the plan. Finally he looked sadly at us, and shrugged, and made the cake, but Madame told us coldly that it was the first time such a thing had ever been requested.

It was a large cake, big enough for ten people, made like a coiled green snake, to celebrate the birthday of the younger girl's pet fetish, a slim reptile of green beads brought once from Mexico, which she carried everywhere with her for many years and which her best friend finally stole. Freud rode roughshod through all the motivations of this strange gift of pastry from the older sibling, and it is no wonder that even the pastry chef blanched a little at her plan.

The result was a reptilian masterpiece, carefully carved in an artful sponge cake and then covered, coil by coil, in a thick layer of green almond paste. There were skin markings of glaze, I remember. A delicate pink fork of sugar protruded between tiny white teeth. The eyes were fierce. A miasma of Alsatian kirsch hovered over and around it.

We never saw the chef again, but guests at the birthday party screamed and then remained polite in our foreign presence, and the whole delicious monstrosity was eaten, and the

next day my little girl succumbed to a semicomatose and ver-
tinginous state called *crise d'acétone* in French and bilious attack
in American. The episode was never mentioned by the wee
lady, so smartly dressed and coiffed, who ran the pastry shop.

The first time I asked her about the beautiful rhythm of the
cakes and fruits and bonbons that flowed through the one generous window of her store, she seemed remotely interested, but
baffled by my own interest.

Why should I bother? What difference did it make? Of
course, of course: reputable confectioners and pastry-makers
always put candied fruits in their windows on such and such
a date, and sugared almonds for the baptismal season and June
brides, and strawberries made of fresh almond paste for this
date and molded painted snails and shrimps for that. Of course;
everyone knew that. If the right things did not appear in the
good shopwindows at their proper time, where would Aix be?
Where would life be? And as for the dates and seasons, everyone knew them.

I flapped oafishly, my accent in lumps and my spiritual bulk
greater than my body's. I tried to explain that to a visitor the
pageantry of the pastry shop windows was mysterious, exciting. It was plainly dictated by the supplies on hand, the new
crop of almonds, the freshly preserved fruits like melons and
cherries and figs, then the deep mysteries of all the different
blends of chocolate at Christmastime, and the purity of Easter
with white eggs and mimosa blossoms and sugar daffodils . . .

She looked firmly at me. "There are always the *calissons*,"
she said. "I see that you are a foreign writer. We shall make
an appointment to show you the kitchens where we produce
the *calissons* of Aix. The best *calissons* of Aix, naturally."

She offered me one, held in a little silver tong. I waved it
respectfully aside, for we both knew that I had sent dozens of
them, boxes of them, to unnumbered friends everywhere in

the world. We both knew they always arrived. We knew too
that they were delicious, and that I never ate them.

I assured her once more that the little pointed ovals of artfully blended almond paste were a superb confection, part
pastry, part candy, light but rich, not cloying, haunting and
delicate, old as the Romans or perhaps Jeanne the second queen
of King René, a regal tidbit . . .

"Yes yes, and thank you again," I said in my stolid Saxon
way, "but I should so much like to have you tell me about the
calendar that you as the leading pastry shop follow here in
Aix . . . the set days for producing all these other specialities
for the town . . . "

She shrugged elegantly. "It is routine," she said. "We all
do it. Everyone knows when it is time to start the chocolate
fish for April Fools' day. But the *calissons* are a specialty
unique to Aix. I shall arrange for an appointment with our
kitchens."

The ugly truth is that I did not keep my date. I sent a note.
From then on I sent my children or friends into the shop across
from the Deux Garçons . . . there were two or three things
there that I felt it almost to a duty to enjoy while I could, like
the little oblong slabs, each made in its own pan, of a kind of
thin solid sponge cake called something like "paving blocks."
In the other town, Dijon, they had been round and called
Genoa bread. In Aix the taste and smell of them crept into
my private map, so that even now I can eat one on the terrace
of the shadow-café, while I wait for six o'clock and the end
of the children's schoolday and a drink with them . . .

Often, after I left Aix the first time, I thought of the book
about the brilliant sights and smells of that rhythmic parade
through the pastry shop windows. It was exciting. It was
based on the main supplies of the strange rich dry land; the
almonds, the colors of all the fruits and fishes, the spring floods
of eggs and cream and syrups. Religion took it over, with

pagan rituals behind the altars: spring, marriage, birth and re-birth, the miracles of Christmas and Easter. And through war and plague and near-starvation the pastry cooks and the candy-makers molded and melted what they had, into the right symbols always.

I decided to try again, and in 1960 I went back to the stylish tiny woman whose stronghold was on the Cours across from the Deux Garçons. She remembered me, with a small unsur-prised smile, and offered me a *calisson* from silver tongs. I thanked her, and because of the passage of time I ate it while she watched.

My accent seemed somewhat less lumpy, thanks also to time and perhaps a vermouth-gin at the café, and I explained once more about my wish to write a kind of calendar, with reasons and dates, of the beautiful procession of sweetmeats in her fabulous windows and in those of all the other good pastry shops in Aix.

She bowed, and I bowed.

Then she tapped a bell beside the cash register, and informed the apprentice who popped in from the odorous rear of the shop, breathing with panic under her sugary smock, that I wished to see the *calisson* factory.

I was a foreign writer, Madame said. I wished to study the art of making the famous *calissons* of Aix.

An appointment was made for the next week.

As I went out, helplessly, to cross the Cours for another vermouth-gin, I arranged in my head to go to Marseille for three days, and I silently composed a regretful letter to Madame.

From the Deux Garçons I could see the windows of her shop. They were a blaze of brilliant fish shaped in replicas of all the mean, bright, fanged, horny, spikedy things that go into a real *bouillabaisse,* painted on artful molds of pure almond paste, spilling from nets and from reed baskets onto the wide window shelf. Seaweeds shaped from tinted sugar caught them. Tiny mussels and urchins tangled in the shadows. There was not a *calisson* in sight.

And back in the depths of the kitchens the next candies were being readied.

Was it for the Rites of Spring, the coming of the first straw-berries, gleaming tiny *fraises des bois* looking more beautiful than possible in their little straw baskets, all made of sugar and vividly painted almond paste? Or was it time already for the cherries? Then there would be candied cherries as deep and translucent as the stained glass of a cathedral window, piled like symmetrical rubies upon silver platters. There would be one or two enormous willow-wand cornucopias, spilling out rich chocolate-covered cherries with their stems still sticking through to prove their race: cherries soaked and floating in the finest marc or kirsch, and then coated delicately with a fon-dant before the final imprisonment of the chocolate. And in Provençal pots and jugs among the glossy bonbons would be cherries of every possible hue and size, realer than life and artfully painted to out-mimic Bings, Royal Annes, and every other kind that ever grew in orchard. Cherries were ripe . . .

Or brides were. Or new babies were. Or it was time to be confirmed, and be given a little prayer book made of fine pastry frosted with white and gold. Or it was Carnaval, and hideous masks of frosted sponge cakes were dusted with edible confetti over their leers. Or perhaps it was simply the time when every pastry shop in Aix was filled with round high cakes covered with sugar made to look shockingly like ripe Gorgon-zola or Roquefort cheese, with one slice cut out and two or three little sugar mice popping in and up mischievously. The more mice, the higher the cost, and for me there was never the real reason for this annual invasion, for I never got any kind of calendar of these tides and rhythms.

I followed them dumbly, perhaps as a fish follows the currents that push it here and there, and make it hungry one time and amorous the next and never more than protestingly wondering.

I sat in a kind of quiescent pet across from the shop on the Cours, mapping a revenge that always fizzled into another order of *calissons* to be mailed to Hong Kong or Pacific Palisades when I next went in for some apple tarts or *brioches*.

"When is Madame going to visit our *calisson* factory?" the tiny owner would ask me perkily now and then.

"Soon, soon," I would say with utterly false warmth.

Then she would offer me one of the bland little sweetmeats with her silver tongs. I would bow. She would too.

And here is the recipe, all positive that I have culled, so far, about the mysterious pattern of the pastry shop windows of Aix, which is apparently as irrevocable as the passage of time itself, and which does not deviate one day, one hour, for generations and even centuries, nor for war, pestilence, invasion, nor even peace.

CALISSONS OF AIX

Grind one pint of blanched almonds very fine in a mortar, with one pound of fine white sugar. Pass them through a sieve and put back into the mortar.

Mix into them a few tablespoonfuls of apricot or peach syrup, and then dry out over a slow fire in a heavy casserole. Spread sheets of sacramental paper-bread on a marble candy slab, and then spread the almond paste about one-quarter inch thick over it.

[This paper-bread is the kind that makes communion wafers in church and that is also fed to goldfish. I do not know where it can be bought except perhaps in pastry supply stores. MFKF]

Over the top of the *calisson* paste spread a Royal Glaze, which is made by mixing two whites of egg with one scant cup of powdered sugar with a wooden spoon until they form a smooth glossy syrup. Cut the whole into pointed ovals about an inch and a half long, and bake them in a moderate oven for a short time. They keep well.

This basic recipe, which is ageless, is varied by the pastry cooks of Aix to have a distinguishing taste of orange in one kitchen (probably the zest added to the almond paste), and hints of anise in another, but the flavor of fine fresh almonds must always predominate.

The Din

'Tis not enough no harshness gives offense;
The sound must seem an echo to the sense.

Alexander Pope, *Essay on Criticism*

T HE second time, it lasted longer. For more than a week
before the official opening of this extraordinary rout,
called the Carnaval d'Aix, the Midway was open, and instead of
fleeing its insane noise after a few days we stayed the whole
ten, mainly because Anne and Mary were old enough to be in
it for themselves, without me alongside.

The day it opened I sat in a kind of inner ague waiting to go
down to the Cours for lunch, I remember. I was almost over-
come with apprehension, not yet quite aware of how much
my girls would like everything this time, which of course
would make it tenable for me as well. At exactly eleven that
morning the music had been turned on, and I knew that it
would hardly cease until the fireworks had died down and the
grand ball was in full swing, the night of Mardi Gras.

I could hear it at my desk, high in the Hôtel de Provence,
and I knew that it would pour from every one of the dozens
of large blue loudspeakers spiked onto the trees nearest the
street, along the sidewalks of the Cours Mirabeau. I felt a
little sick. I did not want to meet the children for lunch in that
gross blare of piped music, which would never cease except
when one of the innumerable local and visiting bands blew its
way with bleary prancings down the street. A wave of
foreign-ness chilled me, not the kind that would make me too

American in France, nor too much a ghost in reality, but something nightmarish that made the threat of too much noise a danger.

And it was more than the noise, I knew. Perhaps there was a Freudian timidity mixed in with it: one or two things that had happened the first time grew clearer suddenly to me. And meanwhile I must go to lunch, and try out the decibels of the hideous blue disks that were already rattling out their first day of canned gaiety.

A few days before, Mary and I, after a poor movie, walked down the muddy Midway, which was along the Avenue des Belges instead of Victor-Hugo as before. It looked more tawdry and sprawling, without the respectable façades of the apartment houses to contain it. There were several other changes, but even so I felt that I had seen some of the stall-keepers before, especially the short strong impassive women, the kind who seem to marry into that tough business.

There was the same big "ride," called something like "The Flying Snow," where a couple of long cars filled with people sped up and down on a track which was partly covered over, so that the passengers could snatch a quick pinch or kiss and emerge tittering, or perhaps even abashed, before the others waiting for the cars to stop.

There was a small ferris wheel, and there were several rinks, instead of only one, of the little padded cars whose drivers crash them loudly together at what seems fantastic speed, with screams and giggles.

Then there were endless booths that sold nougat, and the oblong waffles called *gauffres*, with or without a gob of imitation *crème Chantilly*, and of course fried potatoes. There seemed to be fewer of the sugared peanuts, purplish and brown, that men had made in big copper kettles with charcoal burning under them, but they were still making potato chips and twists

of fried batter in the kettles, so that the air smelled more of cheap hot fat than of the burning sugar of before.

A new thing this time was an electric gadget with a plastic container of hot frankfurters and then three or four deadly-looking spikes, apparently heated from within: the stall-man would cut off the end of a plump roll, stab it down over one of the spikes for a minute, and then dab a sausage into a dish of mustard and screw it into the hole in the bread. My girls ate these later, and reported that the sausage seemed to have been steamed to complete inanity and that the roll was sweetish and not crisp, obviously made by the same company that sold the gadgets. They were, they said, *deceived* . . .

There were of course a lot of shooting galleries. One, for a change, had a big crate of live beautiful pigeons to win, and another an impressive cage of all kinds of wild game like pheasants, exotic dappled guinea fowl, quail. It was sad to see them so pressed together.

Most of the shooting galleries that year had very tall staring dolls as their *Grands Prix,* all blank and blue-eyed but dressed as Spanish dancers or Brigitte Bardot, and everywhere the second prizes and below were dead-black Negresses in plaster bas-relief or in the round, with long necks and scarlet pouting mouths.

On the up side of the Midway were the merry-go-rounds for children, most of them with streamlined buses and sports cars instead of the old dromedaries and zebras and chamois. One had a queerly sentimental coach, pale blue and crested, with two fairy-tale horses pulling it, wearing plumes on their fore-heads. All the other things were sternly chromed, very 1961. There were only two children riding, that afternoon Mary and I watched, and one was inside the fairy coach for round after round, and one was riding the front horse that pulled it . . .

And there was one small drab ring with live donkeys in it.

It was doing the best business. It sported no blast of canned music, either. It could have been a hundred years ago.

Every other stall seemed to have its own loudspeaker and its own supply of worn records, with at least one tired blonde woman or poker-faced, gravelly-voiced man muttering into a little speaker fastened against their faces. It was bedlam, and I kept looking down desperately into the puddles with lottery tickets floating on them, as if to stop my ears with water.

On the children's side of the street there was one mirror house, of course, and across from it a single shoddy peepshow instead of the old row of them. A man in a strange striped coat promised hopelessly that a red-haired beauty would cut off, any minute now, the head of a black-haired beauty, both of whom stood there waiting for some tickets to be sold, as remote as cobras or plow horses, with fairly good bodies but venomously dead eyes.

So Mary and I saw all this, and I tried not to say much, for I could see that she dreamed passionately to return. And that was what she and Anne then did, all week, with or without other girls and boys. They brought back their prizes to me, mostly of bright dyed chicken feathers: one was a little paper heart, one a queer cutting from an old postcard of a man and woman about to kiss or be sick, encircled with fluffy lavender feathers and pasted for some reason to the end of a stick. I never questioned the allowances I kept advancing them. They were having fun.

I was not. It was probably not because I was so much older, either. Perhaps it was the new noise coming from all the loudspeakers at once? I used to like going to little fairs with my father in California, before there were radios. It was the onslaught of sound that made me afraid to go down to the Cours to lunch, I knew . . .

. . . and it was what had driven us away from Aix, six years before.

I had to walk through it and past it several times a day, and at night it seeped down the Rue Cardinale and up into our rooms at Madame Lanes', and I became inwardly fretted by it, worn by it.

The whole town seemed to be caught up in a kind of tarantella of sound, whirling faster and faster, and there were hundreds of Gypsies and carnies camped around the edges of their caravans and stalls, whipping the receptive townspeople into the nearest thing I have ever seen to a mass frenzy.

The staid Cours was decked out like a dignified brothelkeeper of advanced age and prestige, in colored lights and huge painted Mickey Mouse characters which hung across from one wide sidewalk to the other, and swung sickeningly in the wet winds that had blown since the Carnaval opened. The lesser streets along the route designated for the two grand parades were only slightly lesser madams.

Sword swallowers, trained poodles, and a handful of rather cautious or perhaps only tired belly-dancers performed in the stands along the Avenue Victor-Hugo and sometimes on the sidewalks of the Cours, and on corners big bubbling copper pots of sugared nuts and potato chips sent up almost unbearably fallacious fumes into the cold air. The carnies yelled and pounded drums and cymbals. Fifteen full bands and trumpet groups from every place from Arles to Bordighera banged and blew whenever they felt like it as well as for the official parades and athletic events and races. At seemingly inaudible signals like those heard by great flights of starlings, at least forty thousand of the fifty thousand Aixois shrieked and threw confetti, and popped guns at the clay pigeons and corks in all the cafés, and made noisy love everywhere.

It was to last twelve days.

The first four days were interesting and fun for my girls and me, who had never before been swept along in such a pagan sporting. We too popped both corks and guns, and rode on the latest thing in provincial roller coasters, and ate sugared nuts and potato chips and got lost in the Mysterious Maze of Mirrors and patted most of the trained poodles, and at night shook confetti from our clothes onto the dark sidewalks of the Rue Cardinale, before we tiptoed up the great staircase to Madame Lanes' apartment.

And suddenly the razzle-dazzle, which must have risen audibly a mile into the sky above the lovely old town, became too much.

On the first Sunday, about eleven, I went up to the top of the Cours with the children, and in some ways which I do not remember but which accumulated in my deafened spirit, I was pushed rudely and I was rebuked bruskly for starting to go through the wrong gate at the wrong time, or something harmless like that, and instead of forgetting it I felt weighed down by a listless loneliness. I found a Boy Scout selling tickets to go onto the fenced Cours later, and we went up through the Passage Agard to the Brasseie across from the Palace of Justice, where all the First Grand Parade was to form. We sat in the pale sunlight on the glassed *terrasse*, and I recovered from my depression, but can still evoke it.

The owner of the Madeleine gave us the table in the corner, the best one for seeing the whole assembling of the bands, the clowns, the floats. It was delightful. It was confused, in a way unique to Provence.

Several groups dressed in gawdy matching band costumes, young boys all in natty pearl-gray with scarlet satin capes, older men stuffed into maroon trousers and lavender jackets under their purple faces, everyone with an instrument bobbing alongside, searched nonchalantly, it seemed to us, for their prescribed meeting places.

Hundreds of children in cowboy costumes and frowzled tutus, all heavily made up by stage-struck mothers, ran past our window, and Anne shuddered with envy when two of her

classmates from Ste. Catherine teetered by in real satin opera
pumps to join the court of a midget Marie Antoinette on one
of the floats.

Then the floats themselves lunged and shook monstrously
down the Rue Peyresc from the Rue Rifle-Rafle, past the
Prison, to the first stop on their hazardous creep from the covered market, where they had been built and painted. They
blocked off the ominous Prison completely and stood almost
as tall, it seemed to us, as the Palace of Justice, where they
paused ponderously for the official start of the first parade.

The bands all tooted their own notes.

From where we sat, there seemed to emerge a kind of order.
From above, it must have looked like the concentric crowdings
of a thousand ants around a handful of scattered crumbs. And
then the first bands headed down the Rue Thiers toward the
head of the Cours, and the first great ugly float trundled after
it, like a swollen old dowager resolutely returning, edemic and
doughty, to the scenes of her early social triumphs.

We hurried the rest of our good lunch, and cut through the
middle of the seething paraders waiting to take their places
according to the order in the programs, and got through the
Passage Agard in time to see the head of the procession come
into view: the first of the fifteen bands, and then endless floats
top-heavy with costumed children. We had not bought places
on the ineffectual little camp chairs, but roamed at will up and
down the sidewalks, inside the fences. It was tiring and fun.

The day turned very cold, dark with unshed snow. We
worked our way into the Deux Garçons for a drink.

There were many more bands, and clowns with heads on
long necks swooping and miming, and always the bands of
costumed children waving from the tall floats to their happy
parents, and folklore groups dancing with their strange air of
patronizing enjoyment to flutes and drums, and then it was the
end of things with the grand float of his Majesty Carnaval

LVIII, and the real confetti fight started. Until that moment all that we had seen had been practice and unofficial, even though the streets had been snowed with it for at least four days.

A few genteel people we knew were somewhat timidly tossing little handfuls of confetti here and there near the *terrasse* of the café: Henriette Lanes and Lise, looking almost young in a deliberate way behind their masks, dodged in and out of the people at the tables and then seemed suddenly cross when Anne and Mary recognized them enough to throw a little confetti on their collars. And gradually things grew less well bred.

We went through the fence gates onto the Cours. It was beautiful there, without any cars, under the bare giant trees. Their branches reflected the garish lighting of the decorations overhead, and the people looked tiny on the black pavement, which gradually turned white. Confetti stands along the right side of the Cours sold at recklessly mounting prices, in spite of the official warnings against such profiteering in the program (which started out in red ink: *The Committee declines all responsibility for accidents or thefts which might occur during the festivities*).

Against one of the old trees a man with an enormous flat basket of lavender scooped up what was left of it into a flour sack, and went away, but I could stand there two days later and still smell the faint reminder.

We went back to the sidewalk, and a few little boys ran after Anne and Mary, some truly daring and some only drunk with bravado, and lifted the little black lace flaps of their masks and tossed confetti into their mouths. The girls dodged about, and screamed happily.

From Victor-Hugo I could hear the merry-go-rounds. We headed that way: I had seen enough of the increasingly weary gayety on the Cours. Boys were beginning to scoop up the filthy paper petals from the sidewalks, and throw them with brutality . . .

A slender tall man about my age, or perhaps younger, walked straight up to me, looked searchingly at my face, which was not masked, and threw straight into my eyes and not my nose or mouth a handful of confetti, with what I seemed to remember later as a small happy smile.

He disappeared while I gasped and then almost cried out, for the stuff was violently painful, and as I recovered from my first amazement and began to push it from around my eyes I saw that it was mixed with fine shreds of tobacco from an unsmoked cigaret. It had been carefully mixed. It was hard to get out.

My eyes cried, whether I wanted them to or not, to rid themselves of the cruel stuff. I stood there weeping, with black shapes running and screaming all around me and the music thumping up the Cours. The girls came back and I told them I had got some confetti in my eyes. They had wanted me to wear a mask all along, but it would not have made any difference.

We walked slowly through the thinning crowd to the Glacier. It was packed with people waiting for buses. Ange saw us and somehow he sat us at a tiny table, the kind such restaurants keep to squeeze into the aisles on fat days, and without my asking he brought hot tea for the children and a glass of brandy for me. He seemed to murmur, but it must have been a shout in that hubbub, "You should take the girls home now. Go on home."

My eyes kept crying, and I felt that nothing had ever been more painful to me in a surface way, and no confusion had ever been greater outwardly, nor no silence more complete within.

The people pushed and shouted and drank, released for a time, not happy but freed from all the strictures of ordinary conduct. But I myself did not seem to need or want this scheduled induced freedom. I felt invisible in a wrong way. The children looked happy as they sagged over their tea, their masks pushed back on their foreheads; the confetti caught in their dark hair was beautiful.

"You should go home and rinse out your eyes," Ange stated clearly over the din, and with a look it was understood that I would pay him the next day, and we shoved our way hastily out through the packed café and into the mob around the bus stop on the Rotonde. The noise was wild, and people bumped and pushed ferociously to get to their big cars marked Avignon, Pertuis, Berre, and they yelled in drunken time to a band that still thumped on its biggest drums and played an occasional tipsy fanfare all askew, by the grandstand built around the big fountain.

I lost Anne for a minute. Then she bobbed up like a small navy-blue cork frosted with confetti. Her eyes were enormous ripe plums behind the mask she had pulled down again, and until we could not find Mary I knew that she was really alive and in tune with this compulsive noise that to her was music.

We clutched hands and pushed this way and that as fast as we could, crying out Mary's name into an impossible noise. It was like weeping one salt tear into a sea . . .

Mary was taller than the Aix children of her age, but still she was living below the bleared eye level of almost everybody: it was impossible to see her. I had trust in her good sense, but still I could not swallow a sick fear for her as we called and shoved through the wild mob at the end of the Cours. Now Anne's face under the mask looked gray, and her hand in mine was a desperate claw.

We turned back to the Glacier finally, and found Ange, and I tried to keep fright out of my voice as I yelled at him that Mary was lost.

"But she is here," he said. "She had been here for at least a quarter-hour. Come back with me."

I felt my guts turn over with relief. We went back into the dark corridor between the kitchen and the toilets, and there on a pile of coats against the wall she slept, as comfortable as a fat little mole in its hole, as asleep as a bear in the deep winter. She had got separated from us, and gone back to Ange.

We almost ran home. The Rue Cardinale was empty and quiet. Mary staggered along in her own sleep-world, and Anne grew young again, and that night when she undressed there was some confetti in her panties, which I thought amusing, although she was delightedly prim about it.

At supper Henriette and Lise still seemed genteelly gay, and pretended to be incredulous that "two little rude demons" had thrown confetti at them. We smiled and jabbered, all part of the whirling sound and the foolish yet scheduled cruelty of Carnaval to my tired spirit. I felt dangerously lost, not strong enough to be a good bulwark anymore. And the next day I made plans to go away. We would stay until Lent began, and the confetti was all washed away, and the grotesqueries of the great swollen beckoning floats were hidden for another year behind the covered market. King Carnaval LVIII was dead . . .

. . . and then he was alive again, six years, six centuries older, like me. He was tracing new lines on my invisible map. The noise was more ferocious than ever, thanks to a municipal mal-investment of a modern loudspeaker system for the Cours, and to the little portable radiophones all the carnies wore. People seemed to walk faster, more nervously, along the streets, with all the ambling students gone to earth, and familiar faces absent as we once had made ourselves.

I could not help enjoying, still, the relentless strong squat bodies and faces, and the small hard eyes, of the people who ran the stalls on the Midway. Along the right side of the Cours, all the portable stands that sold confetti and nougat and imitation-felt cowboy hats were up . . . whistles with feathers at the end to tickle people . . . masks of girls for boys to wear, and ghastly imitations of men's faces for girls to wear above their tight blue jeans and their flimsy leather Russian boots . . .

Men were still testing the myriad bulbs on the giant stars strung across the two wide sidewalks and the grotesque bright "theme pieces" that swung at intervals over the Cours itself. This would be the brightest Carnaval ever, the city fathers had decreed . . .

All week holes were being filled in the pavement, so that the cumbersome floats would not topple into the crowds and crush people or break trees, and the electric current had been turned off to try out the possible and impossible capacity of the town's lighting system, and at night the light in our rooms at the hotel was too dim for reading, so that the Midway and the Cours could blaze correctly, and the merry-go-rounds could whirl, and all the loudspeakers could pour out their canned tunes and their commercials for washing machines, gingerbread, and aspirin, and their occasional official announcements.

And all of it, I thought sadistically, was for the last time, according to sour towny rumors. I was glad. Once it may have been delightful, when people were simpler and more truthful about preparing themselves for the long night of Lent by a light tonic of license. By now it had become a travesty, gawdy and not gay at all, nor any more essential to the exploding old/new town than a soporific to an already drowsy convalescent.

I could not envy my girls their fresh acceptance of Carnaval, but as I got ready to leave the hotel for the blasting Cours, I was thankful that I could stay invisible, not run away this time . . .

The Hôtel de Provence

Hotel: later form of hostel; an inn, especially one of a superior kind,
1765.

Shorter Oxford English Dictionary

THE Rue Espariat runs off at a mild tangent to the Cours,
from their starting place at the Rotonde, so that by the
time one is at its end, on the Place St. Honoré, the Cours itself
is a long block to the south, instead of only a few feet.

Two of the most beautiful fountains in Aix divide it into
three sections of small shops and an occasional old town-house
of great nobility.

One is in the tiny Place des Augustins: a Roman column
rescued from some mausoleum, surmounted by a copper star
with six points. Once I slept for almost two weeks in a room
just above it in the Hôtel de France, while I was waiting to
enter Madame Lanes' sedate apartment as a boarder. I was glad
to go, for the sound of the fountain was almost lost in the roar
of two or three Vespa clubs, which met there in the Place at
odd hours of the night, to start out on country rallies.

The other fountain, in a gracious cobbled courtyard open to
the street, faces the town-house d'Albertas, which was built in
1707 by a great family of Aix. It is one of the most harmonious
blendings I have ever seen, of form in its own high basin and
in the ordered subtly ornamented façades of the buildings that
enclose it lightly, and then of sound, and of light itself on the
ever-flowing water which falls from the high basin into the
one below and of more light on the soft rose-yellow stone of

the buildings. Never did I pass this melodious little courtyard without veering irresistibly into it, off the street, to rest my eyes and ears from everything but its beauty.

Between the two fountains stand, on one side of the Rue Espariat the Church of the Holy Spirit, and facing it across the street the fifteenth-century Tour des Augustins. That is very worn now, and the fine ironwork belfry is silent, but the color of it in the sunset is deathless . . . or should I be surer and say only that as long as I myself live I shall see it?

Then there is a little wall statue in a niche, of St. Roch and his best dog, a coyote-faced animal but with trust in him as he leans against his protector. They look down the old Rue de la Masse, which like a few other streets was gradually being res-cued and reformed when I was last in Aix. Beautiful old doors and archways were emerging from the boards and plaster of the last two hurried centuries, and the shape of the ancient courtyards and convents was returning to the intelligent owners and shopkeepers who were, it seemed, feeling a new custodianship. It was pleasant . . .

Espariat climbs just enough to give it a special perspective, extremely beautiful at night when it is empty, or at sunset when the buildings glow with an almost audible vibration of golden light.

On the map of Aix it is straight, but on my private one it curves slowly south again at the Church of the Holy Spirit, so that from the edge of the terrace at the Glacier our hotel is out of sight. At least, I was never able to see it from there, but only to know where I would turn in, off the rough side-walks, which like many in Aix are wide, narrow, high, non-existent, with steps jutting out into them, potholes, cobbles one minute, slick old granite and marble slabs the next, now and then new cement. Tourists and a few elderly ladies com-plain, but after a time there it becomes second nature to know where to put one's feet without consciously watching.

The Hôtel de Provence is about two-thirds of the way up toward the end of the Rue Espariat, then, on the righthand side. It makes up most of an odd little triangle formed where the Rue Papassaudi loops off it to join the Rue Nazareth. We lived there for one school-year with the Segonds who owned it.

Anne's two windows gave onto Nazareth, and at night she could hear the beautiful fountain in the Place d'Albertas, a hundred feet or so farther east. Mary and I slept in a larger room which was the family center, and our three windows opened mostly onto rooftops. Across the narrow Papassaudi we looked down into the dim room of our only visible neighbors, although sometimes we could hear the little son of Monsieur François the tailor roaring in what seemed a life-rage, in their apartment above the shop across from Anne.

We were on the top floor of the hotel. Sometimes the stairs were longer and steeper than others, but our big room was always one of the most welcoming I have known. It had the right feeling to it.

We were too high for the radiator to work well, but in the little toilette at the end which had been made by squaring off the point where the hotel fitted into the triangle, so that it was itself a small agreeable triangle filled with cupboards, there was usually hot water in the basin and the bidet.

There were almost plenty of bookcases, and two beds that looked like couches, and two good tables for my work and for the children's homework and for countless picnics, feasts, and other ceremonies. On the marble mantel under a big dim mirror there was the perfect place for our record player and a changing parade of animals carved from olive wood, of *santons*, of shells from Porquerolles, and masks and fans from the Carnaval . . . immediate treasures. The floor was red tiles, and the wallpaper was bright pink and yellow, but we did not feel anything more than an affectionate disregard for them:

they seemed exactly right, if we had been questioned. Colors in Provence are not like any others . . .

I was never happy about Anne's room on the Rue Nazareth, which had a subtle gloom about it that probably contributed to one or two periods of strong depression in her. Dr. Vidal called them School Blues, and once we simply walked off from her work at the Lycée and Mary's classes at the Bon Départ, and went to Porquerolles. It worked well, but still I always wanted Anne to move, and always she resisted me fiercely. At least she could hear the fountain, I would try to reassure myself.

There were five rooms on each floor of the hotel, not counting the first where there were the offices and where once had been an elegant dining room. Its walls were covered with enormous dim panels of Provençal scenes, probably of little value except that they had been done long before auto routes and oil refineries changed the outlines of the land. Above the door was a large vignette of Frédéric Mistral: the owner's father had been a "Félibrige" member, one of the poet's disciples, and the good restaurant he ran there had long been a gathering place of their local enthusiasts, pledged to sing and write and speak the pure tongue of Provence.

There was one sign left of their ardor, a handsome shy boy who stayed overnight on the floor below us, every two weeks. He looked at us without a word, and Anne and Mary shuddered with a pleasure which I could still understand. Outside his door would stand his tall laced tambour. Inside by his bed, we were sure, lay his fife.

My girls called him Lou Tambourinaïre, and because of the *santons* and a few folklore celebrations we had seen, we knew that he would be the most beautiful one for at least a century. He would wear a broad-brimmed blue hat straight on his head, and a black coat and white canvas pants. The drum would hang from a thick strap over his left arm, and he would beat its slanted head with a little stick in his nimble right hand, and with his left play the thin short fife.

We always hoped, for our own reasons, that Madame Segond would introduce us, but she respected his dignity as the most famous *tambourinaire* of his age in all the Midi, and only told us once of a radio program we might listen to, if we but had a radio. For us he was the last of the Félibriges, and naturally the noblest.

Next to us on the top floor lived a dry silent man who for a long time had been a colleague of our friend Georges at the University of Dijon. He taught at the Law School or the Faculté des Lettres, I forget which. He was a good friend of the Segonds too, and she teased and pampered him with equal malice, and enjoyed forcing him to exchange more than a nod on the stairs: he plainly recoiled from so many females at once.

I wished that he would go away and let Anne have his room, but it was sacred to him, his home, although from what I could see when the maids were cleaning it with the door ajar, it could as well have been empty: he did not smoke, cough, even breathe, as far as we knew, although occasionally there was a book left precisely in the middle of the otherwise bare table.

Many people who came for a few nights to the hotel were old customers, and it sounded gay and smelled good when we went past the Segonds' low apartment back of the first landing and heard them all together: they still knew how to eat well, even though the breakfasts served at a few tables in the dismal back end of the old restaurant were perhaps the worst we had ever tasted.

The first morning there, I arranged to have it in our new room, which looked big and bright. It seemed a fine way to start the children off to school: hot milky coffee and fresh rolls and butter. But it was long in coming, and when it did get up to our level, I knew I must never try it again, for the old man who climbed trembling and wheezing up with the tray was, as far as I could tell, ready to die. It was dreadful.

The next morning we ate in the dim hideous screened-off part of the old restaurant, which had a few armchairs and two writing desks up front. I had thought that the breakfast was bad the first day because it was cold and mostly spilled, but it was simply *bad*. The coffee was thin and bitter. The butter was old. The milk was bluish, good only to make a thick skin on itself. The *croissants* were faintly rancid, and like wet felt inside. This is something that was always a puzzle to me, for we got to know the Segonds and to call them good friends, and knew of their gastronomical backgrounds as children of famous restauranteurs and brothers of great chefs.

I decided, fairly soon, that the best answer might be the old man who had first served us: it was he, the night watchman, who made the coffee and heated the milk on a two-burner stove in a tiny cupboard behind the desk where he sat up all night, copying out the accounts in a fine hand and opening the huge front door for a rare night owl among the staid clients. He was the most exhausted old man I have ever seen, and the frailest, although he did not seem to have a cough or to wince or limp. He was very small, and weighed perhaps sixty pounds.

Gradually we learned that when he finished his night's work at the Provence he went home and took care of a bedridden wife. At the hotel he also took care of the furnace. We never saw him anywhere but bent over his bookkeeping, at night, but hoped that in the small hours he might fold himself into one of the furiously uncomfortable chairs in the old restaurant.

Madame Segond was disappointed when after two breakfasts I told her that because of getting the girls off to school I felt it best to walk up the Cours with them for a quick *café au lait*. I could never tell her, of course, that in the hotel we seemed to be eating the old man, for that was what it amounted to: the dreadful coffee, the thin lukewarm milk, even the bread were a kind of summing-up, in cup and plate, of his infinite weariness.

Now and then people would stay for a week or two, waiting for a house to be painted or a job to be vacated, but in general we were the only regular lodgers, with the inaudible professor.

Once about fifteen English boys came for some courses at the University. They were very loud and dirty, and I was relieved that they were not Americans. (This was part of my conditioned pattern: I was hyperconscious of the fact that very often noisy people in restaurants and trains and so on were my compatriots, and that even if they weren't, many French people would scornfully assume them to be, from habit. This depressed me. Often it made me what Madame Lanes would call a little *neurasthénique* and defensive. I could not repress a triumphant pleasure when occasionally a Frenchman would outshout-outboast-outbully any Yank I had ever heard, even the occasional Western politicians who stamped through the Midi now and then wearing their loud-mouthed naïveté and their high-heeled boots.)

Next to our big room was the only bath in the hotel, so that by law we could not keep it to ourselves. A bath cost about ten cents, as I remember. The few people who used it evidently felt that this price included full maid service, but the two overworked slaveys in the hotel did not, so that I usually cleaned the tub in self-protection. I decided then that many people are latently swinish and that I would rather work anywhere than in a hotel.

Next to this little room, which I always wished I could paint and make into my own idea of how to enjoy a toilet and a tub, there was another of about the same size, shaped like it to fit into the triangle. At one end it was perhaps five feet wide, and at the other about seven, so that it was tight indeed for a narrow bed, some shelves, and the tiniest washbasin I have even seen except at the end of a third-class French train.

This room too made me want to pull down the dingy faded *tissu provençal* that tried to cover its shelves and spots, and slap some paint around, and make it mine. I could put Anne and Mary together in the big room, I thought. I could type and sleep in this little cupboard, fresh and clean and with the sound of the fountain at night.

But Madame Segond was almost aloof about it: she must keep the room for servants of her friends, sent in from the country on errands. Later I understood that she must keep it so that at least one room in the little hotel could honestly be rented, now and then, for the lowest price marked in the ratings in the guide books. As she knew us better she let our friends stay there now and then, especially if I told her they were poor artists, which often they were.

The lodger I remember most in that tiny room I saw only for a moment, the morning after I had listened all night to heartbroken sobs from it. He was a short strong man of about twenty-two, dressed in farm clothes. He looked angrily at me as he dashed down the stairs. His door was half-open, and as I went to wake Anne I saw that the bed had not been turned down, but was rumpled as if a child had played on it.

Toward the end of our stay at the Provence, the Segonds told us that they were in the process of selling it. He was far from well, a gray-faced man with a bad heart, and a very sensitive man, to make it worse. She was no longer young enough to cope with the whole strenuous business of maids-linens-repairs-taxes-correspondence. They were negotiating with "a blackfoot" from Algeria, a wealthy widow who would make the hotel her French residence and keep up its good reputation.

All this seemed wise, but we felt strangely distressed and knew that we would never return, even before we met the new owner. The moving was painful: Monsieur had another heart attack; Madame wept quietly for days; the two maids wept; Anne and Mary tried not to cry when they saw the heavy Provençal furniture being carried down from the Segonds' little apartment; I tried not to feel panicky, and resisted my usual impulse in such moments to snatch both girls from school and flee to Porquerolles.

The worst part was taking down the wall pictures in the old restaurant. I flapped around, helpless, while they were cut down and peeled from the walls: they belonged to the new owner, Monsieur said quietly. I asked if some of the Félibriges knew. He said that he had spoken with them, and with two or three of the art dealers, and that this had only made the new owner firmer in her wish to keep them.

They were of little value, but she would not know that. Why not ask to buy them for the canvas, I asked . . . young artists needed good old canvas, and that could be used as an excuse to keep the huge paintings . . . perhaps Monsieur Segond's brother who was making the Château de Meyrargues into a fine small restaurant-hotel could hide them, perhaps even use them?

It was hopeless: Segond was too weary, and he was not, he added delicately, used to dealing with people like the new owner.

The children and I went away like sick dogs for a weekend, and when we came back Mistral and all his countryside had gone, and striped wallpaper was being slapped over the scraped plaster. And although we stayed on for two or three more months, Lou Tambourinaïre never came back.

The new owner should be mentioned as little as possible, probably: life is too short. Two things were enough to fix her on the map for us: the maids and the ancient night watchman stormed off or vanished silently, according to their strengths; in one of our few conversations the woman told me that she had felt it in the wind to sell everything in Al-

geria and buy a hotel near the Coast, so that when her coun-
trymen were forced to flee, she could charge them double in
their panic.

We stayed until time to leave, but the big room did not
seem so bright, and we were seldom in it unless it was the
time to be. It grew to feel like a chore to pass the low apartment at the first landing, where once good sounds and smells
had cheered us: now it was a bower of silver and pale blue
satin, half-filled by an enormous bed piled with tiny pillows,
on which lay the small fat woman who had kept the paintings.
She had perhaps been pretty once, and her hair bubbling from
under her lace "boudoir cap" was bright red, and her skin
was very white, and she was afraid of the whole world. She
was impossibly rude to almost everyone but us, which was
what sickened us the most.

We stayed away all we could, for I was determined to make
every minute that was left to us a good one, and so we did.

Men and Women Mendicants

> . . . at last, little by little, in battles,
> sieges, attacks, campaigns, yes, and in
> their winter quarters too, soldiers per-
> ish, they die, they rot and consume
> away, save but a few, who in their old
> age do furnish us with the best of all
> beggars and vagabonds.
>
> H. J. C. von Grimmelshausen,
> *The Adventurous Simplicissimus*

i

ONE cold twilight of mid-January, with no sunset but no real rain or snow, I heard over all other sounds, of cars and footsteps and an occasional child's calling, a thin accordion song. I knew who was playing it and I felt depressed. I had seen the man often before, with his two little dogs; one day he would be by the Little Market, then down on the Cours, then other days at the Big Saturday Market.

The first time, I felt guilty at not putting something in the little baskets his patient dogs held in their mouths as they sat on a soft pad of old carpeting he laid down for them. The second time I stopped, put down my own baskets and hand-bag, and got out an inadequate number of coins. I divided them, half for each basket. The man behind his dark glasses, even before I had put them in, thanked me, and continued wheezing a dull bass on his instrument. A few paces past him, I heard the sound stop. Vaguely I felt annoyed at him and the puny world.

Later, when I first heard his squeal of sound from my room at the Hôtel de Provence, with somewhat the same impatience at first, I did not think so much about him as about the newsvendor.

He was a man of the same indescribably malnourished twisted non-age of all such physical jetsam being helped by government benevolence, like the one who took tickets at the municipal theater and the one who sat waiting to polish shoes in the public toilet in the Herbs Market. He had a thin dark-eyed face, with several teeth lacking and the rest black and doomed.

I liked this man, at least as far as our current relationship went, and when we passed on the street we usually smiled. I forced him to meet my eyes, and then we smiled. It was a form of lovemaking which did not at all bother me, but of course it would be impossible to explain to my children.

In cafés and restaurants, when the newsvendor came in, I sometimes let my eyes meet his, and then we would salute each other thus, or I very consciously did not look at him and then would feel a slight jar of loss, of disappointment. It was a small connection, but good, like two rocks falling down a cliff together to join the sea.

Once in a restaurant Anne and Mary said, "Oh, here comes that man. I suppose you'll smile at him again. Why, why?"

I said, "I have only bought three newspapers from that man in six months, but we like to smile at each other, that is why."

And when they asked me, half-teasing half-frightened as such young females can be, why I enjoyed this occasional deep unquestioning fleeting communion I seemed to have with the instant of our eyes meeting, our lips grimacing, I said, "Perhaps it is because he has only two teeth and I have never before known anyone with only two teeth who could smile at me so sweetly, so unquestioningly."

"Oh God," they cried, and flapped sideways limply on walls, the way adolescents and great comedians do.

One day, then, I was going down the Cours, after having seen the little man and his two dogs at the Friday Market, and there he was standing by one of the benches with his blindman's black glasses pushed up on his forehead, and he was cutting neatly at the ends of a piece of rope.

Beside him stood the newsvendor, holding the two patient little dogs who always sat with the baskets in their mouths for pennies and their behinds on the piece of clean old carpet, but this time in the arms of a friend, and licking his face and shaking with joy. He looked very happy too.

I did not think it proper to intrude. But there for a flash it was the same as usual: his small black eyes met mine over the heads of the dogs and we all, I was certain, felt fine about things.

I went on down the Cours.

The little dogs undoubtedly went home sedately with their master, at the ends of the new rope leashes, and he was neither truly blind nor truly an accordion player, and later the newsvendor came into the place where we were eating lunch and I looked only at his back as he left. Perhaps in the same way he did not see me.

Late that afternoon I heard the first squeal from the street below our rooms, and I wondered if the little dogs could be there too, in the cold, but I did not look. And the next day he seemed to be settled there on his little folding stool, at the corner of Nazareth and Espariat.

I made myself lean out of our toilet window, to prove to myself that this sour music was as unmistakably his as I had first feared: it was indeed he, in the soft drizzle, with his helpers sitting on the small old rug beside him, holding the little Easter-egg baskets for chance coins.

His playing was dreadful, heard steadily and not in a quick

snatch. He seemed to know only one position in the left hand, so that although he could give out a strong and well timed if mistaken air with the right, there was always the same surly chord underneath. What was worse, the accordion had many exhausted flattened notes.

He played with what seemed almost enthusiasm, even at the end of a Saturday, when I knew he was always in the Big Market early and long. I wished he would go away from our corner: he had a strange tragic habit of wheezing through three old movie tunes, always using the same bass and quite often not remembering whether he was playing "Never on Sunday" or "Around the World in 80 Days," any suite of three such songs, and then, as if he were Larry Adler on the stage of the Alhambra, or Charles Trenet, a proud grand flourish.

Silence, except for the feet hurrying past.

Then he would play three more almost-tunes and end with another flourish, like a soprano hitting her high C and holding it.

Silence.

I did not want to look down from the toilet window. The dogs would be staring straight ahead over their little baskets. The man would be bent over his accordion. I dreamed vaguely about throwing down a handful of bills, ten francs, a hundred francs, everything I had. But the dogs would not know why I wanted them to be picked up, and the man perhaps could not see them . . . or even coins that none of them could pick up or see, or a note saying "Please go away" wrapped around a banknote and a stone. Who could read, who understand?

Certainly not I if I were the man or one of his gentle uncomplaining dogs . . . and how could I, if I were the man or the dogs, comprehend the tragedy in that evenly spaced finale?

It was always three tunes, played with the stolid dutiful concentration of a man who had probably never even whistled straight until they taught him to play an accordion in the Military Hospital when he lost his eyesight, and then, like a sugar cube to the deserving horse, he must always toss himself a suddenly professional one-two-three-hoop-la before the silent applause . . .

I felt sickish, so high above him, guilty for my dread at always having him end thus. I wished that he could at least not finish his dreadfully cheerfully hopeless meaningless almost musical din with this catastrophic smirk of self-approbation. I was ashamed of myself.

I wished it would rain harder, so that he would slowly fold the little soggy carpet and pour the pennies into his pocket from the baskets and tie the new ropes around his dogs' necks and go away.

Go where?

Away.

Surely it was a question of not knowing more than one chord in the bass?

ii

THERE WAS ONE old woman with an empty can, the kind that in America would have held salted peanuts. Someone had bent down the edge clumsily for her, so that it did not cut into her thin papery skin. She stood without a sound at the corner on the Rue Espariat and the Rue Nazareth, across from the beautiful Albertas town-house, and now and then she seemed to seep a little eastward as the sun sank and left her colder against the wall.

She was small, and like many women in her circumstances she may once have been beautiful, with fine withdrawn nose and mouth and eye sockets. She was always dressed in the shapeless coverings of the very old when they are poor and do not have proper shawls and bonnets.

The thing about her that got under our skins, and began to trouble us where, we all knew, we had earned the right to be troubled, was that she simply stood. She did not move in any way at all except now and then to edge toward the sun. She stood.

She stood in the rain . . . not the hard mean kind but the warm kind that was paid little heed in Aix. She stood in the heat of the first summer days when the street seemed to be ready to crack open.

And she never asked for anything. Her blind large eyes were half-closed as if in sleep. Her mouth was softly shut, and her nostrils did not seem to flutter with her invisible breath. Her hand, moreover, did not shake. But when we put something in that artfully arranged ugly little can in her unfaltering hand, we all, Anne and Mary and I and perhaps countless others, felt a terrible slow anger because it was so plain to us that she had been put there like a doll, placed there, shaped into the image of an almost invincible human being. The people who made the can fit her hand had fitted her also into the corner of the streets where Espariat met Nazareth, and we felt, without active rage but with sorrow, that she was left to stand there, blind and beautiful, until someone came to count the money and lead her back to wherever she lay until she went on stage again.

Now and then her lips would smile a little when the coins sounded like more than a penny. That was part of what she had been instructed to do and be.

She was not like the other one who used to come up the Rue Nazareth from the Cours. She was ferocious, not gentle. She fought every inch of her loud rhythmic way.

She was perhaps six feet tall, which in Provence is gigantic for a woman. Maybe she was from the North, or perhaps even from Burgundy where Rude made the heads of those magnificent women who scream down from the Arc de Triomphe in Paris. She had the same majestic stride and the same turn to her neck.

But she was the shambles, the ultimate wreck of a woman. She was diseased, so that her legs were grotesquely swollen and decaying under her. Her body too was grotesquely puffed out here, bitten into there. One of her eyes lay forever open on her cheek. Her mouth gapped with empty holes. She was a human mess.

She would start singing as she turned off the Cours. (Only once did I see her there, and she was not welcome because of her enormous female decadence. The waiters pushed her along with a kind of compassionate speed toward the corner where she would leave.)

In my room at the hotel I would hear her, and part of me would die off, because she was made as many of the women of my family were made, with long thighs, strong necks, small high-arched feet and wrists. I could look down at her from the toilet window, as I tried not to do, and see us there, all of us sisters . . .

The last time I heard her singing, a little girl went ahead with tutored patience and martyrdom and picked up the pennies that people threw onto the streets in front of her, for nobody wanted to risk touching her, and she was almost blind and too enormous to lunge and grope toward any café table. The girl was dressed in what seemed to be a neat blue school uniform, which showed up like a scream to the tawdry haphazard clothing of the magnificent wreck of a woman.

They came on up the Rue Nazareth, as usual. I could see from the little window where I kneeled on the toilet that people were throwing coins down, rather than descend and touch this creature. The little girl from the school, going through who can tell what private hells of embarrassment and even dutiful boredom, skittered along before and behind, picking up pennies from the relatively clean street.

The woman strode on, and her head was thrown back, and she sang in a way that I have seldom heard in my life. It is called, I think, belting it. She sang from down where her belt might have been, once, when she was younger, and from where most of her breath used to come when she worked in the fields, and made love. Her voice suddenly rose to me, straight to me, as strong and clear as I have ever heard any voice in this world. She lifted her haggard monstrous face, and the sound came up like a bolt of lasting lightning. (The little girl looked up too, and her face was like a custard.)

It was a song for pennies, but I did not throw any down. I felt as if I had been sent some kind of message. Later I dropped some, wrapped in a sheet of typing paper, on the roof of a car, and the little girl in the uniform darted out and got it. She looked up at me and waved, and I liked her better, but I never saw her or the woman again. If she has not died, I am sure she is there in Provence somewhere, still singing her strange sweet triumph.

iii

A PERSONAL MAP, one like mine of Aix, has places on it which no printer could indicate, for they are clear only as a smell, or a sound, or a moment of light or dark.

My whole map has a special smell, of course, apart from a few localized ones like the firm delicate fishiness on Fridays as I walked past the open-fronted stalls piled with seaweed and all the animals of the Mediterranean . . . or like the dark brown greasy smell of the foot-doctor's corridor . . . or the one in the olive oil shop. There is the Aix smell, made up of the best air I have ever breathed, purified by all the foun-

tains and the tall trees and the stalls piled with sweet fresh vegetables in the open markets. I feel quite sure that if I could be teleported, blind, to a dozen places I have known, that smell would be the truest one to my inner nose . . .

It is the same about the whole sound of the place. Jean Cocteau has said that a blind man in Aix would think the city wept, but that is not my hearing of it. Instead, the music of the fountains lies under and in a mysterious way over every other, with a melodious gracious mirthfulness . . . on my own map, that is. And then I hear, always, the street sweeper of the Rue Cardinale, who in the dark of the night turned on the water from the little fountain of St. Jean de Malte and let it flood down the gutters, and then swept them with a broom made of long twigs which scratched forever into the unconscious listener in me. In full moon and dark, in the silent street, this sound became familiar, always almost frightening, always a strange reassurance of order and courage in the face of complete silent loneliness.

The light and dark of a secret map would of course be the most impossible to print. Even more than there is no ink for the smell of the Saturday Market or the sound of a broom in the dark gutter, there is none for some of the colors I shall always see clearly on my own cartography.

Perhaps one day was clearer than any other, for me. It happened about six o'clock. I was standing at the long point of the triangle on the Rue Espariat, in front of the Hôtel de Provence. The most golden sunlight I had seen that year lay suddenly on the old Church of the Holy Spirit, so rosy gold, so pure upon the stone, that I must turn my back on it and hurry up the long flights of stairs to our big room.

Once there I knew that the same light would be falling on all the walls facing the northwest, across from our windows. It caught the edges of the yellow and salmon tiles. It lay over blue pools in the tall shadows of the chimneys. It was, in all,

a profound moment of light itself and its meaning, and perhaps I shall always know when it occurred, if not why.

It seemed to set, to jell, the whole pattern of that day, so
that the lulling trivia fell into their sharp places in the pattern
I must soon break by leaving for California. The moment of
intense golden light fell on them in a way to keep them sharp
always in their proper places for that one day, that one moment, and perhaps the sharpest of all was made at noon, when
the flower-man came into the restaurant and without knowing
it settled a point with my girls.

The settlement was as clear as the crash of a crystal bottle
on a marble floor, as plain to their inner ears as the light was
later on my own vision. It had started about seven years before, when we first went to Aix . . . Then there were more
physically broken people, at least in public.

All, yes, all the newspaper vendors were badly crippled or
maimed or diseased. They hopped and hobbled along the
Cours from one café to another, and I always bought papers
from them, and put coins in the hands and old sardine cans
and laps of the sexless mounds that sat at the edges of the
markets and in the Passage Agard, mounds that in a dreadful
way seemed part of the families of the poor men who sold
papers. It was like the Carnival of the Beggars in a book by
Victor Hugo, so that the gray-blue swaddled baby in a filthy
bitter Gypsy's arms seemed the child or perhaps the great-
grandmother of any one of the newsvendors.

My girls were appalled by them all, not frightened of them
as human beings but as spirits, emanations of war and evil.

I regretted this shock, but I could not hide either side of
it, them from the human remnants, or the omnipresent population of life-in-death from them. So without searching for
the chances I accepted the nightmare, and bought the papers
and stopped to drop the coins.

There was one newsie who gave my girls an especial chill,

mostly because he always shook hands with me. I could not stop him from doing it. He headed straight for me, no matter where we were, and took my hand. Usually before he did so he wiped his dribbling nose with it, or ran it across his crusted eyes. He had only two or three teeth in his mouth, and they were snags, and he bared them at me in a truly horrible grin which was the best he could offer me, and which I recognized as such. But the children were still too young: how could they possibly know yet about the reasons for such ugliness? They were repelled actively as well as instinctively by the creature who saluted me as friend.

They became almost hysterical about it, and would run down dark side-streets to avoid all the quasi-beggars, but especially this most hideous one who never begged, but only touched my hand before he gave me the paper I had bought. Once they swore that they had seen him many miles away, in Avignon, in a café, hobbling along grinning and looking for us . . .

There was another one who sold flowers. He was very bent, as if every bone in him had been crushed beyond setting, and with a sideways walk that got better or worse, so that sometimes his head bobbled like a hunchback's on his crooked shoulders.

Occasionally he could speak and other days he only stuttered, and spit ran out of his very twisted mouth while his eyes, always the same large questioning ones, begged for patience. He was filthy too, and the girls could not bring themselves, even for politeness, to touch the flowers he pulled jerkily from his basket. And I always bought them.

Gradually he seemed, sometimes anyway, to be able to smile at me, and he often added a piece of mimosa or an extra leaf to the posy before he slid crablike out of our view.

Then we began to play a game which upset the children, but I told them why I thought it was a fine idea. The story in Aix was that he had no passport there, but was probably a Pole, escaped somehow from Nazi torture, and that he did no harm, and that although he never replied to questions, he seemed occasionally to speak almost any language a little bit, as if parts of him remembered one at a time what he had once had all in a whole.

He began to look at me, up sideways from his basket of flowers, and mutter a single teasing question at me: "Today are you . . ." and then he would put in any word like Swiss, Italian, Swedish, Dutch. I would say seriously to him, "Today I am Danish," or anything at all, and he would bow a little and hand me the flowers and I would hand him the coin, and if I had misunderstood and it was not enough . . . violets get dearer if it rains, and so on . . . he would stoop sideways a little more and dart reproach at me from his eyes, but now with a strange calmness behind the professional scolding. He seemed, at least to me, to accept me as an equal, a person one could joke with.

But of course all the time he did dribble and mutter, and his poor body looked impossibly warped as he sidled remotely from one café to another along the Cours, and my children hated it when he appeared, whether or not it helped him to try to speak to me. They felt sad and disturbed and repelled, and I understood all of it, but was able, because I had gone so much farther, to make a joke with him now and then and to sense, perhaps to see, surely to feel the look of amusement far behind his enormous glazed eyes.

When we came back, five years later, there were fewer shadowy beggars quavering songs on Market days, and the newsies were feeble but not crippled: dignified men who walked slowly from one café to another as if they had spent a long time in bed.

It was not until one of my girls mentioned casually that the paper-man who always shook hands with me was gone that

I realized that both children had been dreading, perhaps actively fearing, to see him again.

I felt sorry about this, that I had tortured them after my fashion. I still believed that it would have done them infinitely more harm if when the poor foul wretch touched my hand I recoiled from him outwardly. We talked of this, and they were older enough to agree with me and to accept my agreement with them that I too was glad the man no longer hobbled up and down the Cours.

About a few months after we came back, though, the flower seller was there. He looked much better, but was still a bad drawing of a cripple, all bent and fragile.

We were sitting on the terrace of the Deux Garçons with some friends who are impatient of any participation with sidewalk commerce: they consider themselves victimized, conspicuous, in some pernicious way emasculated if they give a Gypsy two pennies or even buy a paper or a flower for value received.

My girls moaned aloud when they saw the familiar flower seller creep toward us, and explained hastily that he was one of my pets, as if I were subnormal. I murmured to be careful, for he might understand English, and then added that he would most surely have forgotten us.

Of course he had not. He came in his painful zigzag to the large table where we sat, and looked up at me slyly and asked, "Are you American today? Or are you Norwegian?"

Perhaps because the children were there, and we were with the friends who could not accept such intercourse, or perhaps only because I was touched to make this strange encounter with a fellow-pilgrim after so long, I took his hand. It was a gray claw. I asked him without any preamble, for it was plain that he knew me, where he had been, and he murmured, "Sanitariums," and slid off, leaving a thin long posy of three cornflowers and some scraggly wallflower beside my glass.

Our friends asked gushingly about him and why he had not asked for money and why I had questioned him, and the children, sensing my wonder, replied gently that he was a man we'd once known.

Before we changed the subject back to genial café chatter, I said that he used not to be able to answer questions but today he'd done so. One of my daughters said, protecting me and not him from the uneasiness of the company, "He looks much better than before." Then we talked about *Le Nozze di Figaro*, I think, which would be given that night in the Archbishop's courtyard: the Music Festival was in its fullest swing.

We saw the little man often after that. Anne and Mary always spotted his painful crawling approach, and said *Again* and froze a little where they sat, and I would know that it could mean only the one hazard.

Yes, he would come gradually and inflexibly toward us. He looked much worse, almost as repulsive as five or six years before. He dribbled, and his eyes were most often unseeing, until he got to us and without smiling looked up sideways at me and mouthed, "Swedish?" or "Dutch?" I always bought flowers, of course, and when I could not get him to tell me the price of them and might hand him too little, he simply held out his hand for another coin, and then added an extra flower to the posy on the table.

I never told my children that once, when I was alone, I asked him bluntly, "Are you all right?"

He looked straight at me for the first time in our relationship, and said, "What do you think?"

"Can you go away again to the san?"

"It is too late," he said impassively, but more clearly than I had ever heard him speak.

He put down his basket, wiped his mouth on his sleeve, and to my astonishment kissed my hand. I was in a sudden daze, partly because I was glad the children were not there, and I do not remember watching him pick up his flower basket and go away. The next time we met, there was hardly a flicker in recognition in his great broken gaze, and he did not ask me what country I came from.

Then, the day of the golden light, while we were lunching at the Mazarin down at the other end of the Cours, he hobbled slowly in, with violets. The girls shuddered invisibly and hopelessly.

As he went past us to some farther tables, I said in what was perhaps a defensive way, "One thing I like about his flowers is that they are fresh and real, not doctored. Those violets, for instance; they smell. They are real, not perfumed."

"Yes yes," the children said with teasing compassion. "But remember that he may speak English."

"He could not have heard, and anyway," I said, "it was not bad, what I said. It was true."

"Yes yes," they soothed.

I got out two francs, which was the last price I'd paid for his flowers, and when he got to the table I said firmly in French, "Good morning. One bunch." I felt bored with my family, tired of the whole grim foolishness of things, things-in-general.

He looked at me and mumbled in his painful broken way, "One franc fifty."

I said firmly, "Thank you," and waved my hand for him to keep the extra coin.

And at that he grinned, a ghastly grin but one that was in his eyes warmly and well, and nimbly took from his pocket a little bottle of violet perfume and dabbed it on the flowers I held.

He did it so fast, and then hobbled off so quickly, that I hardly realized it until I heard my children laughing. They were completely pleased.

"Oh, how wonderful," they exclaimed, full of delight. "He

was teasing you. He heard every word. He is really a wonderful man."

They meant it. I do not know how next they might have
reacted to his appearance if we had stayed longer in Aix and
if he had existed too, but for that one time at least they felt a
complete and indeed almost proprietary pleasure in his odd
little mocking game with me. It was worth much.

For one thing, it made me feel respectful of the map of Aix
which seemed to be drawing itself for me, somewhat as if my
being at that spot of the world was in a way retracing, willy-
nilly, exactly the same lines of streets and buildings and fountains that had already been drawn, but with a different ink . . .

The Outlook Across

Peep-Show: a small exhibition of pictures, etc., viewed through
a magnifying lens inserted
in a small orifice.

Shorter Oxford English Dictionary

i *THE WINDOW*

THE first time I ever looked across and into our neighbors'
window was a Sunday morning, a day or two after we
moved to the Hôtel de Provence from the country.

How nice, I thought, how typically French and simple, to
put a rough table by the open airy window and on it place
some grapes and some bread, four white eggs, and a bottle of
wine with two tumblers! How fine to live near such compan-
ionship, I thought.

It was always impossible to ignore the window, from that
day, for it was only a few feet down from the level of ours,
and the lives of the two people who lived behind it were forever mixed with ours.

That first time I watched, they sat across from each other in
the fine September sun, and slowly ate and drank, with finicky
niceness. Then they finished eating, but they kept on at the
big bottle of wine and by the end of the afternoon had drunk
perhaps two more. Toward evening the man got out a sharp
pocketknife and most fastidiously cut a slice of meat into tiny
perfect cubes, on the windowsill.

Meanwhile they had grown very noisy. They shouted and banged the table, and leaned toward each other as if they had suddenly grown deaf. Often he made menacing gestures with his fists or the knife, and the woman cowered back, but they never touched each other.

We did not mean to snoop into this relationship, but it was very close to us physically, so that we could hear almost every word, even the slow expert clicking of the knife on the window ledge, which was stained dark from many such exhibitions of drunken precision, as we came to know. It was not pleasant at all, to be so near what at first had seemed a dreadful drama induced by too much Sunday wine . . . but all the windows in the town were as open as ours and theirs, and where else could we look, what else listen to?

Gradually our glances across the street became a habit, not inquisitive but fascinated, a morbid preoccupation. Soon I came to feel that I knew almost as much about the people as they did, in their behavior at least, and I regretted that we were always a little apprehensive: if I heard a cry or a crash I looked automatically to see if the woman had fallen, or had been struck . . .

Sometimes she leaned in a staggering heavy way out the window, her elbows askew on the greasy ledge, and I wondered impotently if she might overbalance her poor body and fall out, and split open like a ripe melon, as I had read of Modigliani's girl in Montparnasse long ago. Sometimes the man made such a rough gesture toward her that I was sure he would forget to cut back the speed in his arm and splash her eye out on her cheek, her teeth out on the floor. But nothing happened; they went on living in that one room, sleeping and washing and eating together, in an almost uninterrupted bath of the cheapest wine.

The room was perhaps fifteen feet each way, zigzag like all the attic rooms in the quarter. There was a kind of alcove at the back, with a skylight which I saw yellow at lonely hours in the night. I imagined a bed there. Facing me there was a Provençal chimney and hearth, where often a small fire flickered, and that and a little table burner heated by a can of Sterno or some such chemical were what the woman cooked with.

There was a straight chair by the hearth, where a black dog lay on cold days. I felt that the woman took care of him for one of the other people in the ancient building: I saw her now and then on the street with him on a leash, but I was fairly sure he did not live with her all the time.

There was the table, and then against the only wall I could see there was an ugly old chest of drawers with a gray marble top, on which a few pans and the day's food were put. There were always empty green bottles standing beside the door.

I thought that there was a washstand in the corner between this bureau and the window, for I saw the woman combing her hair there, but I knew that there was no piped water, for it was all dipped from a can underneath the window. I suppose there was some kind of toilet in the hall, or further downstairs.

Things like laundry in such a setting have always interested me, perhaps because for a time I lived in much the same lodgings in Dijon, except that I was young and clean and for the most part happy. Now and then the woman rinsed out a man's shirt and hung with it on the string across the window a pair of dingy pink panties. I imagined that both she and the man had strong smells, probably unnoticed by either of them.

He was bent and thin, with a hawklike face. Perhaps he was fifty, but worn. He was usually unshaven, and judging by his clothes he worked as a hod carrier or a porter. He had a sad fineness that was attractive to me, and although he talked in a helpless impatient way to the woman, in rough words that were limited and coarse, he seemed basically courteous, even gentle.

Sometimes he appeared to be in a kind of rage at the way he was living, the sordid clumsy hopeless filth of it, and he would heat water in a bucket over the hearth flames and splash it onto the floor and scrub with a broom and with dirty rags, all the time snarling at the woman but not touching her, only wrenching the water out of the cloths as if he were twisting a human neck, and kicking at the table leg or even the wall as if they were a body to bruise.

Once, late on a Sunday afternoon, there were cries, and I looked over as if I had been waiting for them, and the woman was leaning out over the foul ledge, half-undressed, her hair down, crying in a wambly voice, "Ah, he will kill me, he will kill me . . . he is taking me . . ."

The man stood close against her and behind, and as I looked, in a glance full of shame at my own peeping, he pulled her dirty hair back gently off her face and pecked once, twice, three times on her neck, in a gesture of passion and pity. I could not look anymore, but closed my window so as not to startle them. I felt somewhat moved sexually, somewhat unstrung with compassionate loneliness . . .

The woman was small, with a shapeless body that occasionally betrayed youth and even grace, as when she stood before a mirror that was invisible to me and pulled the dark hair straight up off her shoulders. There was the remainder of coquetry in her.

Even when, in a flat fumbling way, she slowly peeled a potato or cracked the shell off a boiled egg, her swollen fingers looked as if once they had moved lightly. Her skin was dull, and although I saw her only two or perhaps three times on the street I could guess that her legs were heavy, over inadequate feet, from the way she moved in the dim dingy room.

Once, not long after we got to the hotel, I must have been staring openly, for to my confusion the woman stepped to her window and looked across at me and asked the time, in a shy way. Almost at once I knew that she wanted to speak, to speak to anyone, to speak to anyone who would reply to her. So I replied.

I came to know that this speaking to me was extraordinary, for almost never after that was she able to focus her eyes far enough to see my window, much less the shape of me standing in it, and she never looked our way when the man was there.

That day she smiled in a feeble timid manner with her surprising question, and I was grateful to her to be able to cover my gaucherie at having been caught, no matter how unwittingly, in the act of peeping into her home. I told her what time it was.

She made a wandering gesture toward the back of the room, as if to indicate that she was alone, and leaned over the window ledge and talked to me. I am sorry that I did not conquer my own shyness and lead her on to more words, for I was never to hear her speak to me again except in mumblings once in the street. She said that she was very ill. Her back had been broken while she was in a labor camp during the war. She had been sent far off. When she returned, her kidneys were destroyed. She suffered constantly. It was necessary for a kind gentleman to assist her now and then, she said with a pathetic reaching for gentility, with her daily marketing and her chores . . .

We parted, turning away from each other shyly.

A little while later, perhaps a month, I was walking along the side of the hotel on the Rue Nazareth when I came upon her leaning in a daze against the wall, with the man standing helplessly beside her. She seemed about to lie down. I think she may have recognized me, for there we were, in communion of a kind, with people pushing curiously, impatiently, past us. She whimpered like a child that she had fallen twice in the street, twice, twice in the street. The man shrugged and looked sadly at me, with confusion and acceptance on his bristly face.

"Why don't you go to the hospital?" I asked.

"Yes," he said, and it was the only time he ever spoke to me, although once later he shook his fist at one of my girls from his window toward ours and said a foul word at her. "That's what I say too, Madame. A week maybe in hospital and she'd be all right."

I said, "Or two weeks. Why don't you do that?" I spoke toward the woman, but she was sliding down and down the wall.

"It's my poor poor back. They broke it," she whispered, but we all knew that she was nearly dead drunk too.

"Think of it, the hospital," I said urgently to the man, and I hurried away with what decent slowness I could muster, wondering why I should mix myself in something so obviously not my affair.

But it was hard not to, for the people were always there across the little street. There were times when as a point of honor I kept myself from the mechanical look, the automatic noting of a greasy casserole on the ledge, or a sad pink rayon nightgown hanging tipsily on one clothespin from the sagging string.

Sundays were the worst, of course. They always began fairly well, but the progression toward drunkenness, then quarreling, then copulation, then often a quiet standing side by side at the window in the darkening air, elbows on the ledge, occasionally the slow mincing and trimming of a piece of sausage or meat or even bread with the bright knife . . . all this made it hard not to watch with more than the inner eye. It changed the pleasure of our own picnic lunches in our big airy room, so that whenever we could we spent our Sundays away from there, away from the apprehension and the ugliness.

In the winter with windows closed, and usually with the light on in the room across from us, it was like an old silent film being run over and over. The first time it was fascinating: a realistic German movie, somewhere between *The Cabinet of Dr. Caligari* and Emil Jannings' *Le Dernier des Hommes*. Then it grew dull, like a habit of smoking cigarets or drinking gin, necessary but still boring. The taste was no longer even an unwilling taste, but only a need for one . .

The man would shout angrily, the woman would cower; they would drink and drink and then eat; finally he would try to take her bloated grimy body and she would run dully from him and then submit; afterwards they might get dressed and go out toward a low-class bar, they might simply sleep until early the next morning when he must go back to work: all this unrolled over and over, under our helpless eyes.

It was interesting that the man never missed getting up on Mondays. I too had to do it, to send Anne and Mary off to their schools, and I would see the light on across the street as I dressed, and would notice the man's shadow as he moved silently about the room. Often he would light a fire on the hearth, and fill the bucket with water from somewhere outside. He moved lightly and without fumbling. Mostly, I thought, he had slept in all his clothes except a cap and a thick jacket.

Much later the woman would get up, stumbling like a mole in the light. On warm days she often leaned for a long time on the ledge, her arms on a rag of cloth, and watched toward what she could hear on the street four floors below. She would brush back her dark hair with clumsy tender hands, and occasionally shake her head and talk to herself. Then toward noon she would straighten her back and stand by the stained table, painfully peeling vegetables or stitching string around a piece of meat.

It is a wonder that she never cut herself, nor burned her thickened fingers on the dirty pots which she put slowly off and on the one little burner on the table. When she would lift one off to make room for another, in a dreamlike way, the flame would shoot up almost to her face, but she never blinked or drew back.

She was, indeed, dexterous in her quiet evasion of disaster, and watching it was one sure reason for my inability to stop. I hated this peeping, but I could not deny my horrified curiosity about if and when she would burst into slow bright bleeding, or flame up like an oily rag. It is not that I spent hours looking across the street at her and her man, but I did live in the hotel attic with three wide windows a few feet from theirs, and I did move back and forth, and in my moving I did bow to this occasionally worrisome absorption. How could I have known, anytime in my life, that I would have this strange bird's-view of behavior so different from any I had known? I was not hurting them. I was perhaps learning something from them.

I speculated freely, if only now and then, upon such things as what her thick soups and fried meats tasted like, rather than upon what had made her what she was. They really ate well and decently, those people, with salads and fresh peaches and melons and oranges according to the seasons. And I wondered how they made love and if they thought much about it . . . and how old the woman had been when she was sent to the labor camps . . . and if she was Polish perhaps . . . her accent had not been French . . .

There was detachment in my attitude, and acceptance, as well as compulsive curiosity. There was almost an element of fear, for I knew exactly what was being said for all of us one day when Mary remarked, "He's cutting a piece of sausage on the ledge again!"

We were sitting thinking of quite other things, eating and talking, but this side issue seemed natural. Anne said, "He's practicing."

Mary said, "Some day he'll do *her* in neat little pieces."

"Probably," Anne said without any apparent horror.

I started to tell them about a cook we once had who did indeed cut her mother into little pieces, or rather into strips, with her famous French knife, but I thought better of it, and we went on with what we were doing, which was enjoying our Sunday selves.

Later I noticed that the man had closed the windows and turned off the light, and I felt a slight erotic question, and the next morning was relieved, in a curiously remote part of my daily awareness, to see that he had taken in a piece of washing and gone off to work as if all were well.

Then, in an early spring, the windows of all the town were open wide again, and although I did not hear the woman I was more conscious than I had been for a while of her occasional tottering path across my line of vision. She seemed even less sure than before, but her puffed hands still had a delicate feminine turn to them as they moved mazedly about the table or her own face and shoulders.

She talked to herself. I wondered if she argued with the invisible and distant man, or with all men, or perhaps with a grandmother she knew when she was fresh and unbroken.

Once more I watched her with an open view, working with her strange dexterity, never cutting or burning herself, to make two meals every day for the hawklike man who protected her, and I wondered about the meaning of devotion, and about the limits of it.

ii *THE TROUBLE*

ONE THING THAT indicated boldly the morbidity of our unwilling interest in those two people who lived across the Rue Papassaudi from our big room in the hotel was that when their window was not open at least once a day we watched it with an obvious fear, not of how and when it would open but of why it might not.

Once toward the end of April, 1961, it stayed closed for three or four days, with only a faint light showing from the skylight at night, and we grew conscious of the occasional sound of a dog crying.

The dog might not be the black one I had sometimes seen with the woman. But the sound came from there, there in the closed room, and suddenly I began to wonder, not putting it into words to Anne and Mary, if perhaps instead of the poor dog's having been shut into the empty room while the man and woman were away or in prison or in hospital, the sound came from her, shut there.

I tried not to think this way. But the window stayed shut and the dog howled at night and even in the daytime.

I wrote letters to New York and California, trying not to listen.

I explained that I could not send a birthday box to Norah's children, because they would not be accepted at the post office without being opened to look for bombs, *les plastics*. There was quiet steady terrorism in France, especially in Paris.

On the 23rd of April the news was very bad. Everything seemed stopped, waiting, holding its breath, and my own breath came grudgingly as I read the papers. I tried not to be short and morose with Anne and Mary, at breakfast in the Deux Garçons. I parted from them with vague muted feelings of pain.

On the way home Monsieur François the tailor stopped me. I thought at first it was to ask if I had decided from the samples he had loaned me what kind of suit I would want him to make. Instead, he wondered what results there had been from my somewhat hysterical and fruitless visit to the Police Commissariat three days before, about the continued howling of what might be a little black dog and what, as I had decided to my horror, might be the woman behind the window.

It had been Saturday I decided that; and the shutters had been closed since the Tuesday before, when the sound of the long feeble howls began. Any speculation was dreadful, whether for beast or human, and Saturday I could not stand it longer and on my impulsive but determined path to the police I had met Monsieur François and asked his opinion of whom to call, where to go: he was of the neighborhood and we were friends.

And so on Monday he asked me what had been done, and I had to tell him that I failed completely. I did not tell him that I felt helplessly annoyed with him for not doing more than advise me, even though I knew that like most Frenchmen he preferred not to interfere with anything that might prove distasteful.

Yes, the howling was indeed somewhat worse, he agreed . . . and Sunday night had I noticed a light which showed for perhaps five minutes through the shutters?

I told him that the police had sent me, at first gently and then with patent boredom, from one man and one office to another, until finally I was in the presence of the Commissaire himself, except that he was not there. Every available policeman was patrolling the town, as I remembered when I walked past the two sentinels at the door to the big building. They stood carefully behind their steel boxes, submachine guns on the alert. So a pudgy civilian clerk spoke wearily, insolently to me behind the chief's desk: What was I doing there? Had I gone through this and that formality? Exactly what did I want? What was I trying to stir up in this time of trouble?

All his implications were that I was a gossipy interfering unbalanced neighborhood nuisance as well as a non-French-woman, and by then I was so unnerved that I became pretty much what this lout had implied, and was so helpless with worry and anger that I lost my voice, and shook, and in every way proved his points.

An officer came in, and I tried, apologizing for my shaky state, to tell him what I had by now repeated seven or eight times. He said nicely to me to come back some other day, perhaps on Tuesday.

"And meanwhile she dies?" I asked very tremblingly.

"Who dies?" he asked coolly. "Whom do you really imagine to be dying, Madame? What proof have you of any of this fantasy? Here in France we must have proof before we violate the privacy of a man's home."

Ah hell and damnation, I wanted to cry out. I managed to say a thank you, to the officer and not the clerk, and I fled, sobbing and red-nosed behind my dark glasses. I was in pieces, and all the time I had to ask myself if the police had been right and if I were indeed nothing but a neurotic annoyance in this time of riots and *plastics* and suspicions.

And a couple of days later I managed to tell some of this to Monsieur François (I had told Anne and Mary late Saturday of my ordeal, and then when the dog would howl they would put out various feeble suppositions: the sound did not really come from that closed room, the people must be on a little vacation, and so on), and the tailor and I both agreed to increased alarm and he grudgingly said he would speak to a neighbor who was a member of the SPCA. Otherwise, he agreed with the police, there was no way to enter a dwelling to investigate, unless I wished foolishly to swear out a formal complaint. We worried the subject cautiously and politely; it was a dead rat.

Then I said that I would come across from the hotel later to show him the sample the children and I had chosen for my new suit. He was disturbed, he said, because he had ordered several pieces of cloth and of course no packages were allowed through the mails now . . . and suddenly he was shaking and leaning against his counter and saying, "I've had it, Madame. I've had it, all I can stand. I fought the whole war here. Then I was deported. I was two years in Germany, in Hamburg. I was in Hamburg from the first bomb that was dropped to the last one, the very last one. And now I swear if they tell me to fight again, I'll tell them. Pardon me, Madame, but I'll tell them WHERE TO PUT IT."

"Ah, but will you? You can't choose, can you? Can anyone?"

He seemed to look smaller all the time. He shrugged tiredly. "It's civil war we're all afraid of," he said. "It's what they want. French against French."

Abruptly he bowed to me and I left.

I went up to the room with my heart and head at war. I fought down panicky imaginings, and in spite of myself recalled the faces of my sister and brother as they were evacuated from Berne, on M-Day of the war, while I stayed behind. That time it was because my husband was pinned to a bed. This time, if we were ordered to leave, I would want to stay again, to get through whatever must come, with the French people. But I would go because of Anne and Mary, because we would have no right to take up the space and food and energy needed for French women and children . . .

I looked dully out of my window, and for almost the first time in Aix I saw three, not two, Algerian women dressed in very bright soft robes, walking at their never-hastening speed up the Rue Nazareth. Then there were four more. Did I imagine it because of my inflamed emotions, or were the Arabs more brightly dressed than usual? Did they feel a new confidence in that city where they were a troubled minority? Had they perhaps been instructed to walk thus bravely together down the streets, instead of going out silently two by two to market?

I read the front page of the *Provençal*, and the loud stern words of De Gaulle: yes, barricades were being set up in Paris, especially in the St. Cloud quarters, and yes Paris was alerted to probable insurrection directed from Alger and Oran, and yes the airdromes of France were on guard for possible attempt at seizure, and yes the people were begged to resist propaganda and to obey all and any orders for the government and its loyal soldiers and not from the rebels and their mad henchmen . . .

I had not dreamed all this, nor how we had tried four times at the newsstand before some papers came in from Marseille. Across the street the dog still howled.

The men who for several days had been treading cautiously over the roof next to the empty room with new tiles and plaster called roughly down, in voices that echoed enormously in the street, "Shut up, you! Quiet! Silence!" But it did no good.

I could not say honestly that I hoped it was a dog and not a woman, for atavistically I could not condone the realization that a human being had been chained like a beast in a room, but death would be preferable to any life that I had seen her living, that far. Perhaps she should die, rather than an animal? Either way, the confused surmising was dreadful, and just as I knew that the Insurrection must and would be either better or worse, so I knew that I must do something more to find out where the sounds really came from and what was making them and who caused it all. If I could determine those three things, I thought, I might possibly feel more real.

Meanwhile many other things were taking shape around us, as irrevocably but at the same time as fleetingly as deciding to drop a thousand men by parachute on the airfield at Marignane, or shut up a dog, or tie a woman to a bed leg in a dark room.

On April 20, for instance, a great flight of what I called swallows but what English Humphrey stated were swifts had arrived from Africa.

Perhaps the rumor was right, that they were the vanguard of the invasion? They were larger than swallows, I admitted, and they flew almost like bats in astonishing swoops speedier than my eye could really follow, and always making a high thin scream, also like bats but a scream and not a squeaking sound. They circled early in the morning and then at dusk, most surely to catch insects. They made me know, as I half-saw them against the paling sky, the darkening one, how van Gogh knew about the crows that flocked past his eyes and then into his soul and out upon the mad canvases he painted in the fields near his last asylum. Humphrey said they flew at perhaps two hundred miles an hour. Their cry was almost as inaudible as they were almost invisible.

They had come before the Germans too, we were told . . .

iii *THE RETURN*

TOWARD DUSK of the 23rd of April I looked down into the Rue Papassaudi and there by his door the man was standing uncertainly, with the little black dog, which looked silky and plump from our fifth floor. Later the shutters were opened for a few hours, on the dim window across from us, but no light showed, and before morning I heard again the feeble sound of something howling.

About five o'clock of the next afternoon I awoke from a half-sleep on the bed where I had lain quasi-helpless in an escapist doze, with the sound of the whimpering in my head, but this time leaving a nightmare imprint of words, as if the howl had turned into a call, a call to *me*. I tried impotently to recapture what I thought I had heard, what I had perhaps and perhaps not dreamed . . .

I went to the window, but there was nothing new to see, and with the same hopeless feeling I let fade from the first place of recollection the horrible suggestion of syllables in my dulled brain, in the clear air of the afternoon in springtime.

At about half-past five, when there came the sound of the *Marseillaise* half-sung and half-shouted, the window across from ours did not open, but I hung out of mine with my heart beating and with a kind of desperate human pride surging in me, as perhaps three thousand people flowed like a quiet river down the Rue Nazareth.

They were led by two policemen on bicycles, chatting and skidding one foot along the street to keep at the right speed. Behind them came what seemed like an endless stream of people, not straggling, but not really marching in the orderly sense of that word. There were many women with children. Sometimes they had put the smallest ones on their bikes or vélos and walked alongside. Men and youths and enlaced students came in groups, or beside their women. An occasional band of youths would be calling out in ageless unison *"Sa-LAN aux po-TEAUX, Sa-LAN aux po-TEAUX,"* but without much more real threat and hate than a band of parrakeets.

I was interested to note that during all this slow procession, neither as dour as a funeral nor gay as a picnic, I was seized by the shivers. It was an animal reaction, and I observed it with detachment. It was a kind of funk. It was pure emotion. Quite possibly it acted as a purge, an antidote.

What moved me the most, and at the same time soothed my perhaps neurotic and partly unrecognized apprehensions, was the quiet steadiness of everything. The parade had been called all over France for five o'clock that afternoon, and ten million workers, wage earners, salaried people marched as these Aixois did, from their town halls to their Prefectures if they had them, up their own Cours Mirabeau, to stand calling for the Prefect and then when he did not appear to disband and be absorbed once more into myriad alleys, innumerable rooms. It was unforgettable, that silent strong relentless walking . . .

The next day the air was different, because of the quiet show of strength.

People on the streets looked less harried. In town the café waiters were wary, especially along the Cours, and ready for possible trouble from small gangs of nonchalantly strolling bullyboys, dressed as students but organized in Marseille. There were many more Algerian women, even young pretty ones who before were never seen on the streets. They moved with easiness along the Cours, in their bright soft-flowing dresses, instead of stalking mutely through the open markets and then into their unofficial ghettoes. There was a general air of relaxed but still acute tension.

It was in a strange way like comparing two onions, one of which was without its first layer of skin: we all seemed to have been peeled, that day after the parade, of a layer, no matter how thin, of suspicion and prejudice. I saw this clearly in Anne and Mary. They were looking with new eyes, thinking with unsuspected brain cells . . .

I would like to say that as I stood shuddering and ennobled by the quiet parade flowing down the Rue Nazareth, I saw the poor woman from behind the closed window opposite our room staggering along, supported by her man, a look of rebirth on her puffed face. But it is not so. That night the dog still howled. The next morning the masons who had been working on the roof piled rubble into a wooden trough with an enormous clatter and thud, perhaps with the rumble of a small *plastic*, and along with several others of us on the Rue Papassaudi the man in the closed room slid open his shutters a few inches, and leaned out cautiously to see. He wore his beret, but no coat. He did not look up. He closed the shutters again after a few seconds.

I began to think that he was not at work because he was taking care of the woman, that perhaps she was in a crisis which was familiar to him, and that with his innate tenderness, which

I had long sensed, he was with sad accustomedness protecting her and keeping her caged until it passed. I hoped something like that was true.

That night there was no light on, but the dog did not howl again, and the next Sunday the man and woman sat once more in the window, with the tall bottle between them, and the scene was played again, but this time we were free from it. We had learned how, during the Insurrection, to disengage ourselves, to wear our new skins perhaps. It seemed almost good to know that the woman was well again, returned from whatever voyage she had made.

The Almond Blossoms

Is it so small a thing
To have enjoyed the sun,
To have lived light in the spring,
To have loved, to have thought, to have done;
To have advanced true friends, and beat down baffling foes?

Matthew Arnold, Empedocles on Etna

THERE was one old chambermaid at the hotel, not five feet tall, with a cynical merry grin and rather gruff reassuring manners, the kind of woman I would not mind being tyrannized by, domestically: she would scrub and sweep and scold, in my dream, and there would be mutual amusement. I have met one other such ancient troll, many years ago in Mexico. I forget her name. This one was called Rachelle, but I had great difficulty in ever thinking of her as anything but Babushka, for some reason I can't know.

One day we came in from the country with some sprays of almond blossoms, and she was standing by the hotel desk talking with Madame Segond. We gave them each a branch, with much talk about the unseasonable warmth, the danger of frosts to come, the great freeze of February 2, 1956 . . . ah, the dead olive trees, the almonds, the live oaks . . . and then the freeze of last April 30, which took two-thirds or three-quarters or five-eighths of the wine this year . . .

Then we went on up the winding stairs. Madame disappeared into her apartment.

I looked down from the third floor, into the dark well, and at the bottom Babushka was brushing vigorously at the carpet by the desk, with her branch of almond blossoms held up toward the end of the broom handle, so that it and her white head were the only lighted things, swooping minutely in a little tidy dance. It was perhaps the best thing of a delightful day, which we did not wish at all.

There were some people who lived in Marseille but had a *mas* out toward Vauvenargues. My sister Norah met them the summer before we were in the hotel, when she lived near them, and introduced us first to the daughter Hélène and then gradually to all the rest of the family, before she must leave for California.

Mary and Hélène enjoyed each other. Anne on the contrary, or perhaps because of this, found her pedantic and dull. It is true that Hélène had a way of contradicting or correcting all of us, a kind of supercilious amusement which I think was mostly assumed owing to a hidden jealousy of the girls' greater travels and so on and so on. Whatever the reason, Mary saw much more of Hélène than Anne did.

Even so we lunched together a few times in Marseille, and I kept a very straight face when Hélène asked some outrageously superior question about the pronunciation of an American slang word or something like that. I really enjoyed her, because she had beautiful eyes and hair and skin, and she amused me in an innocent way.

Norah had told me about the excellent cooking in the family, and the droll father, the pretty older sister, the tiny old grandmother who occasionally gave out a chirruping but extremely pointed comment.

I wanted to know all this, but at the same time I did find Madame, even more so than her daughter, rather painfully *instructive*, in a way that is tedious even to try to explain.

It always seemed as if she stood ready to make a hundred corrections, to teach me all sorts of facts about whatever we were discussing, from the weather to the French school system. She explained patiently to me things I had known for decades, like the origin of the Provençal *santons* or the significance of hallmarks on solid silver. I felt that it was unbelievable to her, or at least inexplicable, that plain Americans like us had ever heard of such things as good silver, or would give a damn about such local phenomena as the *santons* . . . and of course as I tried to fight this suspicion of her basic disdain and ignorance of us as a people, I became at once ruffled and clumsy, so that my poor pronunciation grew worse and I made laughable mistakes in grammar.

I had to give myself something of a talking-to, especially when I realized that I was relying upon Anne's overt boredom and Mary's shyness, to get out of the kind invitations that this extremely well read and pleasant family kept making to us, perhaps to teach us more about their country, but really not as patronizingly as I occasionally felt.

That was why, in the face of real annoyance and dismay from both my children, I accepted Madame's suggestion that we go that Sunday, to lunch with them at the *mas*. I was rather blandly pragmatical, I suppose: the prospect bored me, but the weather was supernacular, to put it mildly, and I knew the food would be delicious. I would be polite and would try to be charming, and in return I would take everything I could of this most beautiful of sunny days.

I did, in every sense, and I was rewarded for my basically insolent attitude by feeling almost free from, or at last past, the somewhat similar attitude I had sensed in the French family.

They were open, generous of themselves, very amusing to listen to. We laughed a lot. There was a minimum of the in-and-out complicated manner of After you . . . No I beg of you . . . No I insist . . . After you . . . Please serve yourself . . . No, after you.

The grandmother was just as Norah had told me. She must have been very old. Everyone was thoughtful and affectionate with her. She ate nicely, which is rare at her state of senility, and apparently she heard when she wanted to, for suddenly she would say something in her ancient voice which was sharp and funny, or she would laugh with a fragile heartiness at one of Monsieur's many silly and melodramatic grumblings and growlings.

He too was as I forethought: a tall heavy man, basically neurotic and hypochondriac I'd guess, with a finished way of sneering and mocking everything, absolutely everything. He professed loudly and wittily to detest everything from De Gaulle to poodles; and from the spontaneous pleasure of his family I surmised that he was too good an actor to ruin even a brilliant quip by repeating it once too often.

The whole family was good at laughing, and with real enjoyment, and I liked the way they encouraged one another in it. It is a subtle thing, and rare, the way a thread, sometimes a very thin one too, is kept spinning through one bit of teasing, then an anecdote, then a quick play on words, then another story. I do like that, and they did it.

The older sister, Anne-Marie, was probably the most open and simple of the family . . . pleasant, attractive, impersonal. She talked easily with Mary, I noticed. A friend of hers was there, a plainer girl, perhaps not very sweet tempered, who was a trained nurse in Salon. Anne-Marie worked in a factory as an analyst of soils.

Hélène would be an interesting woman later. Then she was unsure and affected, but also generous of herself.

Yes, it was a good day, and I ended it with a kind of affection, and a fairly unashamed dismissal of my first acceptance of it for nothing but the spring weather and the good meal. As for them, they were both of the best.

All the windows of the simple pleasant house were wide open, a wonderful feeling for us after the winter in a hotel, and the walls were white plaster and the good furniture was dark with age and shining with wax, and the floors were of red square tiles. In other words, it was the kind of Provençal *mas* that I most love. And on the hearth a leg of lamb turned on an old spit: Anne-Marie was the family roaster (and salad maker), and she sent Hélène and my girls out for the first sprigs of wild thyme for it.

In front of the house, about fifty feet away, was an old table made of two solid slabs of stone with a piece of marble laid across them. It must have been almost as old as the great bare oak tree above it. Then there was a thick row of lilacs, their buds swollen and waiting. There was a field sown with oats, now up some four or five inches. It was too early yet to hear birds, and we saw only one ant walking drunkenly across the stone floor of the terrace, but there was the family cat, with a thick blue-gray coat, stalking nothings, and there was also the family dog Bobèche, more or less a gray poodle.

It is almost always the case that poodles bring out the most amusing side of their owners, and this family was delightful to listen to, once started on his subject while we drank coffee.

Among dozens of other things, Madame said that once Bobèche escaped from the apartment in Marseille and ran down the Rue Sylvabelle, nonchalantly turning over every garbage pail as he went, and she ran after him in her house slippers, more and more helpless and furious. Finally she caught him, and just then a man asked her in a very admiring and polished way, after many compliments about the dog, "Is he perhaps a *Griffon d'Autriche* or on the other hand a *pur-sang Tolèdain?*" And Madame was so furious at Bobèche that she said loudly, "*Non, mon cher monsieur, ce chien est un* INFIME BÂTARD." Then Monsieur added, "But the worst was when we took him to the vet . . . another client asked delicately, 'Is this dog perhaps a crossing of races?' and the vet said seriously, '*Monsieur, je dirais plûtot un carrefour qu'un croisement . . .*'"

I don't know if this is very funny in English, but it sounded fine there in the thinning warmth of the February afternoon, after the good lunch.

Before it, I sat in the sun with Monsieur, and we drank a *pastis*. Madame came out and with great finickiness her husband made her a small iced vermouth-gin. She said she loved gin and when I said I did too but for its effect rather than its taste, she said that she really loved the smell of it the best, and that she could hardly tell the difference between it and a good toilet water, so that when she got older she might well confuse them and drink up all her eau de cologne.

That is the way it was, casual and pleasant. The sun was almost hot. The younger girls were here and there, picking thyme, picking violets from a neglected flower bed that was like a mattress, unexpectedly, with deep purple and enormous blossoms which should be almost odorless but instead were heady with perfume. The older girls basted the *gigot*, carried plates and tumblers out to the table . . .

Lunch was long and simple, the way I like it.

We ate Anne-Marie's salad of endives, the white Belgian ones so good that time of year, cut in pieces with a dressing made of plenty of mustard, no salt, and plenty of olive oil . . . very little vinegar. It was delicious.

The lamb was the way I like it, very rare. There were brown crisp cubes of potato, and artichoke bottoms cooked with sliced mushrooms and bits of bacon.

Then there was a good mild but ripe Camembert and a good Bleu de Bresse, the way I like them, and then a rather tasteless *crème* with little sweet *brioches* . . . and fruit . . . and coffee.

We drank a *blanc-de-blanc* from near Arbois . . . it was nice. Monsieur was a little annoyed because he had forgotten to warm up a Gigondas to drink with the meat . . . it had been in the cellar all winter. It did not matter. In the warm sunshine the white wine was the way I like it. I looked about me and missed Norah.

I had lied to Madame in accepting her invitation, and said I had an appointment in Aix at three, but even with my changed feelings about the family it was a good time to leave. Monsieur drove us into town. We walked along the Cours with the almond branches, and I felt a little sheepish, for there in Aix only city slickers picked even twigs from trees that could bear nuts or fruits or olives.

And then we went into the hotel and divided our five branches with Madame Segond and Babushka. Anne put one branch in her room, and I stuck the other two in a jar of deep blue anemones by my desk. In the last bright light coming over the yellow and rose tiles of the rooftops, it seemed probably the most beautiful posy of my life.

I thought I should mention this in my invisible notes on the secret map, but before I could get to it I had to tell myself again about the strange feeling of affection and mystery that came over me as I looked down the dark stairwell and saw the white blossoms sweeping stiffly in the dark, on the top of Babushka's broom.

There was nothing more to *tell*, really.

Correction on the Map

O the moon shone bright on Mrs. Porter
And on her daughter
They wash their feet in soda water.

T. S. Eliot, *The Waste Land*

THE second time we left Aix was at once easier and more prolonged: I knew what I was doing, at least somewhat more clearly, and I could salve myself with the knowledge that I had returned once, and therefore might again.

In between these two leave-takings was one which does not count as such, for it was at the end of a short Christmas vacation there from Lugano, in 1959 I think, when after about ten minutes in Aix, I knew without even looking at my girls' faces that we must come back, leave Switzerland, change every schedule, seize this moment of being at least on the same side of the oceans as Aix then was to us, for as long as I dared make it last.

By then I knew more how to be a good ghost.

As I remember it now, I had remained in pain and bewilderment for a long time before we first left Aix. I wrote about it to a few confidants. I was not sure why I felt I must leave, I said, except that I wanted the girls to stay American. Then I gave reasons like their need to continue the orthodontia that had been skillfully interrupted to last one year, no more, of absence from San Francisco. I mentioned my need to earn money, which of course was a lie, at least in my implying that it was impossible for me to do so in France: I was a writer and could work anywhere, and I need not feel guilty about accepting another country's hospitality, for I paid fat taxes as a foreigner and at the same time kept up equally fat ones at home. No, there was an uneasy ambiguity about my compulsion to quit Aix, the first time, and in many ways it still puzzles me, for mostly it seems ridiculous now.

Should I? Why? I would moan, and a friend would look straight at me and ask gently, "Yes, why should you?" and I would have no intelligent answer.

Now and then someone in America would write sternly, admitting vicarious pleasure in my being in Aix. "Stay. California is far from there. Stay while you are there to begin with." And so on.

And I continued with my plainly masochistic and grudging pattern of return, withdrawal, escape, whatever it was.

A night or two before Anne and Mary and I left Aix that time, we ate dinner at the Glacier. We ordered, I think, a favorite dish of one girl's and then a favorite of the other's, and I drank my favorite wine there: fresh asparagus, tepid and not chilled, with a vinaigrette made at the table; plain boiled chicken with rice and a good sauce, all called Poulet Suprême or something like that; a bottle of *blanc-de-blanc* from back of Cassis . . .

It was a good night, under the leaves beginning to grow heavy with their summer dust.

While the children went in to the toilets I said in a willfully calm way to our friend Ange that we would not be back for a time, that we must go home.

He expressed some trite but real regrets: we both knew that he liked the children and me too, and that we in turn felt reassured by everything we knew about him and by the way he looked, as slim and silvery and histrionic as the oldest trout in a well-fished stream.

He glanced around, his professional eye checking all the terrace before he let down the mask to me. His face was lean

and sad, like a saint's. "Madame," he said in a stern quiet in-
sistent way, his dark eyes linked with mine, "Madame, consider what you are doing. *Consider.*"

I stammered hopelessly to him, "I have. I have. I feel I must
go home with them. I have, Ange."

He was the priest, I the penitent. I was young and tossed,
he the rock.

He looked deeply at me for an instant more, and said again,
"Reflect, Madame," and then he flicked his napkin at a coffee-
filter and was Ange again.

I felt infinitely disturbed. Everything I had been pushing
away from me in a kind of protective bewilderment rose with
the good wine in my throat. I said to one of the other waiters
to tell Anne and Mary that I would return at once, and I
ducked across the circle of endless cars around the Rotonde
and walked into the noise and mist of the great garish fountain,
hearing those quiet doomful words *reflect, reflect* . . .

Nobody could see me there, I knew, and for the only time
in Aix I cried hopelessly, the uncouth sobs of a resigned child,
alone, not terrified but puzzled. I walked furiously, perhaps
three times around, or five. Ange's face bent toward my inner
eyes, and above the sound of traffic and the spouting waters
my inner ears were etched relentlessly by the diamond needle
of his voice: *Reflect.*

Never before had I abandoned myself so trustingly, so shame-
lessly, to the impersonal view of a public place. I could have
screamed safely there in the turmoil of the waters and the cars.
I circled the fountain as fast as if I were fleeing, until it was
safe for me again to cross to the Glacier, and there I got the
children into the dappled night shadows, and we went home-
ward, each of us in a daze of our own pain of imminent
removal.

Ange of course did not reappear on the terrace, and when
we came back again years later and I wanted to show him that

we had indeed returned, he had been fired for arrogance, we were told, and was picking up pennies doing wedding suppers and even mop-up work after athletic club reunions in some of the lesser cafés. We nodded on the street now and then with a kind of nonchalant regret, but behind his cynical weary face, puffier than before, I saw his stern eyes and heard him say, as I shall for as long as I live, "Reflect, reflect . . . "

But the second time it was easier, mostly, as I have often told myself, because I had done it once and then got back to it. And I was much older, and more patient of the improbable.

I could reflect with an almost supercilious compassion upon the old bewilderment of my first flight, and when people still asked me occasionally, "But why did you leave and then return, instead of staying and sparing your children all the confused schooling and so on?" and so on and so *on,* I could shrug and admit honestly, "I do not rightly know." At least I had matured enough for candor.

The second time we must flee I was able, with what might be called either resignation or masochism, to go deliberately from one important place to another in my private city, the invisible one, putting it all into final order on the map.

Tomorrow, I would plan to myself, I must go alone to the olive oil shop near the shady little Place des Trois Ormeaux, and smell it to my own satisfaction, and perhaps buy three or four kinds of olives from the open kegs, just to stir up the cool air toward my greedy inner nostrils . . . And the next morning I would walk up the Cours Sextius and into the gardens of the hotel spa behind the remnants of the Roman walls . . .

For many days and nights, once we knew definitely when we were to leave for home, a word which by then had been shaped into its most essential usage on all our tongues, past any need of explanation, I wandered like this in a kind of trance through my own streets and looked with the most seeing eyes of my whole life, and in the same way heard and smelled, and without question I knew that Anne and Mary were doing it too, wittingly or not.

Perhaps because I was older I knew more clearly than they that for many things it was too late. There was not enough time left in the world to find Brondino alive again, nor even to wait for the night when the priests would stand over the flames outside the cloister of St. Sauveur, to light the holy lamp again for Easter morn.

Never again would any of us watch the five law students teetering on the rooftop across from our windows in the Hôtel de Provence, whispering as the sun went into total eclipse and then in the unearthly dark crying out with cracked bravado, "Encore, encore!"

But there were some small lines I could trace more firmly or even rectify on my map, I thought . . . tidily I could attend to a few small bits of unfinished detail, for my own satisfaction: a measurement here, a dingbat there. One ghost in search of several others, I trotted dreamily about, proving to myself that things were in order: the corners must be sharp and clear, the lines incisive for my future contemplation.

A morning not far before the end of June and the end of the stay, I was sitting alone on the terrace of the 2 Gs, resting my feet from a full morning of this secret ferreting, before Anne and Mary could come from school. I thought of feet in general, and of the Provençal feet, short and high arched and well treated, and of how our longer less solid ones could suffer there on the cobbled streets and the rough stony land.

When we first moved into the country at Le Tholonet, before we left Provence the first time, it had been unbelievable how our feet hurt, after a week or so of going without shoes or with only rope-soled espadrilles.

Mine ached like hollow teeth when I went to bed at night, and burned like hell-fire. I would sit in the middle of my big bed, feeling like a self-indulgent ninny, and rub them volup-

tuously with mentholated salves squeezed from tubes marked
La Baume du Docteur Smythe-Schmidt or *Pied-Magique,
Analgésique Miraculeuse.*

Anne despised such nostrums because of their texture, and
seemed to solve the problem of walking by dancing instead,
along the ground.

Mary, about nine then, was the worst: she literally hobbled
like a crone. It was pain to watch her. At night I would rub
her like a little pony, up as far as she went, with the balms and
with watered brandy. She would purr. And in the morning
she would start up the path to the shepherd's house hamstrung
and hobbling again . . .

After perhaps a week of this I could not stand it any more
for her, and decided to go in to Aix for more help than I had
found at the pharmacy.

I felt many reservations. I knew from what waiters had told
me, as perhaps the worst sufferers from their feet in modern
life, that quasi-doctors and even quasi-quacks fattened everywhere on their torture. I did not want to expose my girl to
such a risk. But it would have taken Dr. Vidal a courteous
three or eight weeks of injections, x-rays, pills, tests, analyses,
to tell me the obvious: Mary's good little feet, overprotected
for some years by leather, were not yet tough enough for the
ancient trails and streambeds . . .

. . . and meanwhile, wincing but dogged, she stumbled slowly
after the shepherd of Le Tholonet, and along the streets of
Aix.

So one day I collected a local friend called SaSa Tailleux,
one of those cultural hybrids with eyes forever to be called
drowned violets, a fine sensitive dangerous child if ever I knew
two or three, and we all caught the market bus for Aix. I felt
braver with more of an audience.

There was a woman on the bus with two bumptious young
dogs she planned to leave at the pound unless some of the pas-

sengers wanted them, while she went on to pick fruit near Avignon. We all helped her on and then off, uncommitted to fosterhood, and when one of the pups threw up on a Gypsy's shoe he laughed and took care of it. SaSa focused her great flower-eyes at me, and if I had looked even vaguely fastidious she would have thrown up too, and then my girls would have, in sympathy.

As it was, I looked as much like an amused Gypsy as possible and we got to Aix all right and started things off by veering a little to the left of the bus stop to one of our several "favorite" cafés, where we downed the necessary tipples for our ages.

We then fused into one, SaSa clutching Anne clutching me on one side and Mary clutching and wincing along on my other, to go up the left side of the Cours Mirabeau, which for anyone who has not done it in early summer can be described as swimming languidly, happily upstream if one is a languid happy fish. The impossibly high plane trees bend over like reeds, like river weeds. The air moves with a mysterious tidal current.

Of course no real fish people could possibly swim up the Cours Mirabeau the way the little girls and I did that day, under the curving haughty gracious weeds, with the many fountains spouting and splashing as if their waters were a part of the air, or the air we breathed was really green-gold water.

An old friend, Armenian like most of the street photographers in Provence then, motioned to us with his camera to his eye and hunger back of his face, and at my nod he snapped us, and later we did look almost but not quite real on the film, with four feet stepping forward, four behind. But the only real thing to me as it happened was that poor old Mary could hardly put one foot or another down at all. In the picture I was smiling, but I remember how sick I felt; she was so courteous about it.

Near the Deux Garçons I'd often seen a badly lettered sign

about foot care. While I located it more carefully in my thoughts, we sat down and had an almost unprecedented second drink. SaSa looked tipsy, sucking away at a tall glass of chocolate milk, and my girls eyed me silently over theirs, sure something was up. I let the false fire of a vermouth-gin warm my timorous insides, and then said, "Come on. I know now where we are going." By that I was committed.

The three tender helpless children stood up, with docility their masks. We left our packages there with the waiter, and a few paces to the north of the café terrace I started up the dirtiest smelliest flight of stairs I had ever climbed in the town. It was next to the shop where Cézanne's father once sold his felt hats, near the mouth of the Passage Agard. Behind me I could feel the children's expressions without looking at them; they were quiescent and repelled.

The building was late seventeenth century perhaps, and the air in it seemed to have been there for most of the time lapse, so that it had a color and texture, both bad. The walls were very oily to touch as we climbed. The newest stains on them were square clumsily lettered posters vaunting the foot doctor's amazing successes, and as I went on and around I read their strange boasts and began to bow to my uneasiness.

What kind of man would quote some other man's word that he was a master, a superhuman healer, God-sent? What hungry miserable egocentric would pay someone to hand paint his marvels? What deity could keep on breathing and performing in this greasy dank heaven?

Behind me Mary thudded, as heavily as an exhausted waitress.

We came to a half-glassed door, well covered with small lettered signs about the doctor, and finally an old woman opened to my ringing, with a relatively fresh puff of air reeling with onions and hot fat.

I asked if we were late, thinking it might be her early dinner hour, but she assured me no, and went into a long palaver about appointments, while SaSa and Anne stood on this foot and that and Mary stood on as little of either as she could. The old woman rapidly closed in on me as a possible new convert to her faith, and gabbled hysterically about her son as she led us down a dim corridor to a room no bigger than a generous bath mat, with two chairs hunched into it and the dark plastered walls covered with framed clippings and photographs. The ceiling was low enough to make me stoop a little.

The mother padded on down the hall toward the sound of fumy sizzlings, the girls looked politely at me, sideways, and I smiled overtly and falsely at them.

"We'll get Mary's feet adjusted and then simply *run*," I said.

We sat for quite a while. I wished I had drunk two gins, and the children's faces looked sunken. A man limped up the stairs and past the door. The old woman yelled out at him from the kitchen about how busy the doctor was. He groaned. She said feet were feet and his were not the only ones, and he went limping back down the stairs, to return for an appointment in nine days.

Mary looked at me impassively, but her eyes said *Nine days!*

We studied the framed clippings, and the pictures of deformed human feet with clumsily typed quotations under them. This is a club-thrombo-disk malformation, or something like that, it would say in French, and the little girls would read it glibly and then say, "Oooh. Ugh. Aach. Look at the knob on the bone." Then they would inspect a picture of what flat feet could do to the posture, and Anne would say that any time now Mary would get that bulge on her spine and never get married, and SaSa would laugh a wild half-French half-Irish laugh and Mary would shrug amiably and read another caption: the doctor we waited for was miraculous, no less, in his healing of all ills, not just plain old bunions and broken arches; he was incredibly gifted; he was, to speak bluntly, Messiah, and so on.

We all grew pale and fidgety, and I wondered if SaSa and Anne might fall over or be sick, in the ancient dank fog of cookery and pain. Mary sat staring at her culprit feet.

Suddenly the old woman crashed into the cupboard of a room, almost over our legs and into our laps: her son, she told me with high hysterical laughing speed, was impossibly busy but might possibly arrange to see us in three weeks to the day hour minute.

The children stared at me, and then Mary looked away, and I thought furiously of how I could not, I would not let her hobble out again to the poppy fields, down to the brook, on her poor little feet, and No, I made it clear, *NO*.

The old woman glared at me with what may have been admiration, and dashed back down the hall and slammed her door on the continued sizzlings.

Somebody else limped up the stairs, banged, and then clopped slowly down again.

We did not look any more at the pictures of bulging growths and deformations on the dark streaky walls. The smell of greasy onions seemed to grow thicker around us, like our silence.

Then in a kind of jubilance the old mother slammed in, to tell us that as a special favor the doctor would see Mary, and soon, that very hour. Ah, no people and certainly no passing strangers, no foreigners, had ever before been so fortunate as to be treated immediately by such a proven master. Ah, what fortune!

And then, as in a nightmare which we could not stop, we listened to her read almost every quotation under the pictures, in her high laughing voice. They were from magazine articles, letters from patients, medical dictionaries, professors in schools of chiropody and divine healing. She read and read, while plates clattered and cutlery clanked against china revoltingly in the kitchen and the little girls nodded politely to her litany.

There was a crash, as if someone had fallen off his chair and pulled the tablecloth down with him. The mother put her hand over her weary adoring face, and then pulled it down past a new smile and excused herself as she ran out toward fearful silence.

The air was now almost too thick to breathe through, as if it were dirty flannel pressed over our faces. The low walls seemed to swell in and out and touch us with swollen toes, broken arches, twisted bodies.

I stood up as straight as I could in the low room. The children wheeled from their hynotized crouches before the pictures of troubles which I had until then considered structural or bacterial rather than of the soul. I whispered, "Help me now. We are going to do something bad. We are going to run away before the doctor comes."

There was no question from them. We flowed down those dank stinking stairs like one shadow, not four. We fled silently out onto the Cours. There was not a word in us as we ran from the sick air and the mad old mother.

I felt a kind of panic that her laughing voice would shriek down at us from a window high in the ancient building. Run, run, I cried silently to the children, but by the time we got to the 2 Gs we were seemly enough on the outside.

We got the packages from the table behind the big room, where the waiters always left them, and then outside we all seemed to want to hurry again without talking. It was not until we passed the last brimming fountain, and were almost at the bus stop on the Rotonde, that I noticed that Mary was prancing along like a little pony. Her fine strong feet were almost twinkling on the pavement.

And years later I thought of all this, one of the last mornings of my own secret verification of the inner map.

It was about the same time, in season and day, with the leaves firm in their new ceiling high above the Cours. Girls walked by in fresh cotton skirts high too on their young legs, high themselves on stilt heels made only for the Cours in that town of cobbles and rough pavements. Youth and vanity, I thought: my own feet were past either, and I knew with rueful resignation that I should treat them better than I had done lately, in the survey I was making of my own streets before we must leave.

In a half-hour Anne would come from the Lycée and Mary from her classes at the other end of the Cours. I would ask Monsieur Barthélémy, the pharmacist, for the name of a good chiropodist.

I must have been dazzled, in my haze of effort to fix things forever with my own ink on the paper, to find myself so surprised when the pharmacist said with professional caution that of course there was a foot-man just a few doors down, who had a certain reputation . . . Somehow I had let myself assume, when I remembered the time we went with SaSa up those fumey stairs, that by now the man must have vanished, if ever he did exist except in the mind of his wildly loving mother. Or perhaps it had not happened at all.

But while Monsieur Barthélémy spoke to me, and gave me the names of one or two other doctors, I knew I must go back at once to the messianic healer we had once read and heard about so intimately. There was still time. There was a place that suddenly seemed blurred on my map, and I must repair it.

I hurried onto the Cours, and then started up the narrow twisting stairs toward the top apartment, and gradually as I mounted and turned, the greasy air seemed to clear my head instead of further clouding it, and I felt a dreadful apprehension.

Above me I saw the half-glassed door, with the same badly lettered signs on it.

If the old woman came again to open it, I would follow her down the reeking corridor, and then sit in the low little room with the pictures of toes and tumorous spines and drawn pain-twisted faces, and from the kitchen I would hear food cooking in rancid fat and then a crash as if someone had fallen heavily from his chair, with all the soiled china crashing down around him. Then . . . what then? Who would come down the hall to the room where I was waiting?

I stood for a moment in front of the door. I could push a button, I saw, or I could knock.

Instead, before anyone could come to open for me, I turned and went down the stairs again toward the pure air, as fast and silently as I could, and then I hurried down the Cours, past the Deux Garçons where Anne and Mary were not yet sitting on the terrace. I tried not to feel real panic that perhaps the old woman would scream at me from her high window with her wild laughing voice . . . Madame, Madame . . . you have not kept your appointment . . . Dishonest, coward, cheat. . . . The fountains would stop to listen . . . the life of the Cours would stop to look . . .

I went into a pharmacy at the corner of the Cours and the Rue de la Mosse and bought a tube of some kind of magic mentholated salve.

I felt quite shaken, but by the time I got back to the café all was well again: the ink had dried, only a little smeary, on my correction to the map, and the sun lay green-gold on the faces of my children. For some reason they had decided to order chocolate milk, which I thought they had long since outgrown. As a ghost, I was free again.

The Royal Game of Tennis

At the beginning of the eighteenth century, the municipal theater of Aix settled permanently into the royal tennis hall, built in 1660. In 1756 the Duc de Villars had it remodeled, and it was decorated again in 1786. At this date it supported two troupes, one for opera and ballet, and the other for tragedy and comedy. There were also two concert societies in Aix, one functioning at the Town Hall and the other at the municipal theater . . .

Jean-Paul Coste, *Aix-en-Provence and Its Countryside*

FROM somewhere in my life I remember the smell, the feel even, of a very old jewel box lined in fat tufts with faded dusty velvet. Or perhaps it was a pincushion, set in a chased band of silver.

This seems vague, but is strong enough in my past for me to have recognized the interior of the Opera of Aix at once: it was the same feeling of dust, of elegance, that I got. I was at home there, rather like a forgotten earring or brooch caught in the frayed lining of the jewel box, or an invisible pin stuck into the fat dingy little trinket that may once have sat upon my grandmother's dressing table.

Over the next years after my first comfortable recognition of the place, I sat everywhere I could in it, depending on how quickly I had got to the ticket office in the Parfumerie Truphème, what seats I had been able to buy for the seasonal "Gala d'Art Dramatique," and the general state of my purse.

Once I sat in the second box, right stage, to watch the long afternoon of *La Pastorale* at Christmas. For a whole season I sat in the fourth row center of the second balcony, for the plays that sifted down from Paris. Once I sat front row center, first balcony, to listen to Presti and Lagoya, who had been rained out of the Cloister of St. Louis during the summer Festival. Once I left at the intermission, a variety show too loud and dull to tolerate, with a "public address system" pure torture there where the sound was so undistorted. And once I went to a political meeting which I did not quite agree with but which was exciting. A few times troupes of dancers did not turn up, and after some bored stampings and boos the thin audience left, to get back their money the next day at the Parfumerie.

The acoustics of the theater were very good, especially perhaps for orchestra, although the proportions of the small building were such that a provincial opera troupe could sound as swiftly mellow as if it were from the Métropole itself. The man who ran the downstairs bar told me that the best seat for listening to tenors was three rows under the first balcony, behind the pillar, but I never tried it. For full orchestra, which ranged from mediocre to very fine according to the available musicians from the Conservatory and "around," I liked to sit in as near the center of the theater as I could get, or else very high.

There were two bars, both of them bleak rooms that had once been fairly elegant.

The one that looked down upon the Rue de l'Opéra had no doubt been built for the genteel occupants of the boxes and the first balcony, and was not always open. I liked the one behind the ground floor seats much better. It had sawdust on the floor, and a good smell to it, and it was run by the frail-looking man who advised me about acoustics. I always wondered how and why he knew so well. But he was too reserved to question, and I never saw him except there, between the acts.

Now and then, for something like the official balls of the

Carnaval, a floor would be laid out from the stage over the pit and the seats, and surprisingly the first row of boxes would be almost at its level, with the dance bands playing at the back of the stage, against one of the familiar shabby old drops showing something like a Venetian canal or a formal park.

I went to one of the children's costume parties, which was held an afternoon during the Carnaval, with a runway for the little Pierrettes and Mickey Mice to walk down for the judges, who sat in the panoplied Mayor's box and kept notes. It was a touching spectacle, complete with essential tears and topplings. Already, over the sound of the bored jazzmen dressed in white trousers and bright blue jackets, there was hammering, and a general bustle for the main ball of the Carnaval that night, and baskets of confetti were being stacked in the corridors, and extra ice in sacks for the champagne, and the children sobbed in the corners and trembled with pleasure.

The best concert I ever heard in the Opera was given by the municipal orchestra in celebration of the 300th anniversary of André Campra's birth in Aix. It was all Provençal music: Campra of course, Henri Tomasi, and then Darius Milhaud's *Le Tombeau de Mireille*, and the *Arlésienne Suite* by Georges Bizet, but played as I had never heard them before, with solos by an old man with bagpipes from the Camargue, I think, and beautiful saxaphone-flute-harp in the Bizet, and the young boy who sometimes stayed on our floor at the Hôtel de Provence doing a long intricate kind of sonata in the Milhaud on his little drum and his tambour. I was put under a spell by it, and so was everyone in the crowded place. I have never felt more real delight come almost visibly from so many people at once.

I was very sorry Anne and Mary had not come with me, but they must study . . .

On looking back, it seems impossible that those two young girls managed to go so often to the theater and still keep up their schoolwork, which of course was all in French and already twice as demanding as it would have been at home in their mother tongue. Their teachers did not approve of seeing them with me so often, late at night, but they could not say that it seemed to affect the children's work wrongly, and I myself believed that as long as they stayed healthy it was an experience that could never happen again and therefore should be seized and savored.

While we lived at the Provence we were within ten minutes' walk of everything we wanted to see and hear, whether it was Josephine Baker doing another "farewell tour" at the Casino down past the Rotonde, or *Zazie Dans le Métro* at the Cézanne, the new movie house two blocks down from the Cours on the Rue Mazarine.

Up the Cours was the dingy old Rex, which showed everything from prizefights to second-run pictures, with now and then an exciting troupe of actors too poor or too late to book into the Opera . . . like one from Paris, most probably starving but gifted and well costumed, which gave a beautiful performance of a Greek tragedy written by Kazantzakis.

And then at the top of the Cours and past the little restaurant, and across from two noble old town-houses called Lestang-Parade and Grimaldi, was the theater, the Opera.

It was squeezed into a comparatively undistinguished block of lesser buildings, and before we left there was increasing talk of the need to build a big municipal auditorium which would do for all such present and future problems as legal congresses, international lunch club conventions, and even the Music Festival. Friends tried to quiet us by saying that such rumors had been thriving for at least one hundred of the two hundred and fifty years since the old royal tennis courts had been officially made the town's theater, but it could not but be worrisome.

The Opera was plainly in a state of alarming if still func-

tional disrepair, and local squabbles and scandals about responsibility (Should Monsieur Truphème act without municipal
consent? Would he answer for the bills?) kept any activity
at a minimum.

The theater was surprisingly clean, probably thanks to the
frail barman who may well have been janitor too. The toilets
were hopeless except in dreadful emergencies, and I was told
that the dressing rooms were shockingly drab and ill lighted.
There was of course no real ventilation at all. The gilt of the
proscenium was dim and peeling. The carpeting was in tatters,
and the upholstery on even the few rows of new seats in the
orchestra was stained and shabby. The stairs and high stools
in the boxes creaked and rattled, and the box doors banged
loudly because all the padding had worn off.

But it was a little jewel box, that theater.

It had been remodeled from the tennis courts in the style of
the mid-eighteenth century, like La Scala, like the Paris Opera,
with tiers of boxes rising straight up its sides to right and left
of the deep stage, and with three balconies curving around
to meet them, steeply, facing the proscenium.

The young and limber, the students, sat mostly in the top
balcony, and it needed a clear steady head to lean without
dizziness over the rails, to listen and of course to flirt. The
balcony below it was deeper, and the boxes were a little fatter,
and it was made for the middle classes in age and station, who
could stand hard uncomfortable seats at a middle price, and
would take a middle view of things. The first balcony was
somewhat more sumptuous, and the orchestra seats were the
most comfortable, the most costly, often the best every
way . . .

As always, the boxes were more to be seen in than to see
from, and we avoided them except for *La Pastorale*, when the
audience, dressed mostly in Provençal clothes and speaking the
language of Mistral, was almost as much fun as the play. It

lasted almost six hours, during at least two-thirds of which we were sure we could not stand to stay another minute, but which were unforgettable for the devout way the story was unfolded, of the birth of Jesus in a little Provençal village.

And here, partly to pamper my own amazed nostalgia, is a little of what we saw one single winter at the theater, not counting four operas given by the regional company, two or three evenings of ballet presented by my girls' old ballet teacher, and about six other evenings of dance, one unusually good by the small American Ballet company . . . and of course several concerts like the one in honor of Campra:

> *The Choutes Sisters,* by Barillet and Grèdy
> *The Year of the Final Exams,* by José-André Lacour
> *The Diary of Anne Frank,* by Goodrich and Hackett
> *Léocadia,* by Jean Anouilh
> *Inquisition,* by Diego Fabbri
> *Hard-Tack Inn,* by Marcel Achard
> *The Doors Slam Shut,* by Michel Fermaud
> *The King's Filly,* by Jean Canolle
> *Electra,* by Jean Giraudoux
> *The Dressen Collection,* by Marc-Gilbert Sauvajon
> *The Nitwit,* by Jean Anouilh
> *Andromachus,* by Jean Racine
> *The Tidings Brought to Mary,* by P. Claudel
> *Rhinocérus,* by Eugène Ionesco
> *The Prisoners of Altona,* by Jean-Paul Sartre

The Ionesco was done by the Odéon-Théâtre of Paris, and *Electra* by the Comédie Française, and almost every play used the talents and occasionally the genius of the best actors and directors and designers in France. It was an exciting example of what touring repertory can do to keep the stage one of the great human expressions.

The Opera is said to have been made the official stage of Aix in about 1765 at the passionate request of a group of graduates of the College, who with a high percentage of the population of the snobbish little city found their greatest pleasure in amateur dramatics. In the schools it was taught, according to the dictum of André Campra himself, that opera, ballet, and tragedy would keep the body supple and light, and breed ease and "stage presence" in even the youngest thespians. Private theaters flourished in many of the Provençal country houses, as well as in town, and when the Aixois were not themselves on the boards they were cheering the performances of traveling troupes from Marseille and Avignon and Toulon, in what had for so long been the royal tennis courts.

There is still a little stone plaque in the corridor of the theater that leads up to the first balcony, stating in thin shallow letters that in 1660 this cramped building did indeed house the royal courts, and it is there that visiting actors played out their comedies and tragedies. Once I watched a real game in just such a place, on the grounds of Hampton Court Palace, and it was easy to see how the net-protected gallery for the ladies could turn into one for noble spectators of a drama, with the groundling let onto what would be the court itself, and then a kind of stage at the opposite end of the gallery for the actors. It had the accidental logic of all good public places.

By the time we got to it, the Aix Opera was still in much the form it had been given by the Duc de Villars, with nineteenth-century incrustations of course, and in spite of its cramped size and its general decay, it was a strong and perhaps final proof that the town was still provincial, and passionately loyal to its own troupes and musicians as well as to the steady flow of talent from everywhere in Europe.

In the theater as in many other things, Aix seemed to be on the world's path: Paris and Lyon to the north, for musicians and companies coming up from Rome and Barcelona and Lisbon and even Malaga and Morocco; Italy and Germany and Spain and Africa, for everything traveling south from the Métropole and even from England and Scandinavia.

At the Opera itself, the performances were most either local concerts and galas or plays from the North.

Most of the chamber music went to the Casino, an elegant and larger room with fine acoustics, and decorated with fairly uncompromising finesse in pale blue and white, with crimson velvet . . . as in the Vienna State Opera, I believe, and Carnegie Hall. Often in the afternoons there were somewhat elegant gatherings for fine chamber music sponsored by little groups like the Dante Alighieri Society, with duos and quatuors up from Florence, Bologna, Rome. . . .And once a month there was, in two performances (at six and nine) in one day, which must have been gruelling for the arts, a meeting of the Jeunesses Musicales.

When we first were in Aix, I could go into the "J.M." with a regular ticket, because Mary was kindly accredited with needing an attendant. The next time I had to get my own card as a member auditor, since I was past thirty and she was past eight . . . but I was given a free and fairly good phonograph record for my dollar subscription, and it was amusing to have to show my card with the little passport picture on it when I bought tickets.

The young audience was vital, teeming, pulsating with life and curiosity: it made me feel more invisible than ever, in a good way. I usually went to the first performance, with my smaller girl, and toward the end of our stay Anne went to the later one with members of her *bande*.

It was lucky for us that the "J.M." was very strong in those days, and I hope it will stay so. Its aim was to "enrich the general culture of young men and women by acquainting them with music" . . . and one winter, for instance, we listened to

and saw the following concerts, all with erudite and witty
lectures alongside:

Romance and Laughter in the French Operetta, with
four soloists and piano.

The Paillard Chamber Orchestra, with twelve musicians and violin soloist.

The Beautiful History of the Dance, with four dancers and pianist.

The Jamet Quintet, with harp, violin, flute, alto and
cello.

Campra and His Contemporaries, with the Provençal
Ensemble and soprano.

Chopin and Schumann, Their Tone and Imagery,
pianist.

Panorama of Jazz, with Claude Bolling and his group.

And besides a gala presentation of Molière's *L'Avare* at the
theater, for the "J.M.," there was a fine rowdy performance,
that same winter, of the Comédie de Provence' *Taming of the
Shrew*, and best of all there was the Comédie itself, always
there in Aix.

It worked out of the Archbishop's Palace. There was a
steady titillating come-and-go, with loads of costumes being
carried in, or screams and slashing sounds in the courtyard,
from the rehearsals. Once Mary helped unload an old truck
filled with props, when she was very little, and later Anne
studied diction with the fine old coach Monsieur Rèbe. We
got to know some of the young actors, at least enough to
smile shyly at them across the café terrace. It was a good
feeling, to have a troupe of real actors there in the town . . .

And of course there were concerts a few times a year in
the Cathedral. They were always especially impressive, with

artful lights focused on things like a great illuminated book on the edge of the pulpit, and the tapestries glowing with night color, and the altar masked. There was a worldly hum in the aisles. It would fall and then rise again with veiled excitement as the Archbishop came quietly into a seat in the side stalls, or the Mayor or an Air Force general walked toward the transept to be nearer the music, in fuller view. . . . It seemed like one of the rightest ways in the world for such a great prayerful structure to be kept alive, by the music that rose from the choirs and the orchestras and always from the organ with Monsieur Gay's white head bent over the console . . . a double satisfaction it was.

And then there was the Festival . . .

The Velvet Tunnel

The Music Festival of Aix-en-Provence, formerly called the Mozart Festival, is held in that city from the 9th through the 31st of July, during which time five operas are usually given some thirteen times, some ten concerts are given by five or six orchestras and chamber-music groups, and three recitals are given by famous musicians. The operas are presented in the courtyard of the Archbishop's Palace, the soloists and large groups perform in the Cloister of Saint Louis, and smaller instrumental groups play in the courtyard of the Maynier d'Oppède town-house. One concert is given each season in the Cathedral of the Holy Savior.

Official publicity folder

Part way up Gaston-de-Saporta, past Brondino's window full of reprints of Cézanne and Modigliano and Botticelli on the left, and across from it the even smaller window where in 1954 there were still a few dried *cigales* painstakingly dressed in Provençal costumes, the Place de l'Archevêché seemed to open suddenly like a window itself, wide into tranquillity.

There was a pastry shop on its farther corner, toward the Cathedral, and now and then in the basement floor of the house where my children first lived was a drowsy collection of modern ceramics for sale. The rest of the façades were closed and quiet and very shabby, with a few beautiful doors ill kempt and cracking in the sun. The tall trees flourish there, and make a fine shade.

The second time we lived in Aix cars were beginning to park there in the Place, where even six years before it was all space or, on Market days, the donkeys were standing, their little carts empty of farm produce, waiting for noon and the quick trot home.

There was also quite often one horse, with a sagging carriage, the last one in Aix. The driver was a fat drunken old man who cursed at Anne and Mary and Henri when their kick-ball rolled under his nag's patient belly. And then he was dead, and so was the horse, and the children in the little Square were gone: my own girls were too old for kick-ball anywhere, even in Aix, and the little boy Henri was a sober grind at the Lycée Mignet, a spoiled prig for all we could tell, planning to be a diplomat. And Chantal and Mireille, the rough kindly girls who sometimes played with them, were married and mothers . . .

On the left side of the Square is a narrow alley, which leads into the Cloister, and where once we watched half-mystified and half-exalted as the priests burned a bright fire (Were they burning the robes of Judas, as in Crete?) in the dark night before Easter morning, and lit our tapers from it, and then led us into the unbelievably black hollow terrifying church.

From the alley to the end of the Square is the house Anne and Mary lived in, on the top floor, with Henri and his mother and two older sisters. It had once been a wing of the Archbishop's Palace, which forms the end of the Square. I suppose it was used by visiting prelates, for the rooms were large and gracious but without the grandeur of the Palace itself.

It must have been adequately elegant in the eighteenth century, but by the time we knew it the walls were cracked and sagging, and the tiled floors went up and down, and the only noble things left were the fine curving stairway with its delicate forged iron balustrade, and the beautiful carved wooden door.

Madame Wytenhove's apartment, the top one in this fairly low three-storied building, was a dazzle of sunlight, a delight.

As I remember it, the kitchen, a short hall, the salon which was also the dining room, and two large bedrooms looked down onto the square through tall generous windows, and for them alone I would love to live there, even with the whole dismal state of disrepair and shabbiness, and the ridiculous plumbing.

My girls slept in a small dark room next to Henri's sisters' room, in a short wing which branched out in back to form one wall of the Cloister. The sexton slept just below them, to keep an eye on his domain, and now and then when he did not feel like going down to the Cathedral to ring a little bell for some religious or touristic purpose he would simply lean from his window and jangle it toward the main building of the church. He was the official guide, to show to visitors the famous triptych of the Burning Bush and the tapestries made for Canterbury in 1511, and the bell they were requested to ring for his services often rang all day in his room while he slept beside it. Occasionally it would sound out with obvious irritation, and the children above his room would hear him chuckle . . .

Mary was about eight then. After a few weeks of living with the family and studying with Madame Wytenhove the older Anne started to go to school with the Dominicans, so gentle with little strangers, and Mary stayed on for a time by herself, the only child in the big apartment.

She would go before every meal for a pitcher of fresh spring water from the Fontaine d'Espéluque which spouts from a remnant of Roman wall between the Cloister alley and the pastry shop, and she began to speak enough words to buy bread and cakes there for Madame, and then for herself. The fat old woman who lived behind the shop with her husband and helped him ice his pastries was kind and smiling with her, as everyone seemed to be.

One time when she was roaming about in the Cathedral, listening to the organ and peering into the side chapels, the sexton scared her by pushing her roughly down behind an altar, until she saw that he was smiling and holding his finger to his lips: she had got mixed up in a wedding somehow. She crouched there until the long service was over and everyone gone, and then the old man came for her and led her across the great silent nave to the door into the familiar Cloister, where she and Henri played every afternoon among the broken Roman and Gothic carvings, when he got home from school.

And another time she saw men unloading beautiful dresses, and fantastic wigs held up delicately on sticks, from an old truck in front of the arched passageway that led into the Archbishop's Palace next door, and being a straightforward child she went as close as she could, to watch. Men ran back and forth with what seemed an endless supply of glittering capes and pantaloons and robes, taking them deep into the great courtyard, for all she could see or know.

She went nearer and nearer, and finally a man smiled and said something to her which she could not understand, and thrust a pile of gauzy bright silk into her arms.

It was natural and right to follow him, through the open gates of exquisite forged iron and around the first corner and then into the dim storeroom where other excited people were hanging the clothes on crowded racks. She made several trips, mute but willing, and when the van was empty she ran up the stairs next door, to tell as best she could the morning's adventure.

That afternoon, well primed by Madame, I could explain to her that she had been helping the famous Comédie de Provence unload its props after a tour through France, and we made plans to see a play sometime in that beautiful courtyard. It took almost six years . . .

In the summer of 1960 we stood again where the Place opened like a window from the dark twisted walls of the Rue Gaston-de-Saporta. It was at night, and soft full lights masked high in the trees made them somehow more than ever like tall sea ferns, with us the fish at the bottom of the gold and green water. Hundreds of other people murmured all around us, and we flowed with their currents about the open gates of the Archbishop's Palace, where the long tunnel of the entryway was lined now with velvet and rich silk.

No light came from the windows where once my girls had lived, but I could see the shapes of women leaning silently on their crossed arms, watching.

We put our empty champagne glasses on the long white-covered bar, and the waiter from the Casino smiled and motioned us to hurry. It was the end of the entr'acte of *Don Giovanni*.

The dry shabby courtyard we had first known was now a most beautiful theater, with rows of seats rising halfway to the eaves, before the enormous proscenium that seemed to disappear when the music started and the singers opened their lips. We knew, as perhaps did few other people there, that under the rich velvet of the entry was the door where Mary had helped carry up costumes into the storerooms with two other offices now, oddly juxtaposed in such a once-revered building, the Bureau of Mental Health and the Aix branch of the Communist Party. And behind the heavy steel bleachers at the far end of the courtyard were the high windows which often Anne and Mary had watched with horror and then murderous delight while silhouetted against a curtain two of the young *Comédiens* would rehearse a violent stabbing, and fine strangulation . . . And then underneath and behind the huge temporary stage, we knew, were the basins of the old fountain, that must once have sounded almost as beautiful as the music the orchestra now played in front of it.

We could remember when a bedraggled tall palm tree (or were there two?) still grew beside the empty pools . . . and the music was telling us that soon we would be not there in the strange theater under the soft sky in the old Palace court-

yard, but in front of the village inn where Donna Elvire waited
so foolishly, so helplessly, to let love trick her again . . .

That was the first night of almost a month of music, in other
places of Aix but mostly there.

The Festival seemed to generate a kind of haze, an enchantment, so that going to the concerts and the operas, and waiting for the music to start and stop and start again, and then
walking through the streets empty of any people but others
in the same dream, and the moon rising over the proscenium in
the courtyard, and the slow glasses of champagne before the
music started and the slow walking away again and sleeping
in strange deeply purified sleep, wrapped that month with
timelessness forever, and made it hard to recall and yet part
of our spiritual marrow.

The first night, as if to try to escape before it was too late
from this magic, we broke off from the main current of people
pushing in a bemused way out through the velvety corridor,
and instead of flowing with them on down Gaston-de-Saporta
past Brondino's dark shop, we almost ran down the one little
street that leads directly into the Place de l'Archevêché, Rue
Adanson I think, to the crooked passageway called Esquiche-
Coude in Provençal because a big man can scratch his two
elbows at once on the sides of it.

It was empty. We staggered, drunk with the music, touching this side and then that of the cool walls, and veering fast
around the gentle corners, and laughing in a stifled way. We
tiptoed, even at that silly speed. Suddenly we burst into the
Rue Gibelin, and then zig and zag and we were in the world
again, with the street lights soft and mysterious under the trees
of the Cours Mirabeau, and the café tables set far out onto the
pavement for the crowds. All of us . . . everyone from *Don
Giovanni* . . . felt and looked elegant, weary, exalted, perhaps
reborn, with no more half-felt urge to escape.

And then, months later, I went alone to the courtyard of

the old Palace. It was dead, and everything was gone: the bleachers, the orchestra pit, the proscenium. The walls looked shabbier than ever. The entryway, stripped of its false velvet skin, was a drab tunnel, with the handsome carved door at the street end, on the Square, and the delicate iron grille at the other, and leading off it the offices to help the Communists, the mentally unwell, and the stage-struck. The one remaining tree, which the summer before had obviously felt sickly and about to lose its prematurely yellow leaves, had been severely trimmed, and would obviously survive another year or two of partial suffocation in the bleachers, which rose each season to its first branches.

I knew that I must turn my eyes, both inward and outward ones, from the notices that had begun to appear everywhere in Aix about the next Festival. If I could stay for even one night of it, I would be lost, never able to leave again. I knew that.

It was inconceivable that sometime I might do as many others do, and be there just for that month, or even a part of it. I must have the whole, and I must have what comes before and then remains, the slow growing excitement everywhere and the repeated climaxes of all the concerts and operas, and afterwards the voluptuous and bemazed exhaustion and fulfillment. It was all as clear-cut in its preparation, achievement, satisfaction as a perfect sexual experience, but lengthened by the necromancy of great music to weeks instead of hours and minutes . . .

I wanted to be able to go again into the bare courtyard of the old Palace, and stand in the thin February sunshine which was still rich and warm from the color of the walls. Two men that morning were slowly lifting old stone vases onto the edges of the ancient basin of the fountain, which had emerged again, noble and silent, on the south wall. In a few more months the same men would drag the vases out of sight once more, and the fountain would disappear in the gradual monotonous rebuilding of the great stage, and the stone basin would again become a part of the orchestra pit. By the first of June rehearsals would start . . .

For a long minute or perhaps second I knew that I must flee while I could, while I was still a ghost, still free.

Some of the lines of my map were still blurred, too, and there seemed neither time nor space, right then, to strengthen them.

The notes, though, the music: they were not blurred at all.

The sudden sure acknowledgment of this as I stood looking at the courtyard made me feel ready again. I would forever hear the little mandolin, plucked in the orchestra pit while onstage Don Giovanni pretended to play to the silent mockery of an inn where his mock-love listened. And I knew in a fine positive way that I could nevermore walk any street in the whole real world without hearing, somewhere up from the immediate sounds, the quiet music of the fountains of Aix.

The map was made, and there was no place to flee from it, if I might ever again walk any street, listen to any melody of strings or water. The outlines might gradually twist themselves, as they had done with that map of yet another town, Dijon, but I would always know where I was there, in dream or waking life.

I was a ghost, most fortunately, for ghosts can be wherever they *must* be.

I rolled the invisible map carefully so as not to crease it, and walked out through the open lacy iron gates of the Archbishop's Palace, and through the cool stone tunnel, soon to be velvety again. The thin light of spring lay like gold seen through water on the wall of the house where Anne and Mary had once lived. The mouth of the short alleyway to the cloister of St. Sauveur was open and silent. Down the street Brondino's shop was as blankly dusty as a dead moth.

When I turned onto Espariat toward the Hôtel de Provence I stopped, listening with my sharp ghost-ears to the sound of the water dropping serenely from basin to basin in the Albertas fountain. This time my children would be waiting for me under the faint returning green of the trees on the Cours. The next time, I knew by now, might be any time at all, whether or not the map was exactly true to scale, and plumb, and legible to other eyes than mine. I need not worry about coming back, for I was there anyway.

1. Fontaine de la Rotonde
2. Le Casino Vendôme
3. La Police
4. Le Glacier
5. Fontaine des Augustins
6. Les Bourras
7. St. Esprit
8. Statue of St. Roche
9. Sous-préfecture
10. Hôtel de Provence
11. The Neighbors
12. Fontaine des Neuf Canons
13. Fontaine Old Mossy
14. Fontaine Roy René
15. Foot Doctor
16. Deux Garçons
17. M. Colas
18. Fontaine d'Albertas
19. Sisters of Charity
20. Faculty of Law and Letters
21. M. Brondino
22. Esquiche-Coude
23. Palais de L'Archevêché
24. Mme. Wytenhove
25. St. Sauveur
26. Mme. Perblantier
27. Ste. Catherine
28. Lycée de Jeunes Filles
29. La Madeleine
30. Bookstore
31. Dr. Blanc
32. Deans' Residence, University of Aix-Marseille
33. Lucien Blanc
34. Dr. Vidal
35. Ecole du Bon Départ
36. Cinéma Cézanne
37. Fontaine des Quatre Dauphins
38. St. Jean de Malte
39. Musée des Beaux Arts
40. 17 Rue Cardinale